D1453089

FILMMAKERS SERIES

edited by
ANTHONY SLIDE

In Preparation:

William A. Wellman

by
Frank T. Thompson

with a foreword by
Barbara Stanwyck

FILMMAKERS, NO. 4

The Scarecrow Press, Inc.
Metuchen, N.J., & London
1983

Library of Congress Cataloging in Publication Data

Thompson, Frank T., 1952-
    William A. Wellman.

        (Filmmakers; no. 4)
        Bibliography: p.
        Includes index.
        1. Wellman, William Augustus, 1896-1975.
    2. Moving-picture producers and directors--United
    States--Biography. I. Title. II. Series: Film-
    makers (Scarecrow Press); no. 4.
    PN1998. A3W467   1983   791. 43'0233'0924 [B]   82-16931
    ISBN 0-8108-1594-X

Dedicated to

CHARLES T. BARTON, who believed in and encouraged me when this book was little more than a twinkle in my eye;

and to

SHERYL O'CONNELL, my wife, without whom this book--or any other of my endeavors--would be worth nothing.

CONTENTS

ACKNOWLEDGMENTS

During the five years or so that I have researched materials for this book, I have had occasion to call on many people for help in big matters and small. My most sincere and grateful thanks are extended to those who arranged screenings for me; who supplied me with 16mm prints and, in some cases, videocassettes; and who helped me locate stills, posters, publicity materials, newspaper and magazine articles, interviews, and other important materials: Lee Tsiantis, William K. Everson, Richard Bann, Philip Jenkinson, Ralph Wells, Maxine Fleckner, Michael Durrett, the late James Powers, and Mike Hawks. My gratitude goes also to the staffs of the following: The University of Wisconsin Film Archive and the Wisconsin State Historical Archive; the UCLA Film Archive; the Library of Congress; the Margaret Herrick Library; the public libraries of Boston, Newton, and Brookline (Massachusetts), Chicago, and Los Angeles; Eddie Brandt's Saturday Matinee; and Films, Inc.

I would also like to thank David Shepard of the Director's Guild, Ron Haver, Richard Schickel, Joseph Youngerman, Charles Barton, Frank Capra, Janet Gaynor, Joseph Biroc, Ernest K. Gann, Mike Mazurki, George Chandler, King Vidor, Iris Adrian, Judy Johnson, and Jeff Lenburg.

My deepest gratitude goes to Claire McCulloch, who tirelessly (and, for the most part, uncomplainingly) dug through town records, microfilm, and old newspapers, thus performing some first-class sleuthing to provide me with vital information about Wellman's parents and their families; to John Tibbetts, without whose encouragement to me and willingness to publish my earliest articles on Wellman in American

Classic Screen Magazine, this book would never have come to fruition; to Kevin Brownlow for generously sharing the tapes of his interviews with Wellman from 1964 to 1971 with me, most of which found their way into this volume; to Tony Slide, who felt (contrary to most editors and publishers) that a book on Wellman was long overdue and who kindly gave me the opportunity to fulfill a dream of some years' standing by providing that book; to John Gallagher (whose knowledge of Wellman and his career is formidable) for the immense aid he offered me; and to Barbara Stanwyck, who said she "couldn't help very much" and then went on to write the warm, touching foreword to this book.

Finally, and most especially, I wish to thank the Wellman family: Bill, Jr., Dottie, and Arthur O. Wellman for their kindness, helpfulness, and hospitality. Getting to know them has been among the project's greatest rewards.

Frank T. Thompson

EDITOR'S NOTE

William A. Wellman's career as a director has been
a long and an honorable one, stretching from the early twenties
through the late fifties and encompassing films as varied as
The Public Enemy (1931), Wild Boys of the Road (1933), A
Star Is Born (1937), Nothing Sacred (1937), The Ox-Bow Incident (1943), The Story of G.I. Joe (1945), and The High
and the Mighty (1954). He had a reputation as a "wild" director of action pictures--and it is appropriate that he should
have directed Wings, the first film to win an Academy Award
for Best Picture--but Wellman was also capable of handling
comedies and sensitive subjects with style and imagination.

Wellman's autobiography, A Short Time for Insanity,
published in 1974, helped readers become a little better ac-
quainted with the man, and now we have Frank T. Thompson's
critical study of both Wellman, the man, and Wellman, the
filmmaker. This first book-length evaluation is impressive
not only because it is a first, but because its author considers Wellman's best-known as well as his minor films, giving
equal attention to both. In addition, Frank T. Thompson has
provided a filmography of extraordinary depth, offering credit
information which has required literally years of research
and a close viewing of all extant Wellman films.

Frank T. Thompson is a Georgia-based author, who
has been active in the field of non-theatrical film distribution
for a number of years, and who is editor and co-founder of
Motif, a magazine concerned with the exploration and demonstration of a biblical view of the arts. William A. Wellman
is Thompson's first book. Later, he plans to reconstruct,
via still photographs, a number of Wellman's lost films, with

the results to be published in <u>American Classic Screen</u> (to which Thompson is a frequent contributor), and also hopes to annotate and edit Wellman's second, unpublished volume of memoirs, <u>Growing Old Disgracefully</u>.

Anthony Slide

"Wild Bill" Wellman, as he was called with affection, was the name that was given to him when he served with honor, as they all did, as part of the Lafayette Flying Corps. He never spoke of what "he" did in that service but always of what "we" did, long before the "we" was made popular by Lindbergh. That should tell you something about the man; he was anything but "wild" when you worked for him.

He was gentle and patient. He didn't really tell you what to do. He took it for granted that you knew your business--but there was an understanding and guidance. Bill did his homework, so to speak, and his direction was mapped out long before he started a film; he knew his shots and paced them and you accordingly. Bill also expected his actors to do the same and although I never saw him in a temper, I imagine it would have been hell.

He loved his work and gave every bit of vitality and knowledge to it. One of Bill's, and my, favorite films he directed was The Great Man's Lady with Joel McCrea. It was a lovely story and difficult to film. I did my own stunts in the film which pleased Bill and helped him as a director. We both loved the film in spite of the fact that it was not a box-office block buster--but it did not take our love away from it.

Even though he had a few marriages his greatest love was Dorothy and the beautiful children she gave him. He once said to me, "Dorothy has made the whole damn thing worth while." And she certainly did. She is a lovely human being.

One of the nicest things that ever happened to me is this: A writer, Ella Smith, was doing a book on my work and she asked him for a quote for said book.   Because of my pride, please bear with me if I tell you what it says. It is framed and in my home.   When Bill died, Miss Smith gave it to me because Bill had written it in longhand--so here it is:

> On one of Miss Stanwyck's interviews she mentioned me as one of her favorite directors and ended with 'I love that man. "   Needless to say I was very proud and had a lump in my throat which does not happen to me very often--Barbara Stanwyck--"I love that girl. "
>
> Signed--Bill Wellman

And so again--

I miss you, Bill Wellman
I love you.

CHAPTER ONE

William A. Wellman and his contemporaries--John Ford, Henry King, Allan Dwan, Howard Hawks, Raoul Walsh, King Vidor--came to Hollywood while they were very young men. Yet, all had lived lives packed with exciting events and each brought to his new profession a unique knowledge of adventure, danger, love, and loyalty. Among them, they had been flyers, soldiers, cowboys, race-car drivers, writers, newspapermen and, in some cases, actors--in short they had personally been involved in the very professions that they would prove so adept at putting on the screen.

Of these movie directors, the most consistently under-regarded critically has been Wellman. Some of his films have individually been greeted with critical and popular acclaim and some continue to be regarded highly (or at least nostalgically), yet there remains little knowledge of his career and accomplishments as a whole.

Perhaps the reason for this lack of attention is the general perception of Wellman as a "studio hack." It is assumed that he simply took the projects that he was assigned and churned them out on the assembly line. This is true to some extent: Wellman was a lifelong adherent to the studio system by choice and he very often worked on assignment. This proved, however, to be his greatest strength. Wellman explained,

> You had stock companies that were absolutely fantastic, and you had a choice of stories. I wanted to make every type of picture that was ever made--

1

> kid's pictures, comedies, westerns; all these dif-
> ferent types.   And when I quit, I wanted to be sure
> that I'd done it.   I had to be a studio director to
> do it, and that's what I was.

His affiliation with the various studios did not stifle
him as was the case with, for instance, Orson Welles and
Erich von Stroheim.   It allowed him to develop his craft,
extend his versatility, and indulge his wide range of tastes
and abilities.   By the time he started filming Wings in 1926,
he had only been a director for three years, yet he had already signed eleven features.   In the period 1930-33, he directed twenty full-length films.   Though he slowed down considerably in the late thirties, by the time he quit the business
after the release of Lafayette Escadrille in 1958 he had man-
aged to chalk up over eighty films to his credit.

Despite the breakneck speed with which he worked,
the unpromising properties he took on, and the interference
by unsympathetic studio heads on those projects that did capture his imagination, Wellman's career is marked by remarkable consistency of quality and viewpoint.   His lean, straightforward style, manic invention, cynical humor (sometimes
improbably coupled with an overt sentimentality) infuse the
least of his films with a nobleness of purpose and a living
complexity and density.

In matters of skill, professionalism, commercial sens-
ibilities, and technical competence, Wellman was among the
best and most respected directors in Hollywood.   If he sometimes approached pretension in his themes, he never let his
own "cock-eyed" aspirations to art become a barrier to re-
leasing successful, entertaining films.   He once told an interviewer, "Hell, you make pictures for the public, not for yourself!" and this disciplined view of his craft was perhaps his
artistic salvation.

Not that Wellman considered himself an artist in any
sense of the word, but he sometimes allowed his own concep-
tions of what constituted "art" get onto the screen in films
he made "for himself," like The Ox-bow Incident and Track
of the Cat.   These films, among his most personal, are,
paradoxically, also among his least characteristic; they are
intelligent and well-made--and often quite beautiful--but somehow the Wellman fire and energy are missing.   As Manny
Farber so perceptively wrote, "... Wellman [is] like basket-
ball's corner man: [his] best shooting is done from the deepest, worst angle."

William A. Wellman, 1926.

This is quite true: Wellman's best films are often
his least promising. Such near-forgotten titles as The Man
I Love, Night Nurse, Love Is a Racket, The Conquerors,
The Robin Hood of El Dorado, The Happy Years, and Goodbye, My Lady have often found themselves being dismissed
by writers who have formed opinions by skimming filmographies rather than watching the films. Wellman's prodigious
talent was stimulated by second-rate material; the less the
project brought with it, the more Wellman was forced to
reach into himself to fill it with skill and imagination.

For this reason, there is not an anonymous "throw-
away" film in the Wellman oeuvre. Even the least of his
films (Darby's Rangers) manages to get some of its director's quirky humor, bizarre visual compositions, and impul-
sive, rugged action onto the screen.

This, finally, is Wellman's greatest accomplishment
as a director: each of his films, despite its origins, is vi-
brant, alive, involving, and personal. His films' concerns,
attitudes, moral perspectives, visual and aural styles are
inextricably tied in with Wellman's tastes, moods, and prejudices. There is a wholeness to his work--in style, quality
and point of view--that separates it from the run-of-the-mill
studio product for which it is so often mistaken.

Wellman's personal involvement in his projects often
went far beyond merely injecting the films with his own sen-
sibilities; Wellman could well have been the most blatantly
autobiographical director of the era. Many aspects of his
private life found their way into his work, especially his
days as a flyer in World War I.

His flying days had a bearing on many of his films
and if he injected nothing literal from his past in Wings,
Legion of the Condemned, or Young Eagles, he at least infused these flying films with his knowledge of the milieu.
In other films about flying, though, the references to his
own life were more explicit: The Conquerors, in which
Richard Dix joins the Norton-Harjes Ambulance Corps, then
transfers to the Lafayette Flying Corps--exactly the course
that Wellman took in 1917; Men with Wings, in which Fred
MacMurray is shown flying a Spad VII with the "Black Cat"
insignia--an exact replica of the plane that Wellman flew;
Lafayette Escadrille, one of the most thoroughly autobiographical films ever made by a "studio director," a film
that poignantly tells of Wellman's own adventures in great,

and usually accurate, detail--Wellman himself is portrayed as one of the film's characters.

These autobiographical touches can be found in dozens of Wellman's films, from the little boy with the "floating black eye" in The Happy Years to the judicial reprimand of Norman Maine in night court in A Star Is Born. ("Word for word, that happened to me," Wellman said.) In fact, Wellman extended his fondness for drawing on his own life and experiences by actually appearing in some of his films, as well as creating roles for members of his family. He is onscreen in Wings and Frisco Jenney; his voice is heard off-screen in The Man I Love, Star Witness, and Thunder Birds; he narrates Island in the Sky and Lafayette Escadrille; and his likeness appears in a photograph and a painting in Thunder Birds (as John Sutton's father, who was killed in a World War I dogfight).

As for members of his family, his first wife, Helene Chadwick, is an extra in A Star Is Born; his second wife, Margery Chapin, and their adopted daughter, Gloria, appear in Wings; his fourth wife, Dorothy Coonan, stars in Wild Boys of the Road and The Story of G.I. Joe. His eldest son, Bill, Jr., stars in Darby's Rangers and Lafayette Escadrille (in the latter, playing his father), his next son, Tim, appears in The Happy Years and Island in the Sky, and his youngest son, Mike, is in Island in the Sky and The High and the Mighty.

Autobiographical detail, of course, does not guarantee good art or good entertainment; in Wellman's case, it simply represents another layer of involvement, another thread that connects the whole of his career. As instinctively as Wellman worked, it is quite remarkable that his body of work has such a multiplicity of personal themes, ideas, and obsessions.

This book is neither biography nor close critical analysis of Wellman's motion pictures. It is a career study, an attempt to pull together the seemingly disparate strands of his oeuvre in order to consider his work as a single unit and, by so doing, to gain a deeper understanding of his unique talent.

Though the book is not a biography it has, of necessity, biographical elements, particularly those pertaining to

Wellman's early life.   The period before his entry into movies in 1919 has been covered at some length, for this is the
period that he most often drew upon in his films.

CHAPTER TWO

The man who won the heart and hand of Celia Guinness McCarthy was perhaps her least likely suitor. Celia imbodied every cliché of Irish girlhood. She had flaming red hair, a strong will, a violent temper, and unwavering devotion to those she loved. Her husband, on the other hand, was quiet, gentle, amiable, a man who made up in alcoholic thirst what he lacked in business sense.

His name was Arthur Gouverneur Wellman. Arthur was born April 8, 1858, in Boston, the youngest of four children of English immigrants. Like his brothers Francis and Joseph Wellman, Arthur attended the Massachusetts Institute of Technology for a time. Unlike his brothers, he never graduated, opting in his second year to accept a position in an insurance brokerage in Boston.

Francis and Joseph did graduate and Francis went on to become a noted lawyer in the area, later writing several popular books on law, including The Art of Cross-Examination and Gentlemen of the Jury. Their sister, Matilda, did not attend college. Nevertheless, she also became involved in the practice of law when she married Samuel Williston, a professor at Harvard and (later) author of such legal tomes as Laws and Contracts.

Arthur never approached the success of his brothers. Though he remained an insurance broker until his retirement just after World War I, he was never able to reach the upper echelons of the corporate structure. His second son, William, described Arthur as "an inner and an outer. One month we

7

could eat beans, not just one night of the week, but two or
three, and if things got really rugged, we had beans every
night."

"Father was a real gentleman," added his oldest son,
Arthur O. Wellman. "He never made much money, but he
was able to provide for us, keep us in a good home and keep
food on the table."

The "ins and outs" described by William can be quite
literally traced by the frequency with which the Wellmans
moved around the Boston area. When Arthur was "in" and
making good money, he would move his family into a comfortable home in a good neighborhood, like that at 49 Hill-
side Drive in Newton. When he was "out," the family packed
up, moved to the other side of the tracks and found more
humble dwellings.

If Arthur's erratic financial status put a strain on his
wife, she never let it show. Celia Guinness McCarthy was
a woman of great strength and will. When Arthur failed the
family as a bread-winner, she went out and found work herself. Celia had descended from the Guinness Family of Dub-
lin, the brewers of Guinness Stout. Her mother had fallen
in love out of the Catholic faith, had married, and was
promptly ex-communicated. The McCarthy's then moved to
Boston where they gave birth to Celia on July 13, 1869.

Celia's first ambition was to be an actress and she
was on the stage when she first met Arthur. They were
married in 1892 and moved to Brookline, Massachusetts to
a small, quiet neighborhood called Lyndon Place. It was
here "in a four-poster bed" that Celia gave birth to both of
her sons. Arthur O. was born on October 31, 1894. He
inherited the more positive aspects of both parents' characters; the high intellect and level-headed business sense of
his mother and the casual, even temper of his father.

The second son reversed those traits somewhat. It
wasn't long after William Augustus Wellman was born on
February 29, 1896, that Lyndon Place began to lose some
of the calm that had previously characterized it. It was
quickly apparent that William had inherited his parents' in-
telligence, but to it was added a wide streak of hellishness,
energy, curiosity, and temper.

"People called us the 'Fighting Wellmans,'" recalled

Arthur. "If they couldn't get us to fight each other, they'd
start us fighting with someone else. Bill was a fine athlete,
afraid of nothing. "

William later wrote that his mother remembered, "a
stretch that I went through with a black eye, for four months.
It was a wandering black eye. The moment the right became
normal I got it in the left. My brother, being shorter than
I and much heavier, lowered his head like a goat, but he had
marbles on the top of his head that I think are still there. "

Appropriately, the mother of "The Fighting Wellmans"
found her true vocation when she became a volunteer at the
District Court of Newton as Assistant Probation Officer. This
post has given rise to one of Wellman's favorite anecdotes.
He told Richard Schickel in The Men Who Made the Movies,
". . . a very dear friend and I used to borrow cars at night.
We always brought them back, but we were caught bringing
one of them back and I was put on probation for six months
and had to report to the probation officer of Newton who happened to be my own mother. "

Only after Arthur's luck completely deserted him and
he found himself unable to hold a job did Celia become a full-
time, paid Probation Officer. In fact, the first time she is
mentioned in that capacity in any Newton city records is in
1925. The story that William ever had to report to his
mother in any official capacity is unlikely, for he left Newton in 1917 and never lived there again.

He never lost his admiration for his mother. "She
was a beautiful woman, " he wrote, "and she loved and understood my rather unreliable father. " She supported him emotionally as well as financially.

When William was a boy, his parents hoped that he
would become a singer. "I was a star pupil of Sullivan Sar-
gent, " he recalled. "He was a great voice teacher. I had
a beautiful voice as a kid, and when my voice broke, it was
a beautiful baritone. " He sang in the choir at Trinity (Episcopal) Church in Newton Center and often entertained at school
and church functions.

Perhaps his musical talent was inherited from his
father. "My father was great on the piano. He used to play
beautifully--but he'd never play for money. " William himself
played the piano "not too good, but quietly and softly"; how-

ever, all hopes of a singing career were smashed with the
roof of his mouth in 1918 in a plane crash.

Not all of his goals, however, were artistic. His
hyperactive character required that William be constantly on
the move, so he became an enthusiastic, if undisciplined,
participant in every sport that Newton High offered. His
energy and wiry strength made him uniquely valuable on
most teams, but his quick temper usually precluded his ris-
ing to the heights of any given sport. Probably his best efforts were in the hockey rink. In the 1914 Newtonian, the
Newton High yearbook, he is pictured with the hockey team.
Opposite the photograph we find an overview of the team's
accomplishments for the year which includes this passage:
"On February 6th, Newton won her first league game by defeat-
ing Cambridge Latin 5 to 2. Wellman was the hero of the game
making all five goals." "I was rover and captain of the
hockey team," he wrote, "and we won the New England cham-
pionship. Rover is the lightest, the fastest skater and the
dirtiest player." In the hockey rink, as in the rest of his
life, he had some trouble adhering to the rules. He was,
however, peculiarly willing to fling himself headlong into any
sort of fracas with little regard to personal injury. This
accounts for his success in the sport, for hockey can be a
violent game; Wellman loved violent games.

The 1914 Newtonian is the first and last time that
William Wellman's name or photograph ever appears in that
school's records. This renders any reading of his scholastic
career quite approximate. It is not known for certain whether
or not he ever finished high school, though it's probable that
he didn't. His brother, Arthur, maintains that William "quit
school to go into the service" but the timespan is wrong.
Probably, 1914 was William's last year at Newton High School
and he didn't "go into the service" until May 1917. William
claimed to have been expelled from high school for reasons
that changed with each telling. The most popular anecdote
had him dropping a stink-bomb on his principal's head which
is, if not factual, at least consistent with his character.

He decided, about this time, to go into hockey pro-
fessionally. He spoke many times of having been offered
scholarships to various colleges, but this is most likely
wishful thinking. His taste of high school celebrity in the
hockey rink was enough to start him on the road to a professional career and, if that wasn't enough, another incident
of 1914 definitely convinced him that he was destined for
Hockey Greatness.

In that year, Douglas Fairbanks was in Boston at the
Colonial Theatre with a show called Hawthorne of the U.S.A.
featuring Fred Stone and Phoebe Foster. Boston was (as it
is now, to some extent) a major "preview city"--a city where
plays were brought to be honed and perfected before they hit
Broadway. Fairbanks was still a year away from his first
motion picture, but he was already popular as a stage actor.

Always an enthusiastic sports fan (and, of course, a
remarkable athlete himself), Fairbanks liked to relax during
his time off by taking in local sporting events. On this particular afternoon, Fairbanks went to the Boston Arena to
watch the Newton High hockey team compete against another
local high school. "I didn't play as much during games as
I should," William wrote, "because of my devotion to the
penalty box, but at least I made things interesting."

He was making himself interesting enough that day to
catch Fairbanks' eye. "Mr. Fairbanks asked to meet me.
I skated over and met him and his party, and was invited
backstage (at the Colonial) the following week. This was
something new for a kid and very intriguing. I made several visits and became very fond of Mr. Fairbanks."

He had no way of knowing, of course, that Fairbanks
was to change his life just a few years later by introducing
young Wellman to what would become his life's profession:
motion pictures. At the moment, his concerns were more
immediate; he was tired of high school and the idea of college did not appeal to him at all. The obvious solution was
to become what his high school friends and Fairbanks believed
he was cut out for: a professional hockey player.

Surprisingly, the world of professional hockey did not
greet this decision with the joy and thanksgiving that he would
have thought appropriate. No offers were forthcoming.
Though he continued playing on a regular basis with ama-
teur teams, William began to look around for a way of earn-
ing a living.

His brother was proving to be quite unlike his "rather
unreliable" father by becoming a budding success in the
Boston-area wool trade. He was doing so well that he and
his parents encouraged brother Billy to give the business a
try. "He didn't do too well," Arthur remembers. "People
liked him very much, he was a very personable young man,
but he never had any business sense."

As William did not want it thought that he was riding his brother's coattails to success, he moved to Philadelphia to tackle the trade independently. He tried, but he failed. In two months, William was back in Newton, looking for work.

Opportunity knocked at a factory that produced a candy called Fish's Green Seal Chocolates. William started work there as a line foreman. "They told me to go up and down the lines of gals [who] were packing and eat as much as I wanted to, which I did. For three days, I would eat candy, and I haven't been crazy about candy ever since." He didn't like being confined in the noisy factory either and persuaded his bosses to put him on the road as a salesman. Unfortunately, by this time, he hated Fish's Green Seal Chocolates, which robbed him of some of his credibility as a salesman. "I never sold a goddamn pound of the stuff."

More to his liking was a job as "lumper" at the Butterick Lumber Company in Waltham, Massachusetts. "I was a big success in the lumberyard. I didn't have to use my brain, and I didn't have to be nice and polite to some druggist or mill superintendent, hoping the son of a bitch would buy a couple of boxes of Green Seal chocolates or a few pounds of wool."

Though the work was rather mindless--a lumper "is the guy that takes the lumber and carries it over to a man named a piler who is piling it"--it was physical and, to William, exhilarating. Still, he was restless. He knew that the lumber business was nothing that he would like to make a career out of, but he didn't know what the alternatives were.

One Sunday afternoon, he drove with some friends to a small air field near Woburn, Massachusetts. The boys were fascinated by watching the planes take off and land and they struck up conversations with some of the pilots. Among the fliers there was pioneer aviator Earl Ovington. Ovington saw how thrilled William was with the planes and offered to take him aloft sometime. They made a date for the following Sunday.

When that day finally arrived, Ovington took William aloft for the first of two flights. William was ecstatic. "That was all that was necessary," he remembered. "I just _had_ to fly." In that one afternoon, all thoughts of a hockey career vanished. William wanted to be a flyer. In 1917, this wasn't such an attainable goal. The relative youth of the aviation industry, the lack of qualified instructors, and the high cost of flight training posed a discouraging barrier to William's hopes.

This didn't quell the longings, though, and he continued to frequent the airfield at Woburn. He questioned the pilots, examined the machines and tried to learn everything he could about aviation, all the while attempting to find some way, any way, to learn how to fly.

It seemed an impossible ideal, but at this moment a grim opportunity opened a way for William to learn to fly. "America's entry into the war was imminent," he wrote, "and being an adventurous young man, I had to get into it. I wanted to fly!" William, like most men his age, was thrilled at the thought of war in Europe. Here he felt, was a real chance for adventure, for breathtaking experiences, for an opportunity to show courage, valor and all of the other storybook virtues. Most important, here was a chance to learn to fly and to get paid to learn!

He recalled, "My family decided that the best thing for me to do, under the conditions of my restless nature, was to get out and do that which I had wanted so badly to do--to fly!"

On Saturday, March 29, 1917, William bounded up the stairs of the Massachusetts State House on Beacon Hill in Boston to enlist in the Naval Aviation Service of the United States. "The officer in charge of the enlistments questioned me briefly about my life, and, when he asked me if I were a college graduate and I answered in the negative, he told me there was no chance for me then, and added that the service was full and probably would be for some time." William was dejected by the refusal. What had seemed such a shining promise had been cruelly snatched away from him.

He talked with his parents about his disappointment. Arthur suggested that William approach his two influential uncles, Francis Wellman and Samuel Williston, to see if perhaps they could pull some strings and get him admitted to the Naval Aviation Service. He did so and each promised to do his best to get William accepted. Though both were formidable string-pullers, they were unable to do anything. Again, the situation looked hopeless.

Unknown to them, another alternative was opening up
in France. Already, prior to America's entry into the war,
many young Americans were flocking to France, eager to get
into a war that their own country seemed frustratingly slow
about entering. Once in France, the adventurous young men
were joining the French Foreign Legion, which allowed them
to fight with the French army without relinquishing their
American citizenships.

Many of these young men, like William, had the yen
to fly and found, to their delight, that their status as Legionnaires made it possible for them to get into French aviation.

Norman Prince, who lived in Pride's Crossing,
near Boston, was attempting to form a group of
American volunteers to fly for France [Wellman
wrote]. Prince was aided by his old friend,
Frazier Curtis, and together with the help of the
wealthy William K. Vanderbilt, they were busy in
organizing groups of young men who were eager to
fly for France since their own country would not
accept them into their own Air Service due to
America's stand on neutrality at that time. Eventually Prince, Curtis and Vanderbilt were successful in organizing what later turned out to be the
Lafayette Escadrille.

Once the French government had accepted Prince's
idea to form an all-American escadrille, the floodgates of
volunteers opened. On April 20, 1916, the Escadrille American (as it was originally known) was placed on the French
roster as an official unit--N. 124 Squadron--and ordered to
the front.

The fame of the Lafayette Escadrille grew rapidly and
William saw his hopes rekindled. If his own Air Service
wouldn't accept him, he would get to France and join the
Lafayette Escadrille. This time his uncles were of some
help, for they told William about the Norton-Harjes Ambulance Corps, a group of American volunteers giving medical
assistance at the front.

"I called Mr. Norton--the American sponsor--by long
distance telephone, explained my desire to him, and asked if
I might see him and be examined," he wrote. "His answer
was a prompt 'Yes!.'"

William went to Samuel Williston and Reverend Edward
Sullivan of Grace Episcopal Church in Newton Center to get
letters of recommendation.   Once these were obtained, William
boarded a train to New York to see Norton.   "He talked
pleasantly with me for a few moments, asked me if I could
drive an automobile and, upon being told that I could, accepted my services.   I signed for the customary six months'
period."

Proudly, William returned to his parents' home and
told them that he was leaving for France as an ambulance
driver.   On May 22, 1917, he boarded the French Liner
Rochambeau and sailed from New York harbor.   He wrote
the following year,

> I had been told by friends that once overseas in the
> ambulance service, the American volunteer had two
> choices at his disposal.   He could either stay in
> the ambulance service or he could join the French
> Foreign Legion and in turn be trained for the French
> Flying Corps.   This was the solution to my problem
> and I decided that I wanted to fly so badly that I
> would serve in the front lines and then seek a trans-
> fer to flying.

On board the Rochambeau his ambitions were altered
somewhat.   He met several other young Americans also bound
for France, among them Reginald "Duke" Sinclair.   William
remembered,

> Sinclair was going over expressly to enlist in the
> Lafayette Flying Corps which was an offshoot of the
> original Lafayette Escadrille (which was taking no
> more volunteers).   He planted the seeds anew in
> me.   During the trip to France, these seeds grew
> rapidly and I was crazy with determination and de-
> sire to transfer from the Norton-Harjes Ambulance
> Corps to the Lafayette Flying Corps.   I had been
> informed that this was done quite frequently and
> that the Norton-Harjes people were only too glad
> to accommodate us.

In fact, he never served a single day with the Norton-
Harjes Ambulance Corps.   Upon his arrival in France on
June 1, 1917, he went straight to their headquarters and ap-
prised them of his desire to transfer.

I went at once into the office and, after reporting
to Mr. Norton's brother there, told them of my
desire and determination. He was all kindness
and released me from my former contract.

Without delay I found my way to 23 Avenue
Bois de Bologne, where I found Dr. Edmund Gros,
who was in charge of the Paris enlistments in the
Lafayette Flying Corps. After Dr. Gros had read
my letters of recommendation, which I had wisely
brought along with me, he said that if I passed the
physical examination, he would accept me.

The physical turned out to be a simple affair, for the
French were very reluctant to turn down any volunteers.
William was in superb physical condition and so passed easily. He returned to his hotel, the "France et Choiseul," to
wait for his enlistment papers to arrive from the French
government. After the whirlwind activities of the past weeks,
this period of waiting and inactivity was maddening to him.
The boredom was relieved somewhat in a singularly unpleasant way. Wellman had picked a "friendly bout" with one of
the hotel valets and, in the course of the fight, cut his foot.
The cut didn't seem serious, but the next day it showed signs
of blood poisoning. Dr. Gros sent him to the American Hospital at Nueilly, outside of Paris, to recuperate.

The hospital stay was much more agreeable to William
than the boredom of the hotel, for the food was good and
plentiful, and he was surrounded by pretty American nurses.
He was discharged as "practically cured" on June 23 and,
when he had returned to the "France et Choiseul," he found
that his enlistment papers had arrived. He formally enlisted
in the legendary French Foreign Legion and, on June 27,
found himself on board a train bound for the French aviation
training camp at Avord, in the south of France.

All the romantic notions of being a Foreign Legionnaire soon surrendered to the harsh realities of Legion life
at Avord. The American recruits found themselves face to
face with hardened criminals and other assorted lowlifes.
Theft was rampant. The dwellings were infested with rats
and lice, the clothes were filthy and ill-fitting and the pay
was but $3\frac{1}{2}$ cents a day. Wellman remembered Avord vividly
years later when he wrote of "using latrines that had to be
whitewashed weekly because of the lack of paper, those finger-
drawn feces paintings, being lousy for months, boils and dys-
entery from lack of wholesome food, greybacks that hid in
your navel."

"I can't describe Avord," he said. "I've been in some
pretty rough places making motion pictures--I've been in
Death Valley making a motion picture--and I'd rather be in
Death Valley than in Avord. That's how bad it was."

His arrival at Avord on June 29, 1917, was lightened
somewhat when he found a friend, David Putnam, already
there. Putnam had also gone to Newton High and had been
in French aviation since May 31. He was already an old
hand at Avord life and was instrumental in getting William
settled in. Dave acted as William's guide and protector until William was used to the vagaries of life as a Legionnaire.
Dave Putnam was destined to be killed in combat on September 13, 1918, at the Battle of San Mihiel. Wellman was to
make this battle the climax of his first great epic of the air,
Wings, nine years later.

Putnam's death was not the only occurrence of those
days that William Wellman would put on film. The few
months that he was in France would color the rest of his
life. The things he saw there, the men he knew, the friends
he made and lost, the beauty of flight, the stench of filth and
death, the camaraderie of barracks life--all these things
would always remain with him. The experiences directly in-
fluenced the many times that Wellman's films dealt with planes
and the men who fly them, but, more significantly, the attitudes about loyalty and friendship and the bonds between men
under duress would come to characterize every single film
he ever directed. After the war, Wellman was never again
to pilot a plane, but he never stopped identifying himself with
flyers and he never stopped celebrating the year of his life
that he was one.

The fledgling flyers of the Lafayette Flying Corps were
trained under circumstances that seem irresponsibly hazardous
today. Wellman recalled, "The instructors just told us how
to commit maneuvers and we had to go up and try to do it."
At no point in the training, from first day to last, did an instructor actually get into a plane with a student.

The training was accomplished in five basic steps.
The first was called "Penguin" class, which involved piloting
an unwieldy aircraft (a Penguin) that was incapable of flight.
The Bleriot plane simply taxied up and down the field. After
the student mastered this difficult step, he was graduated to
a Bleriot with a full wing spread. The engine was regulated
so that the plane would still not fly. However, the tail would

come up off the ground, which made the endless taxiing sim-
ulate actual flying conditions more closely.

The third step was called "Rouler" class. This plane
was a slightly larger Bleriot which would fly to an altitude
of about twenty-five feet. Next came the "tour de piste"; a
flight around the airfield at an altitude of about 500 meters.
This was the first stage wherein the students could actually
turn and bank in the air.

Finally, the recruits advanced from the Bleriot to a
Caudron, a plane described by Wellman as resembling a "flying bathtub." The flight in the Caudron was known as the
"Big Trip" for it not only traveled faster than any of the
previous planes, but they were required to make a series
of longer flights. As Wellman described it,

> The "Big Trip" consisted of triangular cross-
> country flights from Avord to Romorantin to Cha-
> teraux, each one within a 15-mile span. On the
> first flight we flew from Avord to Romorantin and
> return to Avord. The following day we would fly
> the complete triangle, Avord-Chateraux-Romorantin-
> returning to Avord. On the fourth day we would fly
> the triangle in reverse order. When you had suc-
> cessfully completed these cross-country flights, the
> French awarded you the wings of a military aviator
> --and then buddy, you're a real guy!
> Prior to this you're still a second-class soldier,
> and believe me you really are! We would do all
> of our flying early in the morning, before the wind
> came up, so we were off from the docks bright and
> early. Our breakfast was packed under the seats
> of the camions that transported us to the field.
> Breakfast was composed of two things: cheese and
> bread. And that's it! We were always hungry.
> God knows we were half starved until the Armistice,
> but as hungry as we were, we didn't dare to eat
> our breakfast! At least not in the dark. We had
> to wait until the daylight hours so that we could see
> what we were chomping into! There were worms
> in the cheese and the bread was moldy. If you
> were to eat a worm--well, he wasn't going to hurt
> you at all--but if you bit into this bread and get
> ptomaine--you're going to be a sick guy!

After the sun (and the wind) came up, all flights had

to halt and the men came back to "our delightful barracks."
For the rest of the day, there was not much for them to do.
In an attempt to imbue a little discipline and order (and cur-
tail the non-stop gambling that the flyers were involved in),
the French officers required them to execute close order
drills.

This was too much for the free-spirited Americans
and they soon came up with a plan to bring the drills to a
stop.

> Several of our group, Tommy Hitchcock, Duke Sin-
> clair, David Judd and a few others could speak
> French and together with the rest of us formed a con-
> spiracy against close order drill. Our chief con-
> spirators said, "Whenever they give you a close
> order command, do the exact opposite." The re-
> sult was the most screwed up mess you've ever
> seen in your life. The French decided that all
> Americans were imbeciles ... so the close order
> drills were eventually abolished.

This entire incident was carried intact to the screen
forty years later in Wellman's last released film, Lafayette
Escadrille. The scene, like the rest of the film, gets most
of its humor from the dubious premise that speaking French
is pretty funny. So funny, in fact, that few of the men who
came from the states to join the French Air Service ever
bothered to learn the language. Wellman himself never
seemed to have noticed this until years later when he wrote,
"Being the egotistical self-centered American that I was, I
never once entertained the idea that I couldn't speak French,
which was, after all, (the) native language.... I was actually
a foreigner.'"

At this point, Wellman had been made a corporal in
the French army. He was thus entitled to wear a single
golden wing on either side of his collar and received his
brevet and pilot's license, a gold and silver wreath with two
wings.

Since the United States was by now in the war, re-
cruiters from the American Flying Service visited Avord to
try and interest the Americans in leaving the French Corps
and join the U.S. Corps. Wellman elected to remain in the
French Army and complete his training at Avord. "As much
as I disliked the place, the schooling there was the best ob-

The most insistently autobiographical film in Wellman's ca-
reer--and his last released--was Lafayette Escadrille.   Left
to right: Bill Wellman, Jr. as a "nicer" version of his
father; Tab Hunter as Thad Walker, a fictionalized character; Jody McCrea as Tommy Hitchcock; and David Janssen
as Reginald "Duke" Sinclair.

tainable.   I did not want to risk waiting any longer (to become a first-class pilot).   I wanted to fly and to fight at the
earliest possible moment."   So on October 25, 1917, Wellman, Duke Sinclair, and David Judd reported to the advanced
fighter school at Pau.   "And now it began to be fun," said
Wellman.   "We really started to fly.   We were using real
machines, Nieuports of varying sizes and speeds."

     The training at Pau was infinitely more dangerous--
and more exciting.   Again the Americans were taught to fly
without benefit of an instructor in the plane.   When they were
told to execute a maneuver that they did not understand, they
would go to their instructor for an explanation.   As often as
not, his reply would be, "That's up to you.   That's what
you're here for" and the nervous pilot would be left to figure
it out for himself--in the air.

Upon graduating at Pau, Wellman was sent to Plessis-Belleville to await assignment to a front-line fighting escadrille. He arrived there on November 12, 1917, after a short leave in Paris. "(At Plessis-Belleville) you sit and wait until somebody gets bumped off in (one of) the sixty-six fighting escadrilles. And if you're next in line, that's where you go," Wellman said in an interview. "I was sent to the Black Cat group, a very famous group."

Wellman arrived at the Black Cat squadron (Les Chats Noir), Escadrille N. 87 on December 3. The famed group of French flyers was stationed at Luneville, in the Alsace-Lorraine sector. It turned out that he was the first American to serve in the group. He was assigned a new plane, a Nieuport 27. Since it was his first plane, Wellman decided to name it. He asked his mechanic to paint the name "Celia" (after his mother) on the fuselage. Prophetically, the mechanic added the numeral "I" after the name. By the time he left Escadrille N. 87, Wellman was flying Celia V.

On December 10, his friend from Avord, Tommy Hitchcock, was assigned to N. 87. Being the only Americans, the two teamed up and soon became a formidable strafing team. Both were reckless, bordering on foolhardy, and took repeated risks in their competitive missions. Once they found themselves deep into enemy territory and rather than hightailing it for home, they decided to single-handedly wreak a little havoc at a German air field. They aimed their machine guns at the German aircraft lined up on the field and then turned their sights on the hangars. They hoped to hit something flammable and start a fire, but were unsuccessful. Finally the anti-aircraft guns drove them back, but they had left considerable damage behind them.

The remainder of the month of December was relatively quiet. The flyers spent their time doing routine chores, flying occasional patrols, "except when the weather was bad. We had a few occasional skirmishes with the Germans but little else." On January 19, this period of inactivity was to come to an end. Wellman and Hitchcock were flying as escorts to a Letord on a photographic mission when they were suddenly under attack by a German Rumpler. The German pilot brought down one of the Nieuports in Wellman's party, but Wellman and Hitchcock finally brought him down. The victory was Wellman's first and for it he received the coveted Croix de Guerre.

Young Billy Wellman in 1918.

Wellman spoke affectionately of Tommy Hitchcock for
the rest of his life. "After he came to Luneville we flew as
team mates almost constantly. Since he was the only other
American in the Escadrille ... we became chums who were
as close as brothers," Wellman wrote in 1918. "What a flyer
and fighter he was--a sure 'ace' in the making, although his
record was then only two official and two unofficial planes."

In his first volume of memoirs, A Short Time for Insanity, Wellman says this about Tommy Hitchcock:

> We trained together at Avord. Went through acro-
> batics together at Pau. Ended up together at the
> front in Luneville in the Alsace-Lorraine. Flew
> patrols together, shot up enemy airdromes together,
> shot down a German Rumpler and a Fokker together.
> Lived together. Dropped President Wilson's mes-
> sage to Congress on America's entrance into the
> war, translated into German, in the front-line
> trenches together. Went to Paris together. Hell,
> we did everything together, and on two occasions
> he saved my life. Tom was a ten-goal polo player.
> Tom was a ten-goaler in everything. It is very
> difficult to write what you really think of a great
> friend if it be a man ... how the hell do you say
> I love a man?

Watching Wings, one is struck by how like Wellman
and Hitchcock are Jack Powell and David Armstrong (Buddy
Rogers and Richard Arlen). And the list of strong male relationships in Wellman's films is a lengthy one. For all his
rough and ready reputation, Wellman understood the tender-
ness of friendship and put it on the screen many times. It
is hard not to trace that feeling back to Tommy Hitchcock.

On March 6, 1918, Hitchcock was brought down in
enemy territory, with a wound in the stomach and one in the
thigh. He was placed in a German hospital until he recovered
sufficiently to be removed to a prison compound at Lechfeld.
In an incident like that in Jean Renoir's Grand Illusion (1937),
Hitchcock and several other prisoners painstakingly planned
an escape and on the day it was to be executed, they were
transferred to another camp.

During the transfer, Hitchcock leaped from the train
and a week later slipped over the border into Switzerland.

After the war, he returned to the sport of polo, in which he
was an outstanding athlete. He was killed in an aerial dogfight in World War II. Wrote Wellman,

> With Tom gone I felt lost myself, for we had flown
> so much together that I had come to depend on him
> and I trusted him absolutely. Shortly after Tom's
> disappearance I asked, and received, permission to
> fly as a one-man patrol thereafter, except when we
> were called upon for special squadron duty.

Shortly before Hitchcock's capture, Wellman and Hitchcock were given ten days' leave in Paris and $100 each in
prize money for their part in bringing down a German plane.
This small honor was treated with enthusiasm back in Newton
where Wellman's exploits were written up in the papers with
all the pomp due a local war hero. At Trinity Episcopal
Church in Newton Centre, where Wellman had been a member
of the choir, his name was placed on a tablet of names of
Newtonians in the war and a star was placed on the church's
service flag in his honor. In addition, there was a special
feature in the Sunday evening service which celebrated his
achievements.

Wellman's friend Douglas Fairbanks happened to see
one of the articles in the paper and was impressed with Wellman's bravery. Wellman remembered, "I got lucky one day
and the newspapers built it up as they always do and you'd
have thought that I had won the war. And Doug sent me a
cablegram which said, 'When it's all over, you'll always have
a job.'" Even more than Wellman's bravery in the air,
Fairbanks might have been moved by a passage in a newspaper article which read, "It is interesting to note that after
Mr. Wellman was refused enlistment in the American aviation
service last summer, he went across and endured many pri-
vations as a beginner in the French Service, where pay is
but $6.00 and $8.00 per month, and where he lived mostly
on horse flesh and wormy bread." Surely there was a place
in Hollywood for such a man.

But the movies would have to wait, for Wellman's
shining hour in combat was still to come. On March 9, 1918,
he was informed that the Rainbow Division--an American division so-named because of the various cardinal colors that de-
noted many different branches of service--was preparing an
all-out frontal attack on German lines and that he would fly
cover for them as leader of the lowest-flying patrol.

At the appointed time I led my patrol over the front
lines where I could view the trench systems of our
forces and those of the enemy. At precisely 1600
hours the Allied artillery opened fire with a devas-
tating barrage ... suddenly I was filled with an
immense pride and choked (with) emotion for I realized that I was the only American pilot in the air
at the time.

During the incredible battle below, Wellman engaged
in dogfight after dogfight. When the smoke cleared, it was
reported that he had brought down two planes, a Rumpler and
an Albatross I. III. For this impressive victory, he received
a second gold palm leaf to his Croix de Guerre and a second
citation. These two planes were to be his only confirmed
solo victories.

On March 21, Wellman was flying solo patrol when he
was caught in a barrage of German anti-aircraft fire. He
was successful in eluding the shells for awhile but without
warning a shell exploded directly in front of him. At first
he thought that Celia V had not been hit, but it became apparent that shrapnel had done its work and that he had lost
control of the plane. It plunged toward earth as Wellman
helplessly tried to maneuver it out of a certain crash. The
plane dived into a grove of fir trees and Wellman was thrown
from the plane, which was totally wrecked.

He lay on the ground, dazed. Finally, he felt that he
had the strength to try to stand, but when he tried, he was
nearly paralyzed with a severe pain in his back. He was
taken to the hospital and grounded while examinations were
underway to determine the extent of his injuries.

His back was not broken, but was seriously wrenched.
The back injury was also sufficient to cause internal bleeding,
which left Wellman with periodic moments of black-out. In
addition, a piece of shrapnel was imbedded in his nose, about
an eighth of an inch from his eye. Minor surgery was required to remove it.

The injury to his back would trouble Wellman for the
rest of his life, sometimes leaving him bed-ridden for days
at a time. Joseph Youngerman, Wellman's assistant director
at Paramount in the late thirties, recalled taking a diatherm
machine on location for Beau Geste (1939) to give Wellman
treatments each day. Indeed, the pain in Wellman's back,

plus the resulting arthritis, was a prime reason for his relative inactivity in the early forties.

In 1918, though, that cloud had a definite silver lining;
it meant that he was going home. He was given an honorable
discharge from the French Army and the Lafayette Flying
Corps on March 29. He was given leave in Paris to await
a transfer to Bordeaux where he was to board the French
liner Espagne and sail to New York.

Back at his parents' home in Newton, Wellman spent
most of his time in rest and recuperation from his injuries.
He was a popular speaker at War Bond rallies and was treated
very much the hero. The inactivity of those days started to
do its work on him, though, and he began to itch to get back
into action somehow. He was approached by Page Company Publishing house in Boston to gather his recollections
of his experiences overseas into a book. With the help of a
staff writer (quite a lot of help, probably) he soon produced
Go, Get 'Em, an exciting account of "the true adventures of
an American aviator of the Lafayette Flying Corps who was
the only Yankee flyer fighting over General Pershing's boys
of the Rainbow Division in Lorraine when they first went over
the top."

The publication of Go, Get 'Em in late 1918 put Wellman back into the public eye for a while and the constant
topic of war made him restless to get back into the air. His
injuries precluded any more combat, but he soon enlisted in
the U.S. Air Service and was commissioned First Lieutenant.
He was transferred to Rockwell Field in San Diego to become
a flight instructor, where his students included Ira Eaker and
"Tooey" Spaatz, who later became ace pilots in World War
II.

Wellman was ordered one day to put on an exhibition
for a visiting inspection mission from Washington. His commander suggested that Wellman show them "something they've
never seen before." Wellman described the events of that
day ruefully.

> I had a Spad down there and everybody else had
> Thomas Morse scouts--the worst thing that any guy
> ever flew. All these Congressmen were assembled,
> and I took off. Well, I was going to do a barrel
> roll just getting off, you know, but I missed by six
> inches and I cracked up, and I showed them some-

thing they'd never seen before in their lives ... and
ended up in the hospital, fractured skull, knocked
my teeth out. Wonderful.

This nasty accident interrupted a popular period in
Wellman's life. The War Effort still in full swing, who
could be more attractive than a handsome flyer in "a neat
blue uniform, with two pair of wings, French and Lafayette,
a couple of medals, wounded with a slight limp that I never
let myself forget a moment. One of the very first daring
young American fliers to return to his native land. I got attention everywhere." Wellman took advantage of the nation's
sentimentality for its Boys In Uniform and he took greater
advantage of his new location, so close to Hollywood and the
most glamorous people in the world who found him glamorous.
"There were a lot of strange new people there, actors and
actresses, and they liked me and the uniform and the medals;
and I was very humble and my limp was eye-catching."

Before the war ended, Wellman found himself married
to a beautiful young movie actress, Helene Chadwick. Before
the two met, at a dinner given by director Louis Gasnier,
Helene had been making pictures for about three years. Her
career had not really taken off by 1918 and she was biding
her time by appearing in serials and "B" pictures. At about
the time they married, Helene secured a contract at the
Goldwyn Studio at which time she embarked on a period of
middle-level stardom that she would keep up through the
twenties.

The marriage was neither long nor happy, but it lasted
long enough to see Wellman change careers. When they married, he was a flight instructor at Rockwell Field. Six months
later, when they had separated, he was, surprisingly, an actor in a cowboy picture.

CHAPTER THREE

This turn of events had come about as a result of a remembered telegram from Douglas Fairbanks. As the war ended, Wellman began to realize that there was not much place for a fighter pilot in peace-time. His term of enlistment in the U.S. Air Service ended with the war. Again, as when he left high school four years earlier, he wondered just what he was going to do with his life. His brother, Arthur, offered him a place in the wool business again, but Wellman remembered the first time and let this particular opportunity slip away. Things looked a little bleak until Fairbanks' cable came to mind.

Wellman suddenly recalled that Fairbanks had telegraphed a message to him the year earlier, which read, "Great work boy we are proud of you when you get home there is a job waiting for you." When he had first received the cable, he didn't take it very seriously. For one thing, he couldn't imagine himself in the motion picture business. What would he do?

Now, however, things were different. Wellman needed a job and Fairbanks had offered one. Whether or not Fairbanks had just been polite by making the offer was something that Wellman was going to have to risk.

On February 5, 1919, Fairbanks had formed United Artists with Mary Pickford, Charles Chaplin, and D. W. Griffith. The immense popularity and power of these four people made the move toward incorporation a logical one, though it prompted a studio head to remark, "The lunatics

have taken over the asylum." Before Fairbanks could start
to make pictures for the new company, he fulfilled a contractual obligation for one more film for Artcraft: The Knickerbocker Buckaroo.

Wellman could hardly have picked a more appropriate
time to see Fairbanks about that job. The day he showed up
at the set, dressed to the nines in his full dress uniform,
complete with medals, Fairbanks was in the process of casting The Knickerbocker Buckaroo. Marjorie Daw was to be
his leading lady and there was a part, a juvenile role, which
called for a young man to play her brother. Wrote Wellman,

> Meeting Douglas was like old times. He didn't ask
> me what I wanted to do, just cast me as the young
> brother of Marjorie Daw in the western he was
> about to start in a week. He introduced me to Al-
> bert Parker, his director, Ted Reed, the production
> manager, Bernie Ziedman, the publicity director,
> and to the assistant director; and presto, I was an
> actor, playing the juvenile lead with Douglas Fair-
> banks in The Knickerbocker Buckaroo at $250 a
> week. Hell, I would have committed murder for
> that kind of money.

In many ways, The Knickerbocker Buckaroo was a
typical Fairbanks vehicle. The story concerned an effete,
frivolous young fellow named Teddy Drake, who had nothing
better to do with his time and money than to wreak havoc at
his exclusive club. His habit of leaping around the furniture
and creating bedlam among the exclusive members results in
his being expelled from the club and avoided by his society
friends.

In order to redeem himself, he decides to devote his
life to making others happy and, with that in mind, blindly
selects a spot on the map and heads there. He arrives in
a southwestern town, near the Mexican border where he becomes involved with a beautiful young woman (Daw) and her
brother (Wellman) who are being harassed by a crooked sheriff and his gang into revealing where they have hidden a large
amount of money.

The simple plot was probably nothing more than an
elaborate excuse for Doug to leap about, on and off horses,
trains and various other moving objects. Existing synopses
of the film suggest that there were no fewer than three major

DOUGLAS
FAIRBANKS
in
"The Knickerbocker Buckaroo"
An ARTCRAFT Picture
Directed by Albert Parker

6 Months to Make--7 Reels--Cost $264,000

SIX months to make "The Knickerbocker Buckaroo"! That's 184 days!

Seven reels! That means 77 solid minutes of the Douglas Fairbanks brand of entertainment!

"Doug" spent two and a half days making every minute of amusement that you get from this picture!

He's made you wait a long time for one of his pictures but now it's here!

"Doug" thought out a lot of new stunts during those six months. For instance:

He leaves the window of a flying train, climbs over the car's side to the roof, runs along the roof to the mail-coach, is swung from that car to the station by the mail conveyor like a sack of fourth-class mail, dropping onto the back of a horse that gallops madly off.

That's only one of his stunts! That's only one of the laughs! You can't afford to miss all the rest.

chases, which was exactly the sort of thing that audiences
loved to see Doug do.

The shooting schedule was exceptionally long for the
period. In fact, the schedule and the budget became so extended that Artcraft decided that the best defense was an of-
fense; they proudly crowed about the exorbitant cost of the
film--$264,000. A press release trumpted,

> Six months to make The Knickerbocker Buckaroo!
> That's 184 days! Seven reels! That means 77
> solid minutes of the Douglas Fairbanks brand of
> entertainment! "Doug" spent two and a half days
> making every minute of amusement that you get
> from this picture! He's made you wait a long time
> for one of his pictures but now it's here!

The New York Times review of May 26, 1919, claims,
"The photoplay bears out the reports of the cost of its production. It was elaborately staged, where elaborateness
would count and Albert Parker, the director, must have used
his good eye for scenic effects." Unfortunately, we must
take the word of reviewers as to The Knickerbocker Buckaroo's quality, for it, like virtually all of the rest of Wellman's silent work, has been lost.

Wellman loved the experience of making the picture.
He was not quite comfortable with the idea of acting, but this
really didn't seem like acting. The days were busy ones,
"learning how to ride, interviews, rehearsals, photographic
tests, meeting friends of Doug's ... I was living." He spent
the week preceding the start of the picture trying to get to
the point that he looked as though he had been born on a
horse.

He enjoyed the action aspects of this business, but
there were many other things that bothered him. "The toughest thing for me to get accustomed to was this makeup ritual," he complained. "A makeup man slops this yellow crap
on your face; at first it feels kind of slimy then it dries, and
your face starts to pucker up. Christ, I looked like a baby."

Besides the uncomfortable (and, one suspects, the
slightly effeminate-feeling) makeup, Wellman began to ob-
serve the less desirable aspects of stardom. He commented,

> I could see that Doug's life was not his own. He

had to share it with all kinds of people and obligations that you acquire when you work for the public.
Doug was a servant, a well-paid one, but everything
he did or said or thought had to be screened, carefully blueprinted to suit the tastes of the great
American public.

Wellman didn't want that kind of public life. Though
he was very attracted to this business, he had begun looking
around for other options, even before The Knickerbocker Buckaroo had finished shooting.

When the film received its premiere, Wellman went
to the Egyptian Theatre ("I think it was the Egyptian Theatre")
to see how he had done. What he saw appalled him and confirmed his decision to find another job in the movie industry.
"It was so frightful, really, to me, that I just stayed for
half the picture and then I went out and vomited for no reason at all, " he remembered, ruefully.

Now he was sure. He certainly didn't want to continue in the acting profession. Again, he went to Fairbanks
to ask for help. "Doug understood my feelings completely,"
he said. Fairbanks asked him, "Well, what do you want to
be?" Wellman asked how much Albert Parker had been paid
for directing The Knickerbocker Buckaroo. When Fairbanks
told him, he immediately replied, "I want to be a director."
The decision was, he was fond of saying, "purely financial."

Even Fairbanks' sphere of influence could do only so
much with this request. He couldn't just appoint a kid with
one picture under his belt a director, but he did what he
could: he got Wellman a job in the production department
at the Goldwyn Studios. Fairbanks warned Wellman that he
might have to start at the bottom, but both of them had great
confidence in Wellman's abilities to learn and to adapt and it
seemed quite possible that he could work his way up to the
job he wanted: directing.

Before he began work at Goldwyn, Wellman had one
more acting job to do. He had signed a contract at $400
per week to play a British sub-lieutenant in Raoul Walsh's
Evangeline. The film starred Walsh's wife, Miriam Cooper,
and co-starred Albert Roscoe. Though Wellman had a lifelong favorite anecdote about the making of the film, there is
really no proof that he was ever actually filmed in any of the
scenes.

> I got four weeks' guarantee, [the story goes] and
> the first thing I did was to wade out into a very
> easy, very soft surf and take the leading lady in
> my arms and carry her in. I was [wearing a]
> white wig. I looked like a fairy and on the way
> in she smelled so nice, she was lovely, and I held
> her a little too tight, and she liked it, so I went,
> as you might say, on the make. And she was kind
> of cuddling up and everything else. And suddenly
> I kissed her and I walked into a hole. And this
> beautiful little thing became a tigress, because she
> didn't know how to swim. And when she did come
> up, the only thing I could do was to cold-cock her
> and carry her in and deposit her at Raoul Walsh's
> feet. It happened to be his wife. So they fired
> me, you see.

The story is amusing, but, like many of Wellman's
patented yarns, must be taken with a substantial grain of
salt. For the record, both Raoul Walsh and Miriam Cooper
denied that Wellman was ever on the picture at all.

In the spring of 1919, Wellman reported to the Goldwyn Studio's production department. As he had been warned,
he did have to start at the bottom.

He was asked, "What did you get as an actor?"

"I got four hundred a week on my last picture."

"Four hundred a week, huh," came the reply.

"Well, here you are a messenger boy, and you get
twenty-two dollars a week."

Thus, in one fell swoop, his brief celebrity and briefer
prosperity came to an abrupt halt. To add insult to injury,
he was informed that, among the stars on his regular delivery
route was his former wife, Helene Chadwick.

Actually, she was not quite his "former wife" yet.
They had married on December 21, 1918, and had separated
only a month later. There had been periodic stabs at reconciling, but they soon admitted defeat. Chadwick filed for de-
sertion on November 23, 1919. She was quoted in a fan magazine as having "hero worshipped" her husband and only after
marriage found that he was all too human.

His job as a messenger boy at Goldwyn was an un-
eventful one, aside from the indignity of delivering mail to
his estranged wife, now a fairly important star.   Still, he
began to be impatient about becoming a director.   He looked
around at the other messenger boys ("Boys?   Not a one under age.   The head messenger boy was old enough to be my
dad. ") and knew that none of them would ever break out of
their unimportant little jobs.

There was a billboard on the lot that listed all of
Goldwyn's contract directors.   Wellman would often stand in
front of it, gazing at the names "that were doing what I hoped
to do someday.   What had they all within themselves that
made them successful directors?   There was no school for
directors, no particular education that was necessary, no
college degrees, just the complete know-how of making a
picture, great desire, unending work, and the great privilege
of having lived unusual and exciting lives. "   He had already
led quite an exciting and unusual life, but he needed something more; he needed a break.

The break came from, of all people, Will Rogers.
The beloved humorist and "part-time movie star" was on
Wellman's mail route.   They got to know each other slightly
and when Wellman confided to Rogers that he wanted to be a
director, Rogers introduced Wellman to head propman James
Flood, who needed an assistant.

Wellman wrote of their meeting, "Jim walked in; we
shook hands.   He looked me all over and I him.   We liked
what we saw.   I became an assistant to an expert, and I
learned more from Jimmy than from anyone else I came in
contact with in all the forty-odd years of my experience in
the making of motion pictures. "   Flood was, himself, bound
to be a director which he became, ironically, in the same
year (1923) and at the same studio (Fox) as his apprentice,
Wellman.

Wellman worked with Flood on six films with Will
Rogers: Jubilo (1919), Jes' Call Me Jim (1920), Cupid the
Cowpuncher (1920), Honest Punch (1920), Guile of Women
(1921), and Boys Will Be Boys (1921)--all directed by Clarence Badger.

Though James Flood had the head start on Wellman,
they were soon running neck and neck.   Flood became an assistant director in 1921 and director in 1923, which job he

kept except for occasional assistant director jobs with Ernst
Lubitsch on pictures like The Marriage Circle (1924) and
Three Women (1924). He never became a major director,
though, and Wellman easily surpassed him in skill and success.

After working as assistant propman on the Rogers pictures, Wellman received another unexpected boost in his career. He had gotten where he was thus far, not by what he
knew, but whom he knew. His uncles pulled strings to get
him into the Lafayette Flying Corps, Douglas Fairbanks pulled
strings to get him into the Goldwyn Studio, Will Rogers pulled
strings to get him into the actual production end of the business. Now he was to get a hand from most unexpected quarters: no less a personage than General Pershing.

It was announced to all employees of the studio that
Pershing would be making a visit and all ex-servicemen were
"requested" to wear their uniforms for the review. After
having his blue French uniform "rejuvenated" by the wardrobe
department, Wellman assumed his place at the head of the
line (he said he was placed there for "the international fla-
vor").

Pershing arrived and everyone snapped to attention,
for "this general was the general," Wellman wrote. "He
looked over at his motley lineup of ex-everythings, with not
a particular happy expression on his face. He was much
more interested in what was gathered in a sweet-smelling
handful at the end of the line." After the servicemen,
Pershing was to have the pleasure of reviewing the Goldwyn
starlets. Pershing started down the long line, "shaking the
sixty-five hard-worked calloused hands to get to the lovely,
soft, well-manicured ones that awaited him."

Anxious to get the ordeal over with, Pershing shook
the first hand offered: Wellman's. He continued down the
line, then paused and turned back. "Where have I seen you
before?" he asked. Wellman thought back to his first meeting with Pershing, in Paris, in a rather compromising position at a brothel there. He replied, "General, I had better
not say where, right here."

Pershing smiled. "That's it. How have you been?"
The two chatted for a moment and Pershing asked Wellman
if there was any assistance that he could offer the struggling
would-be director.

"You could make me pretty important here," Wellman replied, "if you would take me under that tree for a few minutes and just talk to me." Pershing and Wellman strolled away from the crowd and for three or four minutes of torturous suspense for the studio heads, the two chatted away quite chummily.

"It worked like a charm," Wellman wrote. "The next day I was called into the vice-president's palatial office and taken into the president's super-palatial office and introduced to Mr. Goldwyn, who shook my hand and said in perfect English that I was the type of young man he wanted working for him." He had received what was becoming a characteristic boost from a helpful higher-up. He was now an assistant director.

Since Wellman had been working on the Will Rogers Pictures with director Clarence Badger, it was only logical that he make his bow as assistant director with the same director/star combination. He was assigned to work on The Poor Relation. Of its director, Wellman recalled years later, "Clarence Badger was a man I was very fond of and he had a delightful sense of humor. I learned a lot from him. And yet if you talked to him, or knew him, you'd think he was the dullest man in the world."

He did not remember the next director he worked with in such glowing terms. "E. Mason Hopper could have been one of the finest directors, but he was completely crazy." Wellman worked on such films with Hopper as From the Ground Up (1921), Hold Your Horses (1921), and The Glorious Fool (1922). The first and last of these films featured Wellman's ex-wife, Helene Chadwick. Her presence on the set caused him some disquiet, and that, combined with the personality of the director, caused Wellman to start looking around at other studios. Hopper was, Wellman said, "a horrible little bastard. He was a nut! He'd rather cook than make pictures; he was a much better chef than he was a director. He was a little screwy, but he had great talent, he really did. No one liked him, though."

The exact number of features that Wellman worked on as an assistant director at Goldwyn is not known, though it is reasonably certain that he assisted Alfred Green in Just Out of College and, perhaps, some other titles.

In February 1922, he left Goldwyn to go to Fox Film

Corporation. Probably his first work there was done on Iron
to Gold, directed by Bernard J. Durning. Durning liked to
work fast, and the feature was released on March 12, 1922.

Durning was, perhaps, the greatest influence on Wellman's filmmaking. Though not one of his films survives today, it's most probable that Wellman absorbed more from
Durning's technique than from any other director whom he
assisted. "Bernie was six feet six, and besides being a director he was an actor--and a bad one. He was the hand-
somest guy I've ever seen in my life."

Wellman assisted Durning on such features as Fast
Mail (1922), Oath Bound (1922), Strange Idols (1922), While
Justice Waits (1922), Yosemite Trail (1922) and The Eleventh
Hour (1923). "He gave me two of the greatest years I've
ever had," Wellman said, "and taught me more than anybody
in the business. He made all those thrilling melodramas and
you learned everything from them--action, pacing, stunts.
This was the greatest school a director ever had."

Wellman didn't work exclusively with Durning during
his first two years at Fox. He also worked with men like
Emmett Flynn on A Fool There Was (1922), Monte Cristo
(1922), Without Compromise (1922), and Hell's Hole (1923);
Harry Beaumont on Lights of the Desert (1922) and Very
Truly Yours (1922); and Colin Campbell on Three Who Paid
(1923), Bucking the Barrier (1923), and The Buster (1923).

Already, Wellman's nickname of "Wild Bill" was getting to be well known, as the star of Three Who Paid, Bessie
Love, remembers:

> We went miles out on location, oh ... simply miles
> out from Hollywood ... and I discovered I had no
> spirit gum to fix my wig [the plot involved Love
> impersonating a boy]. Bill said, "That's all right.
> Lepage's Glue will do it." "Oh, Bill," I said,
> "that's for furniture!" "It sticks wigs on as well,"
> he replied ... this was too much for him!
>   Well, I took some convincing, but finally we
> used Lepage's Glue. It stuck the wig on all right,
> but when I got back at night I couldn't get it off.
> It was stuck fast to my long hair which had been
> curled up underneath.

Wellman's love for practical jokes was lifelong and he

didn't care how rough they got. "Whenever I was walking on
the lot," Love recalls, "wherever I was and whomever I was
with, the moment I heard Bill yell my name I'd start running.
I knew if he caught me he'd bring me down with a football
tackle.   It didn't matter what I was wearing.   It was a gag
with him.   He'd call my name and I'd start running.   I knew
what would happen...."

On location in Eureka, California, Wellman was working with Durning on a film called Strange Idols with Dustin
Farnum and Doris Pawn.   It was the story of a lumberjack
who marries a New York cabaret dancer and brings her back
to the Great Northwest.   She doesn't like the rustic life and
eventually goes back to dancing.

The scene being shot on this particular occasion con-
sisted of Pawn dreaming of the Bright Lights from her wilderness home.   As the New York skyline was to be superimposed
on the film, Pawn was to break into tears.   The three-piece
combo prepared to play some heartbreaking melody and Durning gave Pawn her instructions.   Then, Wellman recalled,
"he screamed for quiet.   The world stopped, all except the
fiddle, the cello and the portable organ.   The script girl
sniffed, the wardrobe mistress started to cry softly ... and
Bernie looked at his leading lady with hope in his eyes.
Nothing happened.   She was as dry as a parched throat."

Take after take was ruined due to Pawn's inability to
come up with any tears, until, finally, she told Durning how
to make her cry.   Durning walked over to Wellman with a
concerned look on his face.   "You know what she said?" he
asked.   "She said 'call me dirty names and then hit me.'
How the hell am I going to hit her?"   He brightened and remembered who was the director and who was the assistant.
"Look, Bill.   You do it."

Wellman was finally coerced into telling her off in no
delicate language and capping off his soliloquy with a well-
aimed kick in the ass.   "That pulled the finger out of the
dyke," he wrote, "and she cried and cried and cried, and
the mascara got in her eyes and she cried some more and
the camera got it all.   And when Bernie yelled 'Cut!,' the
troop applauded; the dumb dame thought it was for her and
with bowed head took her curtain call."   Wellman often said
that that was the day he learned how to direct.

Though Durning was large, handsome and energetic,

he was not really the picture of health. By the time Wellman met him, Durning was dying of tuberculosis. He faced the disease by drinking; not constantly, but periodically and seriously. He told Wellman that when he felt a binge coming on, then he would turn to Wellman to get the picture done.

Durning, to Wellman's knowledge, never drank to excess in all of the films they made together, but the dreaded "occasion" was approaching. The film was The Eleventh Hour, which had all the ingredients of a twelve-chapter serial packed into seven reels. A Mad Scientist is attempting to take over the world, but his plans are thwarted by the Chief of the U.S. Secret Service. The denouement comes only after "many complications--wild chases involving motor boats, airplanes and submarines; fights with lions; and a rescue from a threatened descent into a pit of molten steel" (The American Film Institute Catalog of Feature Films, 1921-30).

Wellman, in addition to his assistant director chores, found himself involved in acting, extra work and stunts. Durning was fearless himself and found no reason to exempt anyone in his crew from anything that would improve the picture. Wellman wrote,

> [Durning] once signaled the pilot to take off when I was standing on the tip of the wing [of an airplane], in the middle of the Los Angeles Harbor. [I was] doubling for Walter McGrail, and I became a wing walker for the first and last time. Bernie considered it an added thrill for his picture. He never had the slightest doubt that I wouldn't make it back into the cockpit. Let's put it this way: we just played rough.

The Eleventh Hour was an unusually rugged picture to make, but it was an important one for Wellman, for in the course of its filming, he got his first chance to direct. He told Kevin Brownlow how the chance came about.

> When we were down in San Diego, doing some air stuff at North Island, (Bernie) got one of his attacks. He called me up and told me he was in bed. "It's all yours, Willie," he said. I went out and shot that stuff and saved a day on schedule. When it was all over, we went back to the Fox Studio, and Winnie Sheehan and Sol Wurtzel, who were running the place, ran the stuff in the projection

room. None of the cast or technicians had said
anything about Bernie being off the picture--they
loved him too much. But he was up there in the
theater, and when it was all over he unwound himself and stood up. And, goddamn it, he stood high.
"How do you like that stuff?" he asked the two guys.
      "Bernie, it's as good, if not better than, any-
thing you've got in your other pictures. Congratu-
lations."
      "Congratulations, hell," he said, "I was on a
little trip that I make every once in a while--and I
was in bed all the time. Wellman did it; make him
a director. And by the way, Dustin [Farnum] is
crazy about him and so am I." Then he walked
out of the room and they made me a director right
then and there.

The Eleventh Hour was a beginning for Wellman, but
it was the end for Durning. Before Wellman's first film had
been released, only a month later, Durning was dead. Wellman wrote in the early sixties, "You don't have to write an
epitaph for Bernie, Bernie was his own epitaph. It has been
some forty-odd years since he died, and I still think of him
constantly."

It is appropriate that Wellman's first directoral chore
involved airplanes, for they would feature prominently in his
first great success four years later in Wings and remain a
theme that he would return to no fewer than eleven more
times in the next thirty-five years.

*   *   *

Wellman's first assignment as director was The Man
Who Won starring Dustin Farnum. Wellman knew Farnum
well, for they had worked together on a dozen occasions in
Durning's films and those of Colin Campbell. Durning had
advised Wellman, upon hearing of his upcoming official directing
debut, to take great care that Farnum's toupee never be dis-
lodged. "When you hire your actors," Durning said, "their
acting ability isn't as important as their allergy to that fore-
lock, especially in fight scenes."

Wellman took extra special care to keep Farnum's pate
covered and the film was a successful one. Interestingly, the
Farnum character in The Man Who Won was named "Wild
Bill." The source of the film was Ridgwell Cullum's novel

Twins of Suffering Creek, published in 1912. The title has
been the source of some confusion, for Wellman always listed
a film of that title, starring Dustin Farnum, as his first film
which, he said, was directed in 1920.

Though the film was successful and Wellman got along
well with Farnum, it was their last picture together. For
his second assignment Wellman was given a bootlegging story,
Second-Hand Love, starring the actor featured in The Eleventh
Hour, Charles "Buck" Jones. Though The Man Who Won had
been filmed first, Second-Hand Love was copyrighted first,
on August 12, 1923. Oddly, both features were put into release on exactly the same day, August 26, 1923.

The next five films that Wellman directed were very
much of a piece. They all starred Buck Jones, were all
scripted by Dorothy (Doty) Hobart, photographed by Joseph
August (except The Circus Cowboy, which was shot by Joseph
Brotherton) and featured Marion Nixon (with the exception of
Not a Drum Was Heard, in which the female lead was played
by Betty Bouton).

None of the films have survived and so it is impossible to ascertain what their quality was. Only Big Dan has
some surviving footage--reels 2, 3 and 5 of the six-reel
feature--and what is there looks very tantalizing.

Big Dan was released on October 14, 1923. It is the
story of a boxer who returns from an army stint during the
First World War to find that his wife has left him. He decides to put his skills to use and opens a boys' camp at his
home and trains the kids to be boxers. The existing footage
is fragmented, of course, and has the extra impediment to
the English-speaking viewer of having Czech sub-titles. Still,
August's photography is beautiful in a sun-drenched, pastoral
way and there exists an exciting boxing scene with Jones and
Ben Hendricks. Big Dan is a marvelously relaxed film, the
sort of project that seems to indicate that everyone involved
in the making of it had no illusions about "Art," no intent of
making something big and important. It's the sort of gentle
picture that Wellman had a particular fondness for, especially
later in his career with films like The Happy Years and Goodbye, My Lady.

Cupid's Fireman, released on December 16, 1923,
starred Jones as a fireman who joins the force against his
mother's wishes and who rescues a beautiful woman from a

Charles "Buck" Jones and Marion Nixon in Big Dan. This
is the earliest of Wellman's films to survive in part: three
of its six reels have been salvaged.

fire, later marrying her. Wellman had little to say about
the film except, "Best fire picture I've ever seen ... well,
that's something."

Not a Drum Was Heard, released the next month, was
an early example of Wellman's keen interest in friendship and
loyalty between men. Jones plays Jacks Mills, a man who
loses his sweetheart to his best friend, Bud Loupel (William
Scott). When Bud turns robber, stealing money from the
bank where he works to make up his delinquent house-
payments, Jack takes the blame by holding up the bank and
pretending to rob the money already stolen by his friend.

It is a typical show of loyalty in a Wellman film.
That Jack stands by his friend through all the twists and
turns of the plot confirms Wellman's reverence for male-
bonding, a relationship that he finds, ultimately, more sacred than the sexual union between man and woman. Jack's
beau geste anticipates a dozen more like it, still to come in
so many of Wellman's films. Characters in Wings, You
Never Know Women, Beggars of Life, Other Men's Women,
Central Airport, The Purchase Price, Men with Wings, The
Great Man's Lady, Thunder Birds, and others willingly sacrifice their romantic relationships in order to strengthen and
support their fraternal ones.

The Vagabond Trail (March 9, 1924) anticipates another
important Wellman interest: brotherly love and conflict. In
this one, Jones plays Donnegan, a man searching for his
long-lost brother. To this end, Donnegan becomes a hobo.
When he is thrown from a train by a rail detective, he is
found and nursed back to health by a miner and his daughter.
Donnegan finds that his brother is the dishonest partner of
the miner and is forced into conflict with the brother he has
searched for.

Brothers in conflict show up in several of Wellman's
films, most prominently in The Public Enemy, Woman Trap
and Track of the Cat. More broadly, The Vagabond Trail
shows an early example of Wellman's near obsession with
family. There is virtually no Wellman film that does not
augment the portraits of the main characters by showing
them with their families. Even those that don't actually
show characters with their families send familial mementos
along to make their presence felt, such as the phonograph
record in The Story of G.I. Joe or the everpresent small-
town newspapers in Battleground. Wellman was, despite his

Buck Jones in <u>Not a Drum Was Heard</u>.

Marion Nixon and Buck Jones in Cupid's Fireman.

rugged reputation, overtly sentimental about his family and
this part of his personality, like so many other parts,
started to show up in his films from the very beginning.

Wellman's last film at Fox, The Circus Cowboy, is
not particularly typical of his work (at least on paper--re-
member that none of these films is available for viewing).
The film was released on May 11, 1924, and as the title im-
plies, it is a circus story, which is a location that Wellman
never returned to.   He did direct (uncredited) scenes from
the 1955 Batjac production Ring of Fear, which is a circus
story.   However, it is rather typical of the rest of the Buck
Jones films in its basic premise.   After a two-year absence,
Buck Saxon (Jones) returns home to find that his sweetheart
has married another man.   Jones consistently loses sweet-
hearts in these pictures: in Big Dan he gets back from overseas to find that his wife has deserted him; in Not a Drum
Was Heard he loses his sweetheart to his best friend.

In all of the films, the losing of a girlfriend results
in Jones's finding a new life for himself and, coincidentally,
a new girl.   In this case, he runs off to join the circus.
There is a sub-plot that has him accused of murder, but he
is acquitted through the efforts of a pretty tightrope walker,
Bird (Marion Nixon).

All in all, Wellman's debut films as a director were
successful.   He was already building a reputation as a fast
worker, a director who, more often than not, brought in his
pictures ahead of schedule and under-budget.   He still had
not brought his salary back up to his actor's pay of $400 a
week, though; his salary at Fox after having completed seven
feature films with one of the most popular cowboy stars in
Hollywood, was $185 per week.

He decided that he was worth a bit more and went into
the vice-president in charge of production and told him so.
"I went in and told the guy, 'I think I'm doing a pretty good
job here and I'd like a raise.'   The guy said to me, 'I'll give
you a raise.   You're fired.'"

Wellman had not been prepared for such a response.
Possibly, he could have talked himself back into the job, but
his pride kept him from what he felt would be groveling.   He
told an interviewer, "After [being fired], I couldn't land another job for a year.   No one would look at my Fox pictures.
I used to steal milk off of doorsteps, swipe what I could from

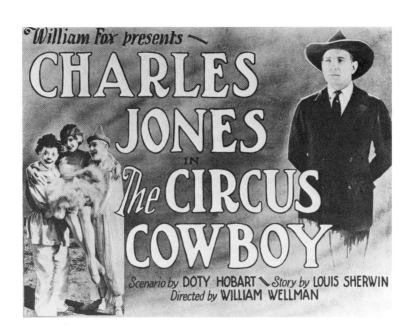

William Fox presents ~

CHARLES JONES

IN

The CIRCUS COWBOY

Scenario by DOTY HOBART ~ *Story by* LOUIS SHERWIN
Directed by WILLIAM WELLMAN

William Fox presents

BUCK JONES

IN

The VAGABOND TRAIL

Story by GEORGE OWEN BAXTER
Scenario by DOTY HOBART
Directed by
WILLIAM WELLMAN

the outdoor stands with which California is blessed, and borrow gas from some other fellow's car for my roadster. ''

Finally, in April 1925, Wellman was signed on at
Metro-Goldwyn-Mayer studios--but as an assistant director.
He was disappointed at the demotion, but he was thankful to
be working again. He was always restless and uneasy when
he wasn't working, but at the moment, he had a more important reason to be bringing home the bacon: he had just
made Margery Chapin Mrs. Wellman, number two.

Margery was a former singer and dancer in the Fol-
lies, but, refreshingly for Wellman, she had no ambition to
be in the movies. He remembered,

> I met her at the Hollywood Hotel one night when I
> was having dinner with my good friend Ward Crane.
> Every time Ward saw me looking lean and hungry,
> he'd ask me in to spend a few days with him.
>   Margery, who was visiting her brother--an as-
> sistant director at MGM*--was sitting at the table
> next to us on this particular night. Ward intro-
> duced me to her. For the next two weeks I enter-
> tained her ... on Ward's money. In six months
> we were married, with a wedding ring I bought
> from the five- and ten-cent store. It was a blaz-
> ing hot day. We drove up to Riverside and were
> married by a one-armed minister. All four tires
> on my car were ready to blow out and, as I had
> no spare, I was pretty worried about the heat.
> Our honeymoon consisted of listening to the organ
> recital in the Riverside Inn, and then, when it got
> cool, we came back to Hollywood.

Wellman was sure that this was the marriage for which
he had waited. Margery did not want to become a star, yet
she had enough interest in the motion picture business to understand the life her husband led and to support him. She
often worked with him as script girl. She seemed to be everything he looked for in a wife.

---

*Jacques "Jack" Chapin. After Margery's marriage to Well-
man, Chapin often worked on his pictures, usually in the capacity of propman, though he occasionally did stunts and, on
one occasion (Beggars of Life) appeared as an actor.

There was one thing that Margery could not give him, something that Wellman desperately wanted: a child. After a year of marriage had passed and she was still not pregnant, she consulted a physician, who told her that she could never bear children. Wellman did not take the news well and this news was the beginning of the end of their marriage. Knowing how he wanted children, Margery suggested that they adopt. Wellman grudgingly agreed.

On March 25, 1926, they adopted a pretty, spirited two-year-old girl, named Gloria. He came to think highly of the baby, though he never really thought of her as his own child, and when Wellman and Margery divorced in 1928, Gloria was given into the custody of her mother. However, when Margery remarried (to comedian Benny Baker), Gloria was shunted off to a series of foster homes. She grew up a bitter, troubled girl and was to live a sad, if eventful, life. Oddly, she later found that her real father had also been a director: Robert Tansey, most noted for his "B" westerns.

Though the future was to be rather troubled, things looked bright in early 1925. Wellman was assigned as assistant director to Edmund Goulding, himself a new director and recent refugee from Fox, on Sally, Irene and Mary. Goulding "had a lot of faith in me and sold me to the officials," Wellman said and he was soon given a real directing job.

The only trouble was, that it wasn't his own film. Robert Vignola had been shooting a picture called The Way of a Girl with Eleanor Boardman and the powers-that-be were not at all pleased with the way it was turning out. Taking Goulding's recommendation, they gave Wellman the thankless job of "cleaning it up." He shot about one third of the film, it was released to some success and Wellman moved up a notch in M-G-M's estimation.

They still were not quite ready to entrust a full feature to him, though, and gave him another "doctoring" job, this time on Josef von Sternberg's Escape (released as The Exquisite Sinner). This time the brass were very pleased and on May 26, 1925, Variety carried this brief item: "William Wellman, assistant director called in to finish Escape which Josef von Sternberg made for MGM, has been promoted to a directorship."

Oddly, after Wellman had done extensive re-shooting
on Escape, Phil Rosen was called in to re-shoot Wellman's
footage.   It is unknown whether any of Wellman's footage
ever reached the screen.

This was the least of his worries, now, for he was
given a picture of his own.   Actually, this film, too, had
been begun by Robert Vignola and then taken out of his hands.
The picture was called I'll Tell the World and starred George
K. Arthur, Lucille Le Sueur (Joan Crawford) and Gertrude Olmstead.   Though it looked at first as though it was going to be
another "doctor" job, Wellman was informed that he would
receive sole credit as director and, as if to prove the point,
he was assigned his own assistant, Nick Grinde (later to become a director himself).   Before release, I'll Tell the World
was retitled The Boob.

In the 1950's, producer Robert Youngson compiled a
feature film of silent comedy clips called MGM's Big Parade
of Comedy.   He inserted about sixty seconds of footage from
The Boob.   It is the only footage that survives from the film.
The scene is delightful.   It takes place in a speakeasy which
is designed to look like a library.   The books on the walls
have names which give a clue as to what's really inside: Old
Crow: Stories of Bird Life, Scotch Essays, Gunga Gin,
Three Plays by Brew.   Joan Crawford is the only star of
the film who appears in this clip; she plays a government
agent on the trail of bootleggers.   As she sits at a table
gathering evidence, the floor show begins.   Six dancers parade demurely onto the floor, dressed in hoop skirts and
carrying parasols.   They dance sedately for a moment until
a stage hand pulls a series of levers that pulls their dresses
off over their heads.   Now dressed only in their underwear
and the hoops from the vanished skirts, the girls go into a
frenzied Charleston.   Another level is pulled, the hoops are
whisked away and the six dancers finish their number as un-
dressed as the censors would allow.

As delightful as this brief clip is (it makes one doubly
sad that the feature is apparently gone for good), Wellman
never had a good word to say about the film.   "When (the
studio heads) saw the picture, they fired me because it was
so bad," he said.   "They changed her name from Lucille
Le Sueur to Joan Crawford.   So I enjoy the distinction, which
I'm very proud of, of having made the lousiest Joan Crawford
movie ever made."   Whether or not things happened as he
said, one thing is certain: The picture was completed in

Wellman goes over the script of I'll Tell the World (soon to be retitled The Boob) with stars George K. Arthur and Charles Murray.

September 1925. By the time it was released on May 17, 1926, Wellman was already signed with B. P. Schulberg's Preferred Pictures.

In fact, not a month had passed since the completion of The Boob when Wellman's next film hit the theaters. The film was called When Husbands Flirt and Wellman had directed it at Columbia Studios for Harry Cohn. When Cohn heard that Wellman was out of a job again, he approached him with a proposition: Cohn had a project, a good screenplay by Dorothy Arzner and some money--but not much. Cohn asked Wellman if he could finish the film in a week. Wellman said that, for a bonus, he'd go Cohn one better: he'd make When Husbands Flirt in five days. As it turned out, he even surprised himself by finishing the feature in just over three days. Cohn gladly gave him the bonus.

> We got six reels out of (it) [Wellman wrote] by bor-
> rowing long shots of big scenes in other pictures,
> by building corners of sets and cutting close shots
> into them, by re-writing to fit what we had or could
> steal, to give the picture production, by working so
> long and so hard that you could sleep standing up
> or sitting down, or lying on the floor or in your
> car with your feet sticking out.   This was making
> them the rugged way and learning the tough way,
> but learning how to put a jigsaw puzzle together
> quickly, cheaply, efficiently and presentably.

When Husbands Flirt was written by Dorothy Arzner, who had achieved some celebrity with her editing of Blood and Sand and The Covered Wagon some years earlier.   She went on to become the only female director working at a major studio in the 1930's.   The picture was a comedy of misunderstanding.   A newlywed (Forrest Stanley) lends his car to his "gay blade" partner (Tom Rickets) who uses it to go joy-riding.   The next day, his wife finds incriminating evidence in the car and prepares for a divorce.   Eventually, all is explained and the fade-out is a happy one.   Wellman, though, remembers the story quite differently: "Old man takes a dose of castor oil, leaves home for office, things start to move."   Since the film no longer exists, it is difficult to know if this decidedly odd sub-plot appears in the film or not.

At any rate, When Husbands Flirt had a happy ending for Wellman, too.   B. P. Schulberg saw the film and offered Wellman a job with his Preferred Pictures.   Cohn, who had been pleased at getting a good feature so quickly and cheaply, wanted Wellman to stay at Columbia.   "So they fought about me and Schulberg won.   He won by ten bucks.   Cohn offered me $200 a week and Schulberg offered me $210."   Wellman signed on at Preferred Pictures, but never made a picture there.   Almost immediately after Wellman signed on with the studio, B. P. Schulberg was appointed Head of Production at Famous Players-Lasky.

When Schulberg moved to Paramount, he took his most popular star, Clara Bow, with him.   Bow had been under a non-exclusive contract with Schulberg for a year appearing in six of his features throughout 1925.   Her roles in Preferred Pictures releases like Capital Punishment, Free to Love, Lawful Cheaters, My Lady's Lips, Parisian Love and The Plastic Age were fast making her one of the hottest actresses in Hollywood.

Schulberg brought his latest discovery with him as
well, but Wellman's name caused much less excitement
around the Paramount lot than did Bow's.   His first assignment was a Betty Bronson vehicle, The Cat's Pajamas.
("One of the most horrible pictures ever made," according
to Wellman.)

Wellman was instructed to bring Miss Bronson--best
known for her delightful portrayal of Peter Pan in Herbert
Brenon's 1924 film--into adulthood with her role in The
Cat's Pajamas.   Wellman complained to Schulberg that he
was asking the impossible.   "You don't want a director,"
he said, "you want a magician."   Schulberg replied, "Do
whatever you have to to make this a good picture.   Make
it tough.   Make The Cat's Pajamas The Lion's Bathrobe!"

"Peter Pan--that's what she was," Wellman said.
"She was a delightful little actress, but that's what she was,
and, to make a long story short, when she tried to be sexy,
she looked like a little girl that wanted to go to the bathroom."

The Cat's Pajamas did not do poorly at the box office
by any means.   To Wellman, though, and to the executives at Paramount, it looked like his first flop.   He
wrote, "It was indescribably atrocious, and the powers
that be took a look at the picture and accused Mr. Schulberg of false representation.   He had not sold them a director, he had presented them with an idiot, and they demanded a rebate."

Wellman was in real danger of being fired.   Paramount, at the time, was one of the top studios, artistically
and financially.   The stable of directors there was an impressive one, including Eddie Sutherland, Malcolm St. Clair,
Gregory La Cava, George Seitz, Victor Fleming, Fred New-
meyer, Clarence Badger, Allan Dwan, Cecil B. DeMille,
Herbert Brenon, and others of like caliber.   One thing Paramount did not need was a director who put out films of the
quality of The Cat's Pajamas.

He might have been fired but for the intervention of
Schulberg.   Wellman wrote, "He had a sneaking hunch that
my exit might well include him, so he fought like hell for
one more chance for his young protégé.   I am sure he
thought I was a bust; but this had to be a shot in the dark,
so they reluctantly gave me another picture.

In a scene from The Cat's Pajamas, Wellman said of star
Betty Bronson, "When she tried to look sexy she just looked
like a little girl who had to go to the bathroom."

The best reason to believe that The Cat's Pajamas was not quite the debacle that Wellman believed it to be is the existence of his next picture, You Never Know Women; the film is very nearly a masterpiece. Exquisitely filmed, beautifully acted and imaginatively thought-out, You Never Know Women is a strong indicator that Wellman was possibly one of the finest, most unique filmmakers of the silent era.

You Never Know Women is about the Russian theatrical troupe Chauve-Souris and is based on a story by Ernest Vajda, who also wrote The Cat's Pajamas. At the center of the story, as in so many of Wellman's films, is a romantic triangle. Vera (Florence Vidor), the star of the troupe is loved by Eugene Foster (Lowell Sherman), a wealthy broker and by Norodin (Clive Brook) a fellow actor.

Perhaps because of its exotic subject matter, You Never Know Women is Wellman's most "European" film. Victor Milner's camera is mobile and expressive, the lighting dramatic, the sub-titles few. The film is starkly dramatic (even El Brendel is relatively subdued) and filled with bravura sequences.

When Norodin believes that Vera loves her wealthy suitor, he makes her believe that one of his daring stunts (an escape from a chained trunk which has been dropped into the river) has failed and he is dead. He believes that this will free her to marry Foster with a clean conscience. The stunt has the opposite effect, of course, and Vera realizes that she can only love her former partner. Late at night after the theatre has closed, she breaks the news to Foster that she is leaving him. Enraged, he attempts to rape her. She escapes from his grasp and runs through the darkened backstage area in search of a place to hide.

She finally settles on the cabinet used in Norodin's disappearing act. Meanwhile Norodin has found that Vera is grieving for him and he has returned to the theatre to seek her. He arrives as Vera runs screaming into his cabinet (she knows that there is a trap door which leads to the other side of the stage). As soon as she is inside, she disappears in a cloud of smoke and, in a flash, Norodin is standing in her place. This, understandably, disconcerts Foster and he is chagrined to find himself being pinned to the wall by several of Norodin's knives. Norodin aims the last blade at Foster's neck and suggests that Foster slink away. He does and all is well at the fade-out.

Florence Vidor and Billy Seay in Wellman's brilliant <u>You Never Know Women</u>.

      This air of magic and skill permeates <u>You Never Know Women</u>. Foster could never have really won Vera's love because he had no idea how to exist in the peculiar world that she inhabits. Vera and Norodin belong together because they both <u>know the rules</u>; they are both theatrical folk and their relationship is filled with unconscious little gestures and tricks that reveal their deep kinship. There is even a suggestion that Vera and Norodin, together, possess real magic. There is a lovely, lyrical scene during one of their performances when Vera leaves the stage and flies over the audience like a butterfly. This spell is broken in Foster's presence, though; during a private performance at his home, Vera stands atop three other performers in a balancing act. She loses her balance and falls to the ground. Here, the pros and cons of her rival suitors are most explicitly displayed: Norodin causes her to soar through the air, graceful and free; Foster brings her to earth with a thud.

<u>You Never Know Women</u> lifted Wellman back into the esteem of his employers.   The film was a commercial and a critical success (Wellman often said that it won "the artistic award" for 1926, but if it did, it is not certain which award he spoke of) and the director got a $25 a week raise, a month's vacation and another assignment: <u>Wings</u>.

CHAPTER FOUR

Wings was the brain-child of author John Monk Saunders, himself a pilot in the first World War. In February 1926, Saunders approached Jesse Lasky with the idea of filming a story about the Air Corps in the war. The project seemed viable in light of the enormous success of The Big Parade and What Price Glory. The public, it seemed, was eager to see stories about the Great War after a long period in which war films were thought to be box-office poison.

Lasky came to share Saunder's enthusiasm for Wings, but felt that in order to do justice to such a picture, great expense would be necessary--and Paramount would not be willing to spend that much for any picture. Saunders suggested that the federal government might put up some of the necessary capital, or at least might provide troops, equipment, and military facilities. Lasky agreed that it was worth a try. "Go to Washington. Talk to the government," he told Saunders. "If they will help us with the picture, we will make it."

Saunders left for Washington immediately and talked with the War Department. They agreed readily to support the making of Wings, but only on several conditions: Paramount would be liable for any damage done to government property during the filming, each military man would be insured for $10,000, and the film would have to provide legitimate training for any of the troops who worked on it.

Paramount agreed to the terms and began to work on the pre-production aspects. Hope Loring and Louis D. Lighton

were assigned the screenplay and the titles were to be written
by Julian Johnson.   B. P. Schulberg was producing Wings
and he thought of giving the picture to Wellman.   Lasky
thought the decision unwise.   Though You Never Know Women
was a success, Wellman was still considered too green, still
an under-tested director.   Schulberg, however, was adamant.
He knew that Wellman was a capable director and, besides,
he was the only director under contract to Paramount who
had actually been a pilot during the war.   "So, they took the
big gamble and gave me the job of directing the first flying
picture (a two-million-dollar item) to be made by the erratic
motion picture business," Wellman wrote, adding that his
salary for heading this mammoth effort was a "jumbo" $250
a week.

Wellman was still on vacation when he received word
that he was to direct Paramount's major production of the
year.   Excitedly, he cut his break short and hurried back
to Hollywood, arriving there in mid-June 1926.   Once at
work, he began the task of casting the film.

The first person cast was no surprise, since Schulberg was the Executive Producer: Clara Bow.   The story
had to be somewhat re-structured to accommodate her, but
everyone involved felt it was worth it; they needed her drawing power at the box-office as insurance against the financial
risk they were undertaking.   As the two male leads, rivals
who become friends, producer Lucien Hubbard wanted to sign
Charles "Buddy" Rogers, a newcomer in Hollywood, and Neil
Hamilton, who had recently appeared in the hit Beau Geste.

In fact, Buddy Rogers had almost appeared in Beau
Geste himself.   He had been studying at Paramount's acting
school in New York and, he remembers,

> At the end of school they told me I was going to
> play Ronald Colman's younger brother in Beau
> Geste and I was fitted out for these beautiful
> French Foreign Legion uniforms.   I had to go to
> California by train; so I asked if I could stop off
> in Olathe [his home town, in Kansas] on my way,
> which I did.   I spent the whole three or four days
> there walking up and down Main Street in my For-
> eign Legion uniform, I was so proud.

When he arrived in Hollywood, however, he was told
that Ralph Forbes had been chosen for the role instead.   He

was "just devastated" and went to Jesse Lasky to ask to be
let out of his contract. "When a person in Olathe says he's
going to do something," he told Lasky, "he does it, and now,
here I am, not making the picture." Lasky told him to re-
lax--they had already cast him in another picture and he was
to have lunch with the picture's director: Wellman. Rogers
said,

> Well, we hit it off well, and I was cast in Wings,
> thank goodness, although Wellman was the toughest
> director I ever had. Most directors would say,
> "Fine, Buddy, that's great!" when they knew and
> I knew it wasn't fine and it wasn't great. They
> just wanted to get it over with. But Wellman would
> make me do it until it really was fine.

Having cast Rogers, Wellman began to have doubts
about Neil Hamilton. He thought that Hamilton was a little
too staid for the energetic role. He began to look around
for someone else to take the part. When Wellman had to go
scout for locations in San Antonio, Texas, he asked his close
friend and (at this time) second propman Charles Barton for
advice. Barton was good friends with young Richard Arlen,
who, up to this time, had had only a few bit parts. Barton
asked Wellman, "Can I test Dick Arlen?" Wellman replied,
"Who the hell is Dick Arlen?" "Well, he's a friend of mine,
you've met him," Barton replied. Wellman muttered that he
didn't want two "goddam unknowns" in the lead and left for
San Antonio. Barton went ahead and tested Arlen anyway.

> No name on the slate, just "Test: Wings." So
> [Wellman] came back from San Antonio--now this
> is just four or five weeks before we left for Texas,
> that's how close it was--and Wellman started run-
> ning all the tests and he saw Dick Arlen. And he
> says, "Jesus Christ! Who's that good-looking son
> of a bitch?" He didn't see his name on any of the
> slates. So I said, "Well, give me five minutes
> and I'll find out." I didn't want to tell him who
> it was, cause I knew this would build him up. So
> I came back after a few minutes and said, "That
> was Dick Arlen." And Wellman said, "You dirty
> son of a bitch. I'll kill you." But he fell in love
> with him. Dick Arlen got the part.

San Antonio was chosen as the location of Wings because of its proximity to both Army bases and air fields. It

was decided to base the bulk of the operations at Kelly Field
and Wellman summoned flyers from the Air Service Ground
School at Brooks Field in San Antonio, the First Pursuit
Group from Selfridge Field in Detroit, and several other
air bases from all over the country.

The climax of Wings was to be the massive Battle of
St.-Mihiel, the battle in which Wellman's friend Dave Putnam
had died. He chose a location outside San Antonio, which
was about a mile long, and had the army bombard the ground
with field guns. That done, he had trenches dug by teams
of Mexican laborers. The result was so eerily effective that
several of the fliers who had flown in France confessed to
Wellman that just flying over the location made them nervous.

Interestingly, the Wings company was not the only
group of motion picture people in San Antonio at the time.
Victor Fleming was making The Rough Riders in the city and,
according to Wellman, staying at the same hotel, the Saint
Anthony. "San Antonio became the Armageddon of a magnifi-
cent sexual Donnybrook," Wellman wrote. "The town was
lousy with movie people, and if you think that contributes to
a state of tranquility, you don't know your motion picture
ABC's." He claimed that all of the Saint Anthony's elevator
operators, all young girls, were bearing children by the end
of the shooting of Wings, and the fathers weren't San Antone
boys, either. "They were replaced by old men, and the company's hunting grounds were barren."

Wellman was given orders by the War Department that
granted him authority to request whatever assistance he needed. He was not shy about using them and he was resented
by some of the officers. No other military film ever made
was to have such complete cooperation by the Armed Forces
and Wellman didn't want to waste a thing.

Though the bulk of Wellman's reputation was based on
the fact that he shot quickly (he claimed to be of the "Woody
Van Dyke school"), Wings is one instance where he took his
time, shot scenes over and over, and waited until all the conditions were favorable.

After two months of shooting, Wellman decided that he
couldn't use anything they had filmed. The flying scenes
didn't look right and the methods of filming the actors in
flight still weren't perfected. Producer Lucien Hubbard recalled,

We had cameras shooting both forward and backward. There were many scenes when we shot over Arlen's head, as he dived to earth. You put that much weight in an unaccustomed place, and you're courting a crash. You're doing something that has never been accomplished before, and to do it so you don't crash and still get your picture, is really amazing.

Wellman insisted that all scenes of the actors flying the planes be shot in the air, so complicated camera mounts were placed on the front of the planes, the actors would go aloft with one pilot and, when they got to the right altitude, the pilot would duck down and the actor became, as Buddy Rogers said, "The photographer, the director, the actor, everything ... for five hundred feet."

Harry Perry was the director of photography and it was he who developed the methods for shooting the aerial footage. He had an enormous crew of photographers, including E. Burton Steene, William Clothier, Faxon Dean, Paul Perry, Bert Balbridge, Cliff Blackston, Frank Cotner, Russell Harlan, Ray Olsen, Herman Schoop, L. Guy Wilky, and Al Williams. Cameras were mounted on planes, on platforms, and in various places around the locations. There was even a tower built that was a hundred feet tall from which the impressive panoramas of the big battle scenes could be shot.

Wellman's responsibilities on the location were massive. Motion Picture Magazine wrote in the September 1927 issue,

> When the director was not working on the picture, he and the producer were settling the difficulties that arose because of army politics, smoothing over jealousies between different branches of the service, pacifying the impatient troops with barrels of beer and motion picture entertainments, giving the aviators dinners and dances and conciliating fuming officers with a diplomacy that would have avoided the World War. The Government cannot be hired, but at the close of the picture, Wellman handed over fifty thousand dollars as a gift to the mess funds.

[Opposite:] Dick Arlen and Buddy Rogers in the emotional climax of Wings.

Wellman had his problems with the crew, as well. Charles Barton was promoted from assistant propman to propman to assistant manager to assistant director while on location in Texas. "I got promoted three times," he said, "I became the assistant manager and when they found out the unit manager was skimming a little off the top, I got promoted again. When he found out they were gonna build a set, he'd go out and buy the lumber and sell it to the studio at a higher price. He was doing pretty good. I think they asked him to quit."

About mid-way through the shooting schedule, the weather turned on the company. The sky was a constant, dingy grey and there was frequent rain. There were still a lot of aerial scenes to shoot and Wellman refused to do so without the proper lighting and, more importantly, without clouds. He explained,

> Say you can't shoot a dog fight without clouds to a guy who doesn't know anything about flying and he thinks you're nuts. He'll say, "Why can't you?" [First], it's unattractive. Number two, you get no sense of speed, because there's nothing there that's parallel. The clouds give you that, but against a blue sky, it's like a lot of goddam flies! And photographically, it's terrible.

So they waited on the clouds to come. They waited for over a month. Barton remembered,

> He got to a certain point and wouldn't go on until the clouds were there. And he was so right. But we tried everything. I admit he just didn't sit on his ass. Wellman said to Harry Perry, "Try any-thing!" Well, Harry got little pieces of cotton and put them on the thinnest thread that he could find and painted them to look like clouds. But it didn't work, cause when the camera moved, the clouds would go right along there. But he tried a million other things. He tried skywriters; he sent up these planes to try and make it look like clouds, but.... Well, he knew exactly what he wanted till the day he died.

The rigors of shooting in San Antonio was sometimes rough on the actors, too. Buddy Rogers recalls,

I had to learn to fly for that movie. I got terribly airsick at first, but I stuck with it, and I had a good flying instructor. I just knew him as Van, but he was Hoyt Vandenberg, who later became head of the Air Force. After the movie was finished, I kept up with my flying and logged 800 hours on my own, so that it was easy for me to join the navy as a pilot in World War II.

During the seemingly interminable days of waiting out the cloud situation, the crew amused themselves by playing football ... on the runways. Someone suggested to Wellman, "Uh, this is a cement runway. We'd better play touch." "Hell, no!" Wellman replied. "We play tackle or nothing!" Barton recalled, "Next thing I knew, he had Buddy Rogers and Dick Arlen in the game. And if either one of them had broken an arm or a leg, it would have set back production and caused chaos. But that didn't bother Wellman. We played football."

William Clothier, Faxon Dean's assistant cameraman also remembered the football games. "I was the center and [Wellman] was the quarterback on the team. We played the Army and the Air Force and we beat 'em every day. I had cleat marks up and down my back. I'd pass the ball to him and he'd run right up my back."

The government officials began to grow impatient. They hadn't put the entire Army at Paramount's disposal to play football all day. The support of Wings became a political subject and many people believed that the movie company was squandering money and time. Paramount decided to send down their top financiers to try to talk sense into Wellman, to get him to finish shooting this picture.

Meanwhile, he was planning the biggest sequence in the picture: St.-Mihiel Offensive. Since he knew he had to get the entire battle shot in a single day, he spent ten days rehearsing the 3,500 troops and sixty planes that would be used that day.

The scheduled day dawned dark and cloudy, just as every previous day for a month had done, but Wellman decided to chance getting enough sunlight to try the shot. Wellman and Hubbard had planned the battle as carefully as though it were a real military maneuver. They met with the officers

in charge of the troops to map out the activity with maps and
blueprints. They appointed every man who was to "die" and
relegated junior officers to handle the various squads. Wellman said,

> We had dozens of cameras. On the big scene, we
> fanned out a series of camera parallels, and had
> about twenty-eight Eyemos, hand-held 35mm cam-
> eras, stuck about. I played the explosions from a
> detonator keyboard on the third level. I wouldn't
> allow anybody up there. I kept the barrage ahead
> of the advancing troops. A guy came up to me to
> ask me a question and I pushed the wrong button.

When Wellman pushed the wrong button on the keyboard,
he saw a couple of bodies fly up into the air, "and they weren't
dummies. I kept on pressing buttons, but I said, 'You son
of a bitch, you get off this thing, whoever you are, or I'll
kill you!' " The man he kicked off the parallel was Otto Kahn,
a major financier for Paramount who, with Sir William Wise-
man and William Stralem had arrived in San Antonio that
day to see about the delays in shooting.

The sun had lasted just long enough to get the shot
and, to Wellman's relief, no one had been seriously injured
during the few minutes of chaos.

There had only been on unscheduled airplane crash
during the shooting of the battle scene. Wellman had watched
the erratic actions of the pilot from atop the parallel. He
was "knocking the helmets off the advancing waves of dough-
boys. The bastard was going nuts, he was slowing us down,
screwing up the whole carefully planned advance, and then I
saw him crash, and his plane rolled over and over, and I
was almost glad."

In the midst of the euphoria of completing the chancy
scene, Wellman suddenly remembered the crash and went
toward it to check on the pilot. He wrote,

> When I got there, the plane was demolished, but
> the pilot was leaning against an ambulance with a
> bandage around his head. He was dazed, but not
> from the crash, and I suddenly realized that in all
> my planning, I had forgotten one terribly important
> factor, the human element. This pilot had flown at
> the front. He had been decorated. He had flown

Buddy Rogers (left), Richard Arlen (center) and Gary Cooper
in Wings.

missions just like this one.   For five minutes it
was not 1926 to him; it was 1918.   He just stuck
out his hand and said, "I'm sorry."   C'est la
guerre.

Wellman was sure that his gruff talk to Otto Kahn had
finished the picture for him; calling your studio's main financier a son of a bitch and offering to break his neck is not the
recommended way to get ahead in the movie business.   That
night he was alone in his room in the Saint Anthony getting
"lonesome drunk."   The three money men came up to see
him.   "I came out of the shower to open the door," he said,
"and there were these three guys.   I thought they were going
to fire me."   He thought, "But at least if they fire me,
they're going to have five minutes that they'll never forget
as long as they live."

Wellman said to Kahn, "I'm sorry, you want a drink?
I'm a little loaded but I can't help it."

Kahn replied, "I don't blame you, but all we want to say is we've got to go home, we're on our way back to New York, and you can have whatever you want, for as long as you want it. You're a very, very wonderful man."

"With that," Wellman said, "they went out and I fell down on the floor and cried like a baby."

Charles Barton remembered, "I was the first one he told. He came running down the hall with a towel wrapped around him, yelling, 'We're gonna go on! We're gonna go on!' like a little boy."

For the number of planes and fliers involved, it's somewhat amazing that there were as few crashes during the filming as there were. Just the three that occurred, however, was three too many for the Air Force officials and Wellman was warned that one more crash would cause all military assistance to be removed from the project.

From that point on, Wellman was quite careful, even going as far as faking one crash (Arlen's crash into the French farm-house at the end of the film) with miniatures. This particular crash, the last one to be filmed, had to be faked because Wellman's ace stuntman, Dick Grace was in the hospital with a broken neck. "He got hurt doing the simplest thing in the world," Wellman said. "Instead of turning his plane over, he <u>almost</u> went over--and snapped his neck."

Charles Barton was there the day Grace crashed:

> In the scene, the Fokker plane is hit from above by an American plane. Dick had to slide the Fokker across the muddy battlefield and flip it over on top of a shellhole.
> Before performing the stunt on film, Dick came over to me and said, "You're the first person I want out there after the stunt, just in case anything goes wrong."
> I said, "Well, how will I <u>know</u> if you're okay?"
> "I'll flip the tail rudder."
> Good enough. Wellman was ready and so was Dick. Action. The plane came in as smooth as a dove ... soldiers were running all over the place. Grace zeroed in the plane for a crash. It hit the ground. He did it! I anxiously watch for the rudders to flip. They didn't.

Wellman was still filming while the soldiers
ran across the field. The rudders still didn't move.
I started running in.

Bill shouted, "Get out of there you son of a
bitch! What are you doing?" "They didn't flip!"
I shouted.

Wellman jumped out of his chair and we ran
out to the crash site where Grace was hanging up-
side down. We carefully removed him from the
wreckage. He had broken his neck.

Dick Grace wrote of the account,

When I awoke, I was standing in front of a battery
of cameras. I had passed out on my feet! Two
days later I collapsed again, and when I was taken
to the hospital at Fort Sam Houston, it was found
that the first and second cervical vertebrae were
crushed together; so also were the fourth and fifth.
The sixth was dislocated. There was a slight frac-
ture of the big bone in my chest. Of course,
bruises didn't count.

Wellman added,

They put a big thing on his neck and sent him to
the hospital, and I went to see him every day. He
was supposed to keep that cast on for at least a
year. He had it on for six weeks. I happened to
be dancing at the St. Anthony's Hotel, San Antonio,
and I saw this guy Grace dancing with a dame.
He'd gotten a hammer and broken the cast and escaped through a window. He never went back and
he never put that thing back on his neck, either.

There was still the final crash to be done and Grace's
contract stated that he was to be responsible for all crack-ups
in the film. When Barton went to visit Grace at the hospital,
Grace asked, "What is Wellman planning to do about the crash
into the house?" Barton started to hem and haw and Grace
broke in, "I'm going to do it, you know."

"I don't think so, Dick," said Barton. "I think Bill
has other plans."

"He'd better not! You better let me talk to him."

Wellman went to the hospital and said to Grace, "No, I'm not going to let you do it.   We'll fake it."

"If you do," replied Grace, "I'll sue you."

The crash was faked and Grace sued.   And won.

After the visit of Kahn and his fellow money-men, the tension was substantially reduced on the <u>Wings</u> location.   The remainder of the shooting schedule was considerably more light-hearted and characterized by an easy camaraderie. Wellman tried to get as many of the crew in front of the camera as possible.   He himself plays a doughboy in the final advance.   He advances doggedly, is shot by a German in a pill-box, twirls once and falls.   When Rogers' plane swoops in and wipes out the pill-box, Wellman looks to the sky and says, "Atta boy, them buzzards are some good after all!"   Charles Barton plays the soldier who is hit by Clara Bow's ambulance and who, in order to be caressed and kissed by Bow, pretends to be badly hurt.   His revery comes to an end when a gruff sergeant barks, "If you guys want kissin', I'll kiss ya....   Wit a gun butt!"

Also in the cast (in cameo roles) were John Monk Saunders, Dick Grace, and several of Kelly Field's officers. For the sequence near the end in which Arlen dies in the French farmhouse, Wellman chose his wife, Margery, and daughter, Gloria, for the roles of the peasant woman and her small daughter.

Gloria was, Wellman said,

> the belle of the army.   Gloria was always on the field.   Whenever she wandered off we'd find her in the arms of some big, husky sergeant.   We spent Christmas in Texas--such a Christmas as I have never seen in my life.   The soldiers set up a huge Christmas tree in our hotel suite and brought pres- ents by the hundred.   Gloria knows them all by name.
> [He continued,] Of course, everybody's baby is great, but ours is the greatest yet.   We're letting her go her own way.   She is fascinated with the movies, has seen me shoot many a scene and played a part herself.

As the shooting neared completion in San Antonio, Well-

man shot a brief scene with newcomer Gary Cooper. This
near-cameo was to be quite important in launching Cooper's
career. Cooper is, in fact, visible earlier in the film as
Rogers and Arlen are in basic training, but his big scene
comes when Rogers and Arlen first arrive at their camp
and find that Cooper is their tent-mate.

The titles given for Cooper's dialog are surprisingly
prescient of his later screen persona. Such lines as "Luck
or no luck, when your time comes, you're going to get it,"
and "I've got to go up and do a flock of eights before chow"
have that terse, laconic attitude that Cooper was to become
so identified with.

Wellman always told the story of shooting this scene
in rather self-congratulatory tones ("You keep on picking your
nose and you'll pick it into a fortune"), but it seems clear
that Wellman saw how unique Cooper was.

> All Coop had was a very small scene, but at the
> end he had to turn as he left the tent and he had
> to look at [Rogers and Arlen], and that look, every-
> body in the audience would have to remember. To
> get someone to do that was kind of rugged. I looked
> at eight million people. I suddenly saw Coop. That
> wonderful smile. That funny, odd, indescribable
> something or other, and I took him. I kept him
> down in San Antonio for weeks, because he was a
> nice guy, getting nothing, but he was broke and he
> needed the dough. I kept him there as long as I
> could, but finally I had to do his scene.

By the time Cooper's scene was shot, most of the company
had already gone back to Hollywood and Wellman wrapped up
the production in San Antonio.

The final scenes shot were the various interiors, the
framing actions of the film which were shot at Busch Gardens
in Pasadena (where Wellman was to film Beau Geste twelve
years later). About midway through the final shooting, Wellman's contract ran out and Paramount did not renew it.
There was a great deal of bitterness toward Wellman among
those who ran Paramount; he had had them by the throat in
Texas and they resented it. Even Schulberg had turned against
Wellman.

Wellman had decided that he needed an agent and ap-

proached Myron Selznick to see if Selznick would take him on
as a client. Selznick agreed; he was a fledgling agent and
needed all the clients he could get. Besides, Wellman was
a good friend of Myron's and his brother David. Wellman
went to Selznick and told him of his contract predicament.
"What do I do?" he asked. Selznick replied, "Just keep
your mouth shut. You've got 'em where it hurts." He
worked for six weeks on cutting Wings and preparing it for
release--and the entire time, he received no pay.

Wings received its premiere in July 1927. The ani-
mosity toward Wellman was so great that he was not invited
to the premiere. This attitude changed after Wings's smash
first showing. The film was incredibly popular and Paramount, which had been prepared to write the whole thing off
as an expensive mistake, found itself raking in the cash.

For the roadshow engagement of Wings, the film was
accompanied by an orchestra playing a specially written score
by J. S. Zamecnik. In addition, from behind the screen
came "cockeyed" and synchronized sounds of airplane engines,
machine guns, and bomb explosions. As was quite common
at the time, portions of the film were tinted in atmospheric
colors (for example, red for battle scenes, blue for night
scenes).

As a final blockbuster, Paramount used the large-
screen process Magnascope for Wings's original showings.
Here is another example of Wellman appropriating the credit
for something he had nothing whatever to do with, for he
often told reviewers, "I got a screwy idea that if the picture
could just enlarge itself as the dawn patrol took off, it would
be something unforgettable. And, by God, Roy Pomeroy did
it." In fact Glen Allvine developed Magnascope--which was
not a wide-screen process, like CinemaScope or Panavision;
it simply enlarged the entire frame to several times its normal size--and before Wings, had already used it in Chang
and Old Ironsides and was to use it once more in Four Fathers.

Wings played only the roadshow engagements for the
remainder of the period 1927-28. It was widely released on
January 5, 1929, with the added attraction of a sound effects
and music track for those theaters equipped for sound. The
picture was a smash success critically and commercially.

On May 16, 1929, Wings was presented with the first

Academy Award ever given for Best Picture. In addition,
Roy Pomeroy received the only Oscar ever given for "Engineering Effects" for his work with Magnascope and the synchronized score. Wellman was not invited to the Academy
Awards ceremony that night. By this time, the Paramount
brass were convinced that he had known what he was doing
during those long months in San Antonio, but they still didn't
like him.

In early 1928, it was widely announced that Wellman
was to direct Beau Sabreur, starring Gary Cooper. The film
was intended as a cheater, a way for Paramount to cash in
on the huge success in 1926 of Beau Geste. There was still
so much good footage left over from Herbert Brenon's film
that it seemed only logical to follow it up with another adaptation of a P. C. Wren novel. Wellman balked at the assignment. He had just directed Paramount's biggest hit of the
year and he saw no reason to direct a little quickie.

When the good reviews and (more significantly) the
box-office receipts began to pour in from Wings, Schulberg
realized that Wellman was going to be an important director.
He called Wellman into his office and told him that he was
being withdrawn from Beau Sabreur (the direction of which
would go to John Waters) and that he would be given a pet
project, Legion of the Condemned, instead. Legion had been
written by John Monk Saunders and Paramount planned a big
publicity campaign centered around the two Wings geniuses
getting together again on another epic of the air.

Wellman smiled. "There's just one problem, Mr.
Schulberg."

"What's that?"

"I've been working for Paramount many weeks now,
and I haven't received a cent."

"There must be some mistake," sputtered Schulberg.
He called the studio manager, Mike Levy on the intercom.
"Mike, Wellman tells me that we haven't taken up his op-
tion."

Levy started to reply, "Well, you remember, Ben,
you told me to--" and Schulberg switched off the intercom.
He looked up at Wellman. "Well, Bill, you've got a great
talent and we have big plans for you...."

Wellman cut in, "Yes, I've got a great talent and there's a guy outside who wants to talk with you about it. His name is Myron Selznick."

Schulberg sighed and signaled his secretary. "Send Selznick in." Selznick heard him and said to the secretary, "Tell Schulberg that I'm taking Mr. Wellman somewhere else. We've got other people interested in him."

Selznick and Wellman went to see Otto Kahn and told him of the situation. Kahn still greatly admired Wellman and was instrumental in getting him a new, more favorable contract with Paramount.

A week later Wellman signed a contract "for seven years and I hate to tell you what I got the seventh year of that contract. I never knew there was that much money. I jumped from $350 a week to $1500 a week. That was the first jump, the first year and it went up in that way until the end of the seven years."

After a well-deserved vacation, Wellman started work on Legion of the Condemned, starring Gary Cooper and Fay Wray.

Ironically, Legion of the Condemned turned out to be a "cheater" like Beau Sabreur. Schulberg rushed the film into production and urged Wellman to use as much of the flying and battle footage from Wings as possible. Since the movie no longer exists, one can't be quite sure how much (if any) new aerial footage was shot for Legion, but it is probable that none was.

Though Wings had benefited from Wellman's experience as a pilot, Legion was actually closer to the actual locale of his World War I stint. Most reviews actually name the Lafayette Escadrille as the flying unit depicted in the film, though Eustace Hale Ball's book (based on John Monk Saunders' screenplay) never really clarified what squadron is supposed to be represented. It is certainly a Foreign Legion-like troop, for there are men of varying nationalities involved in the story.

At about the same time as Legion of the Condemned was being shot, Wellman was instrumental in getting David O. Selznick a job as producer at Paramount. Selznick and Wellman were close friends and enjoyed working together; in fact, Selznick was hired because Wellman convinced Schulberg that Selznick was the only producer he could work with.

Selznick did not work on Legion, but he remembered it years later in an interview with Kevin Brownlow:

> The opening sequence of his Legion of the Condemned I've many times quoted as one of the most brilliant uses of film to tell a story that I've ever seen. He told the story of four individual men in, I think, less than one minute each. He was really a remarkable talent.

The review by The New York Times also singled out this section of the film for praise.

> The best chapter in the film is the first one. Here are given the reasons why some of the fliers don't care a rap about living. There is an Argentinian (Francis MacDonald) who is depicted on his native heath in a pistol duel over a girl. From there you turn to London where a young Britisher (Barry Norton) through reckless driving is the cause of a girl's death.* There is the gambler in Monte Carlo [Lane Chandler] who, after throwing away bills and gold on the green baize tables, walks out to the balcony to put a bullet through his brain. A laugh, supposedly cruel, stays the trigger and the gambler turns his eyes on his mistress who, according to George Marion, Jr., the title writer, says: "Don't try to blow out what you haven't got."

The film is a spy story. Gale Price (Gary Cooper) falls in love with a beautiful young socialite, Christine Charteris (Fay Wray). When he finds that she is a spy and, on top of that, is sleeping with a dangerous German agent, Von Hohendorff (Albert Conti), he joins the Legion of the Condemned, a squadron of flying men whose only aim is to die in combat.

Christine turns out to be an allied spy (surprise!) and

---

*Wellman obviously remembered this bit, for it's the same reason that Thad Walker (Tab Hunter) joins the Lafayette Escadrille (1958).

Gale finds the will to live again. When he helps her on her
mission, and has to drop her behind enemy lines, they are
caught by the Germans and sentenced to death by firing squad.
The rest of Gale's squadron, their will to die momentarily
surmounted by their innate patriotism, rallies to their rescue in what The New York Times called, "quite a rousing
climax, what with the dropping of bombs and the enemy
troops dashing to cover."

Fay Wray had come to Legion of the Condemned directly after finishing The Wedding March with Erich von Stroheim. She and Gary Cooper made such a hit in Legion of the
Condemned, that Paramount tried for a while to build them
up into a major romantic team, like Ronald Colman and Vilma
Banky.

Fay Wray spoke of working with Cooper:

> He was very quiet, quite shy. There was a curious
> thing about Gary, he dozed a lot, he had the capa-
> city to fall asleep in between shots. I think that
> Legion of the Condemned was his first leading role.
> William Wellman had good energy, good drive. He
> loved his work and therefore he was exciting to
> work for. Everyone liked the film, so Paramount
> began to focus on Gary and me as a team. They
> decided we would be "Paramount's Glorious Young
> Lovers."

After shooting was completed on Legion of the Condemned,
Fay Wray married John Monk Saunders.

Saunders had written the original story for the film
but he collaborated on the screenplay with Jean de Limur.
Count de Limur had a somewhat interesting film career: he
acted in a few films in the early 1920's, is listed as "Re-
searcher" on Chaplin's A Woman of Paris (1923), wrote several scenarios and later was to become a director, most
notably of the Jeanne Eagels films The Letter and Jealousy
(both 1929). He claimed to have flown in the Lafayette Escadrille which, if true, would make the aerial knowledge behind
the camera of Legion of the Condemned formidable indeed.

Legion of the Condemned was released on March 10,
1928, to generally good reviews and very good business.
Wellman and Saunders began to work immediately on their
next picture, Dirigible. After some weeks' work, the pair

was abruptly pulled from the project (it is not known why)
and Wellman was assigned Ladies of the Mob, which was to
star Clara Bow and Richard Arlen. Dirigible was later sold
to Columbia. Frank Capra directed a film of that name in
1931, though it is not certain how much of Wellman's and
Saunders' ideas remained in the story.

Ladies of the Mob was Wellman's first foray into the
world of crime, a milieu that he would make his own in the
early thirties. Clara Bow played Yvonne, a girl whose father
died in the electric chair, an experience that turned her to
crime at an early age. She becomes involved with a small-
time crook, Red (Richard Arlen), and together they alternately
try to make the Big Score and attempt to go straight. At the
fade-out the two are taken to prison looking forward to the
time when they are released, when they can live without the
shadow of guilt.

The New York Times called Ladies of the Mob "gloomy,
artificial and undefying," though this opinion might have come
from a certain squeamishness on the part of Mordaunt Hall.
He describes with barely concealed disgust "the depressing
suggestion of a murderer expiating his crime in the electric
chair and, although the unfortunate criminal is not seen,
there is quite enough detail to satisfy morbid curiosity."

Since Wellman always sported enthusiasm for sensa-
tionalism and tragedy, it is regrettable indeed that Ladies of
the Mob is lost to us. He takes such grim pleasure in the
execution scenes in his other films (most notably the remarkable hanging of the outlaw gang in The Conquerors) that one
would be "morbidly curious" to see what "details" he essayed
in the prologue of Ladies of the Mob.

There is a sequence near the end of the film that
sounds tailor-made for Bugs Bunny. Mordaunt Hall explains:
"Yvonne and 'Red' are in a house alone and, to deceive the
police, who have surrounded the dwelling, bullets are put into
pots and pans on a lighted gas stove. The gullible detectives
are supposed to think that the gangsters are in the house because the cartridges are heard exploding."

Ladies of the Mob was based on a short story by Ernest Booth, an inmate in Folsom Prison, a fact that was certainly not lost on the Paramount publicity department. The
scenario was written by a young Australian, John Farrow, who
had been friends with Wellman since the latter came to Para-

Clara Bow in <u>Ladies of the Mob</u>.

mount. On the night of <u>Wings</u>'s premiere, Farrow cabled
Wellman:

> Up to last night I'd received one big thrill in my
> life. That was from a Portuguese lady in Shanghai.
> I thought that was the climax of emotional thrills
> but last night I saw your picture <u>Wings</u> [and] that
> beats any lady or boy, white or colored. When I
> say that, you know what I mean, Billy Boy.

Farrow was to work mainly as a writer until the mid-1930's,
when he became a director at Warner Bros. and Paramount,
producing such films as <u>Two Years Before the Mast</u>, <u>The Big
Clock</u> and <u>Wake Island</u>. He later "produced" (with his wife,
Maureen O'Sullivan) Mia and Tisa Farrow.

Farrow was also to become a converted Catholic and
a respected writer on Catholic history. But while he worked
with Wellman, Farrow was, if anything, wilder than Wild Bill.
Wellman called him "a wonderful guy, a brilliant writer. Not
a good director. How the hell he got that cable through, I
don't know."

<u>Ladies of the Mob</u> would be the last time that Wellman
would work with the "It Girl," Clara Bow. Her immense
popularity was on the wane even before sound came in and
by the late thirties she had retired from the screen. However, Wellman's next leading lady was one of the most remarkable women he ever directed: Louise Brooks.

<u>Beggars of Life</u> was Wellman's next film at Paramount.
It was loosely based on the novel by "hobo author" Jim Tully
who co-scripted the film with Benjamin Glazer. It is the
story of a girl who kills her foster father when he attempts
to rape her. She runs away from the scene with a young
tramp, becomes involved with a group of hoboes and, eventually, escapes with the young tramp into Canada, having convinced the police that she is dead.

Louise Brooks was signed on as the girl, though Wellman was skeptical of her talents and her willingness to work.
Brooks wrote,

> Billy Wellman came to the unfortunate conclusion
> that, since I did not follow the pattern of the actors
> who haunted the studio, panting after film roles, I
> did not care about making films at all. This con-

clusion set up a coldness between us which neither
of us could dispel because he did not know that
sycophancy has no merit in the New York studio
[Astoria] where I had begun my career and I was
unaware that prudent Hollywood actors wooed producers, directors and writers with flattering attention.

More to Wellman's liking were his two male stars,
Wallace Beery and, again, Richard Arlen. Beery played
Oklahoma Red, a gruff hobo who has eyes for Brooks ("When
I'm in a gang, it's my gang," Red says. "And if there's a
girl, she's my girl."). Arlen took the role of the gentle
young tramp who yearns for something better than a life on
the road.

Most of the filming was done in Jacumba, California
near the Mexican border. The movie company virtually took
over the resort town of four hundred inhabitants and the sixteen days of filming Beggars of Life was a riotous period of
fighting, drinking, and carousing. The stuntmen spent much
of their free time challenging the local talent to foot-races
down the main street of Jacumba and the sporting events
usually ended in brawls.

Wellman liked location work, possibly because the outdoor camaraderie was so similar to his days as a flier, but
it could be trying for actors who did not share Wellman's
rough-housing nature.

Though his marriage to Margery Chapin was now on
the rocks, she accompanied Wellman to Jacumba and acted
as script girl on the film. In addition, her brother Jack was
signed on as an extra. Perhaps she had made the trip in an
attempt to rekindle their eroding relationship, but it didn't
work; upon their return to Hollywood, Wellman and Margery
were divorced.

While in Jacumba, though, Wellman was in his element. He had picked a long stretch of railroad track on the
line between San Diego and Yuma for shooting the crucial
train scenes. Since only four trains ran on the track daily,
Wellman and his crew were allowed many hours of privacy
with which to shoot their scenes. Louise Brooks wrote lov-
ingly of the train, Locomotive 102, that was used in the film:

An indulgent train, she let us ride all over her--

astride the cow catcher, in the engine cab, atop
box cars, inside gondolas and on flat cars. I chose
to ride in the caboose with its cozy bunks and fat
little black stove which glowed red in the cold
mountain nights. When everyone was accounted for
by the assistant director [Charlie Barton], after a
warning ring of her bell, away she skipped up the
canyons on the hour trip to Carrizo Gorge which
was the central point from which we operated.
      She was a train to make her engineer, her fire-
man and her brakeman proud. Under Billy's expert
guidance she learned numerous tricks of changing
speed and direction, of starts and stops with perfect timing.

Locomotive 102 is featured prominently throughout the
greater part of the film; indeed, the train is so versatile that
it plays a multiple role--it impersonates three separate trains.

Some of the scenes shot on the train are reminiscent
of Wings, for Wellman and photographer Henry Gerrard
strapped the camera to the end of a boxcar and let the actors play the scene while the train is plummeting along the
track at top speed. Like Wings, Beggars of Life is a testa-
ment of Wellman's exhilaration with movement. All of the
characters are constantly in motion either walking down the
road or riding on trains, in cars, on a bread-cart.

In fact, at any given time in the film, when Wellman
wants to express to us what a character is feeling, he shows
us their feet. Our first glimpse of Arlen, as he walks toward a farmhouse to ask for a handout, is of his feet, tiredly
tramping down the road. When he arrives at the house and
finds the farmer sitting at the kitchen table, dead, our first
view is of the farmer's feet; his shoes are streaked with a
stream of blood and the camera pans up from the feet to the
head, which contains a bullet-hole.

When the girl comes downstairs and explains how she
came to shoot the farmer, the bulk of her story (shown in
flashback and superimposed over her face as she talks) is of
his feet advancing, her feet retreating, until her hands find
the rifle in its place on the wall.

When the girl and the tramp leave (she dressed in
men's clothes) each scene of the two walking down the road
begins with their tramping feet. It is clear that Wellman

appreciates their locomotion more than their brains, more
than their faces. In Beggars of Life, he made a film about
movement, about people who are bound to advance constantly.
In the final analysis, Wellman seems to treat the actors no
differently from how he treats Locomotive 102 or, for that
matter, the planes in Wings. The story and the acting are
simply the catalysts that make the motion occur.

After the sixteen days in Jacumba were finished, the
company returned to the Paramount studios to shoot the interiors, close-ups, and so on. In just over twenty more
days, Beggars of Life was completed--or so Wellman thought.

B. P. Schulberg had become infatuated with sound.
Already Roy Pomeroy had added music and sound effects to
some of Paramount's major releases, but the studio had not
yet followed the lead of Warner Bros. by inserting dialog sequences in otherwise silent pictures (a process that was known
in the trade as "goat-glanding"). Schulberg decided that Beggars of Life would be an excellent film to try out the various
possibilities of dialog.

Wellman was skeptical. He felt that the intrusion of
sound into his carefully constructed drama would be out of
place and prove disturbing to the audience and the mood. He
was overruled, however, and Schulberg instructed Pomeroy
to supervise a scene which would feature a song by Wallace
Beery.

This scene was to be Beery's introduction into the film.
He comes upon the hobo jungle where the girl and the tramp
are taking refuge for the night. Pomeroy wanted Beery to
enter the scene, stand in the midst of the hoboes and sing
his song, "Hark the Bells!" Wellman thought that the scene
would be static and unnatural. He wanted Beery to come
walking into the jungle, carrying a barrel of moonshine and
singing his song. Pomeroy insisted that the microphone could
not, under any circumstances, be moved. "That burned me
up," Wellman said. "You can't make a picture that way.
You've got to have some flow. So I came in and I said,
'I've got news for you soundmen this morning. I'm moving
that goddamned mike.' " David Selznick recalled to Kevin
Brownlow,

> I was also present on the stage when the micro-
> phone was moved for the first time by Wellman, be-
> lieve it or not. Sound was relatively new and at

that time the sound engineer insisted that the microphone be steady.   Wellman, who had quite a temper
in those days, got very angry, took the microphone
himself, hung it on a boom [actually, he put it on
a broom], gave orders to record--and moved it.
That was the end of what had been a complete loss
of cinema.

Beery also recorded some dialog, probably only one
scene.   A review mentions, "One also hears, through the
medium of the Vitaphone, Wallace Beery as Oklahoma Red,
refer to his companions as 'Jungle Buzzards.'"   Sadly,
though the film exists, the soundtrack has been lost.   Possibly, upon hearing Beery sing, angry villagers tossed it into
the sea.

This song and brief dialog sequence was the first recorded vocal for a Paramount feature and it is interesting to
point out that the first time Wellman used the microphone,
he used it in conjunction with a tracking camera.   The man
just wouldn't stay still.

CHAPTER FIVE

The coming of sound didn't appear to affect Wellman one way or the other. His brief experimentation with dialog in Beggars of Life had shown him that the panic about sound was a little exaggerated and he was anxious to move on to full talkies.

What is most interesting about his first sound films at Paramount is the air of prescience with which they are imbued. Every one contains the germ of an idea, an expression, a characteristic trait or a theme that would later be developed in his more mature period. This is not to say that the early sound films are worthwhile only as stylistic blueprints; they are fine, tough films that need no apology. Certainly there's not a masterpiece among them but there is in each much to admire and much to learn about their director's interests, flaws, strengths, and obsessions.

The films--Chinatown Nights (1929), The Man I Love (1929), Woman Trap (1930), Dangerous Paradise (1930), and Young Eagles (1930)--are virtually unknown today as are the great majority of the films produced in that turbulent era. Perhaps this is because the early sound film strikes people as being rather more archaic than just about any period before or since. Much is written in the film histories about the "static, stage-bound" qualities of the early sound cinema; the "microphone in the bush" stories are widely regarded as the state of the art of the late twenties and early thirties, but looking at these films quickly erases most of those biases. Among their most striking qualities is their movement. In fact, these five films probably make wider use of tracking

shots and dollies than any of Wellman's later motion pictures.
He stubbornly held on to the beauty of the silent film, while
he carefully and intelligently went about augmenting the images
with dialog, music, and sounds of all sorts.

"Camera movement I loved," said Wellman, "and then
I got awfully sick of it." In fact, the rest of his career
seems to have been spent in honing down his style to the
bare essentials. After the mid-thirties, the camera movement in a Wellman film is used in a manner more utilitarian
than stylistic.

But at this period, he pulled out all the stops. His
camera movement was born equally of ego as of artistic con-
siderations. An arrogant man, he seemed out to prove that
nothing so inconsequential as a little microphone was going
to hamper his work. If everyone else was nailing his camera to the floor, then by God, Wellman would track till the
cows came home.

Wellman was among those directors who claimed to
have been the first to use a boom microphone and he seems
to have excellent ground for his claim. Whether or not he
was actually the first, it is true that he was among the first
directors to resume more-or-less normal filmmaking technique after the sound panic hit. He took sound in stride and
used it naturally and unobtrusively just as he was later to
become an early master of new processes like Technicolor
and CinemaScope.

About sound he "didn't have an opinion one way or the
other. My reputation was based on making films very quickly.
Whether a film talks or not is immaterial anyhow. I hate
the word 'film'--I prefer (the term) 'motion picture'--a picture that moves, and movement is the most important thing."

His pictures certainly did that and his early sound
films moved just as much as his silents. In fact, the major
stylistic difference one finds in the sound films is the lack
of close-ups. With the new informational possibilities of dialog, he could dispense with what he considered an over-used
technique. To Wellman, close-ups were exclamation points,
elbow nudges to the audience. While very necessary in silent
films where the face and eyes bear so much dramatic responsibility, the close-ups could be used with more discre-
tion when dialog was available.

He explained, "You use close-ups to bolster a sequence, to get a point over.   Cut in to a close-up and it
means something. " So relieved did he seem to be when rid
of the necessity of the constant close-up, that his films are
almost completely devoid of them.   Rarely, particularly in
his early sound films, does he move in closer than a medium
shot, even in the most dramatic moments.

Wellman wanted to evoke emotion, not from tight close-
ups of tear-stained faces, but from the skillful manipulation
of the camera, editing and dialog.   No matter how unjustified
his faith turned out to be, Wellman always trusted the story
and used his skills in ways that best told it.

> I don't know what made me begin to move the cam-
> era around.   I'd seen fights and I wanted to get
> closer to them so I'd move forward.   Then I thought
> I'd do that with the camera.   But what I loved most
> was composition.   I used to get some wonderful odd
> angles, but then everybody started using odd angles
> --shooting through people's navels--so the idea was
> destroyed.   Then I realized that the best thing was
> to make pictures the simplest way you could; if you
> wanted movement or anything like that, use it where
> it really meant something.

Though he never completely shook his penchant for
"odd angles" Wellman spent his years at Paramount unifying
his vision and reconciling the extremes in his nature.   While
still a sucker for a good tracking shot, one notes from film
to film that he tried to simplify things, to make his direction
invisible.

A celebrated bit of Wellman technique is the tracking
crane shot through the Paris cafe in Wings.   The camera
moves with ease and precision over the tabletops and one is
carried along with the momentum.   The shot is brilliant and
Wellman knew it.

In The Man I Love, there is a scene of greater virtu-
osity.   The camera follows a boxer (Richard Arlen) into a
locker room, staying with him as he crosses the room and
enters a dressing area with his manager.   It waits outside
the door of the dressing room as the two men argue, each of
their faces periodically appearing in the round window in the
door.   When the two men emerge, the camera moves with
them back out of the locker room, into a corridor, through

another door and into the boxing arena. As they walk down
the aisle, acknowledging the cheers of the crowd, the camera
tracks steadily along behind them. The men enter the ring
and the camera continues to track along the front row all the
way around to the other side of the ring to bring the boxer's
girlfriend (Mary Brian) into a medium shot. The entire sequence is accomplished in one shot!

The length and complexity of the scene is breathtaking
and, as an example of Wellman's skill, exceeds the Folies-
Bergère shot in Wings. A shot of this type would have been
formidable in a silent film (it takes place in three different
rooms and goes places where it would seem impossible to lay
track); with the added ingredients of dialog and sound effects,
it seems nearly superhuman.

The most important point about the scene, though, is
the matter-of-fact way in which it is accomplished. The
scene is strictly functional. It was done in one take, not
because Wellman felt like being brilliant that day, but because it was the way that the story could best be served at
that point. It is a tour de force which puts the lie to all
stories about the static condition of early talkies. As Wellman said, he used movement where "it really meant something."

His progression toward a simpler style had farther
reaching effects than a mere paring down of his visual virtu-
osity; it also affected his choice of stories. The personal
story in Wings is vital, of course, but the real star of that
film is World War I, not "Buddy" Rogers.

With the coming of sound, Wellman was forced to
work on more intimate stories. Characters and relationships became the theme and performances became more
subtle and nuanced. One remembers the dog fights and
massive battles in Wings, but the strongest aspect of The
Public Enemy is James Cagney's riveting performance. The
progression is an important one. The period from 1929 to
1930 at Paramount is where it evolved.

Obviously, at first glance, there seems to have been
a regression. Woman Trap, on the surface, must seem a
step down from Wings. A modest story of two brothers on
opposite sides of the law, Woman Trap runs an efficient hour
in length and has all the appearances of being just another
programmer. Yet Wellman's career is full of such apparent

contradictions: How does one explain a film like The Ox-Bow
Incident being followed up by Lady of Burlesque? Surely the
former is an important statement and the latter is frivolous
filler. Yet to approach Wellman's career in this way is to
deny his wide range of concerns and to ignore his position
as a contract director.

First and foremost in importance to Wellman was his
need to work. "Now, Frank Capra can take a project and
start working on it, get a good writer and work on the script,
get everything all ready, do the casting, make the picture
and almost a year's gone by. I couldn't do it. I'd be so
damned bored. One time when Frank was making a picture,
I made six pictures."

But he always did right by his films. Whether studio
assignments or personal projects, Wellman's career is all of
a piece. Woman Trap is as close to the essential Wellman
as Wings--closer perhaps, since the smaller, more unassum-
ing project almost by definition leaves more room for the director's personality to project itself. In fact it demands the
director's personality for it to be transformed from assembly-
line product to a grudging work of art.

No matter how slight the film seemed to be, no matter how trivial the subject matter, Wellman was able to leave
his personal imprint on the finished product. In his truly
self-depreciating way, Wellman confirms this: "Frankly, if
you review my whole background, it isn't very good. I can
tell you that for every good picture, I made five or six
stinkers. But I always tried to do it a little differently. I
don't know whether I accomplished it, but I tried."

He succeeded better than he knew, perhaps. The way
Wellman did things "a little differently" translates to style.
How strong and original was that style becomes more appar-
ent with every viewing of one of his films.

Charles Barton contested Wellman's above statement.
"Well, I'll tell you something. I don't think Wellman ever
made very many bad films. I really mean this. Even at the
start, he always had some little thing in his films. He was
real, he was honest."

While describing Wellman, Barton describes his films
as well. Sometimes shaky in premise, underdeveloped,
poorly motivated, the films still work. It's as if they are

propelled forward on the strength of Wellman's convictions. Where the scripts provided no originality, when the actors brought no life to their roles, Wellman infused his own into the films until they whirred along with pace, energy, and enthusiasm. What Barton said about Wellman can be equally applied to his films: They are real. They are honest.

Wellman had finished his second film with Wallace Beery, Chinatown Nights, as a silent film in late 1928. Encouraged by the success of the part-talkies being turned out at the time, Paramount decided to put Chinatown Nights back into production to add a few talking scenes. Wellman and producer David O. Selznick, felt a little more ambitious, however. They talked it over and decided to convert Chinatown Nights into a full-sound picture.

The process of adding a sound sequence or two to a silent film was known derisively in the trade as "goat-glanding" and neither Wellman nor Selznick liked that idea too much. In addition to some dialog scenes, they went back to several other sections of Chinatown Nights and dubbed in the dialog and sound effects. The outcome was quite remarkable; it had the popular novelty of sound, yet it retained all the fluidity of the silent cinema. William K. Everson has written, "Chinatown Nights is a perfect example of what Hollywood directors themselves envisioned as the talkie of the future. In pacing, mobile camerawork, and overall design, it is essentially a silent film, still using a constant musical score and narrative subtitles."

Looking back, David Selznick remembered Chinatown Nights as "an awful attempt at melodrama." He wrote, "I thought that a picture about a tong war would be exciting, but somehow it didn't come off." Still more recently, historian Kevin Brownlow characterized the film as "the worst film by a major director that I've ever seen." Even contemporary reviews were hostile toward Chinatown Nights. The New York Times critic called it an "absurd story from beginning to end."

The film is not quite the horror that these quotes might lead one to believe. Chinatown Nights is quite a curious film, rather an inverted, nightmarish Broken Blossoms. It concerns a society matron (Florence Vidor) who becomes involved with the white leader (Wallace Beery) of a tong faction in San Francisco's Chinatown.

Wallace Beery (left) as Chuck Riley, a white tong leader in
Chinatown Nights.

Wellman proved far better at creating a mood than in
conveying much sincerity in the rather hysterical plot.   The
events are cursorily told, the acting is widely variable, and
the ending lacks conviction.   Yet, Chinatown Nights remains
consistently interesting.

Its added sound is, curiously, its greatest asset.   The
somewhat disembodied dialog, caused by dubbing onto a scene
shot silently, adds greatly to the film's overwhelming sense
of isolation and confusion.   Undoubtedly coincidental, the use
of sound (and the quality of that sound) could hardly have been
used in a more appropriate vehicle.

The theme of the picture is dislocation.   The characters are depicted as being incongruous elements in the Chinatown atmosphere.   Beery is the white leader of an Oriental
tong faction and is involved in a war waged entirely by Chinese.   Florence Vidor is a woman of means who develops a
masochistic need for squalor and brutality through her attraction to the villainous Beery.   The emphatic, deliberate rhythm

of the dubbed speech heightens the hallucinatory mood and lends a sense of ritual to the proceedings.   Dark and ugly and good in ways that Wellman probably never intended, Chinatown Nights has the essence of a nightmare. Two years later at Warner Bros., Wellman returned to this location and theme in his much maligned The Hatchet Man.

The new sound edition of Chinatown Nights was released on March 23, 1929.   Only two months later, on May 25, Wellman's first full-talkie was released.

The Man I Love has all the trappings of a routine and forgettable little feature.   The story is time-honored--boxer gets to the top with the aid of his faithful wife, dumps her for an exotic mistress, comes to his senses, wins the Big Fight--but Wellman infuses it with wit and imagination.   What emerges is a truly delightful film.

Richard Arlen in The Man I Love.

Dum-Dum Brooks (Richard Arlen) is a perplexing protagonist for a film, mainly because he so thoroughly lives up
to his name.   He is quite stupid, arrogant and a rank oppor-
tunist.   He dumps his wife at the very first opportunity and
only takes her back after he's been rejected by his mistress
and the "respectable" society of which he longs to be a part.

Though the plot is moth-eaten and the hero is something less than sympathetic, the film is engaging on many
levels.   Much credit is due Herman Mankiewicz's witty
script, for the dialog has a low-life charm and more than
its share of crisp lines.   More importantly, The Man I Love
is perhaps the first film that is truly representative of Wellman.   It contains in total the characteristic touches and tics
that will define the remainder of his career.

One of these characteristics is the provocative suggestion.   Wellman would prefer to allude to something rather
than show it.   One example is the climactic fight.   Dum-
Dum's wife, Celia (Mary Brian), listens to the fight on the
radio and it is through her reactions that we follow what is
happening.   The camera cuts from the ring-side announcer
to Celia at radio-side and only incidentally shows the action
in the ring at all.   When Wellman does deign to show the
fight, it's apt to be shot from the ceiling, as though from
the point of view of a light bulb.   Earlier in the film, Wellman uses the element of suggestion to depict Dum-Dum and
Celia's wedding night.

Unable to afford the train tickets to New York, Dum-
Dum has arranged with a friend ("a fight bug" with Wellman's
voice) to ride in a boxcar that is transporting race-horses.
Celia is being a good sport about the less-than-desirable circumstances (the scene recalls Louise Brooks and Richard
Arlen's ride on the bread cart in Beggars of Life) and Dum-
Dum tries to create a romantic mood with the Victrola that
is her wedding present.   He plays "their song," "Sweetheart"
which they have renamed "Celia" and she sings along.   Dum-
Dum kisses Celia in mid-verse.   As he does, the camera
rises discreetly above this action and focuses on the sober
face of a horse.   He seems completely uninterested in the
scene on the floor and, for a full minute, until the song
ends, the horse simply stares out of the screen.   When the
song is over, the camera cuts to a shot of the spinning turn-
table until we realize that no one is thinking of turning it off.

Dozens of eccentric little touches like this color The

Man I Love. Though we are always a step ahead of the plot,
we remain amused and interested.   Where a film like Wings
was the product of a gifted young man with the resources of
a huge studio, a phenomenal budget, a squadron of photographers, and an entire army base (complete with army) at his
disposal, The Man I Love is a good example of his ability to
make something of nothing.

In addition to the stunning tracking shot alluded to
earlier, The Man I Love is filled with interesting camera
angles and movement.   In the latter portion of the film,
Dum-Dum is at a party thrown by his new mistress, Sonia
(Olga Baclanova).   Her previous lover, Carlo Vesper (Leslie
Fenton), has made it his business to get Dum-Dum as drunk
as possible.   These tensions set up another quite remarkable
shot.

The shot begins by showing Dum-Dum sitting in a
drunken stupor.   The camera backs up to record Carlo's
walk to the telephone where he sits down to call Celia (and
flubs a line which goes uncorrected--apparently, Wellman
wanted to go through this once), then follows him as he
strolls back to the party.   The camera tracks past Carlo
and up to a full-figure shot of Dum-Dum standing next to
Sonia and weaving to and fro with inebriation.   The camera
again backs up as Dum-Dum walks toward a chair in which
he collapses.   He is holding a glass and a bottle enters at
the side of the frame to fill it.   Dum-Dum looks up and
says, "Hey, you've been my private butler all night," and
this remarkably long shot ends.

Also in the cast of The Man I Love is Jack Oakie,
making his second of four appearances with Wellman.   He
had played a conniving newspaper reporter with a pronounced
stutter and a talent for stirring up the tongs in Chinatown
Nights.   Here, he is Lew Layton, the cynical henchman of
boxing manager D. J. McCarthy (Pat O'Malley).   The role
allows Oakie some of the better lines in the script.   Upon
Dum-Dum's first sight of the exotic Sonia Barondoff, he
asks Layton "who the Million Dollar Dame" is.   Layton replies, "She's the hottest thing in New York society.   Why,
it ain't legal for a tabloid paper to be printed without at
least two pictures of that dame."   Dum-Dum indicates Sonia's
boyfriend.   Layton replies in exasperation, "How did you ever
get so old without the truant officer catching you?   Why that's
Carlo Vesper.   He's the new expressionistic poet."   Dum-
Dum is puzzled.   Layton tries again.   "He writes the new

kind of poetry," he says, fluttering his eyelids.   Even Dum-
Dum gets his meaning now.

Olga Baclanova is also given some choice dialog, but
her greatest asset is her frankly sexual gaze and erotic
"body English."   The New York Times said, "It is certain
that when she portrays a character there is going to be
trouble.   Heroes are supposed to give one or two sighs and
then become victims of Baclanova's beauty."

Carlo Vesper tells Sonia, "If I ever thought you didn't
love me, I'd kill myself."   Sonia replies, "Of course you
would.   That's the way I like to be loved."

Richard Arlen makes his fourth appearance with Wellman in The Man I Love.   Unaccountably, Arlen seems to
have been a favorite of Wellman's.   In the first three films,
Wings, Beggars of Life, and Ladies of the Mob, Arlen was
good enough.   These were all silent films and Arlen was
handsome enough to get by, but his "audible" performances
are sadly lacking in skill.   At least in The Man I Love, he
plays a dim-witted character, so his wooden performance is
not altogether inappropriate.   But when he is called on, in
Dangerous Paradise, to act the part of a world-weary intel-
lectual, he is nearly intolerable.   Wellman was fortunate in
casting Arlen opposite an impressive array of leading ladies.
Even Arlen is hard-pressed to look bad with partners like
Louise Brooks, Mary Brian, Nancy Carroll, and Clara Bow.

Luckily, too, Dangerous Paradise has much to divert
our attention from Arlen.   The enchanting Nancy Carroll is
a major asset, but the film really belongs to a movie full of
some of the slimiest villains on record.

In an apparent attempt to deflect criticism from its
rather cavalier treatment of Joseph Conrad's novel Victory,
Dangerous Paradise carries a credit that reads, "Based on
incidents from a novel by Joseph Conrad."   This never fooled
anyone and Dangerous Paradise is usually regarded as bad
Conrad and bad Wellman.

It is neither, in fact, for Dangerous Paradise is quite
successful in creating a Conradian atmosphere and many of
the characters are pictured quite accurately.   The muggy,
heavy tropical atmosphere is brought off beautifully and shows
again how much care Wellman could put into the background.

Richard Arlen and Nancy Carroll in a posed scene from Dangerous Paradise, based on "incidents from a novel by Joseph Conrad" (Victory).

William Everson wrote, "It's a comic-strip adaptation of Conrad--yet, at that, it automatically contains more built-in values than similar comic-strip movies without such distinguished ancestry."

One of the enormous riches of Dangerous Paradise is its vast assortment of villains. In what must be the most lecherous cast ever assembled, the slavering honors are tied between the eternally weaslly Clarence H. Wilson as Zangiacomo, leader of an all-woman orchestra, and the fat and oily Warner Oland, in whom lust and drool are synonymous, as the hotel-owner Schomberg, in whose hotel the orchestra plays.

Nancy Carroll plays Alma, a violinist and singer with Zangiacomo's orchestra. This unfortunate girl gets it from all sides; not only is there an intense competition for her favors by Zangiacomo and Schomberg, but she is also constantly verbally and physically (her violin case is slammed violently on her fingers, at one point) harassed by their respective wives. She is treated kindly by a guest at the hotel, Heyst (Richard Arlen), and hides aboard his boat as he is heading back to the secluded island where he lives. As she is leaving, both Zangiocomo and Schomberg are converging on her room with hopes of consummating their lusts for her. When they find each other in Alma's room, a fight breaks out.

Wellman's trait of alluding to action characterizes this conflict. With a grunted threat, Schomberg hulks toward Zangiacomo, who screams with fear and picks up a large candlestick to defend himself. The candle falls from the holder and lies, still lit, on the dresser-top. Instead of following the action of the fight, the camera continues its slow track toward the candle. When the candle fills the frame, we hear a scream ... the sound of a body falling downstairs ... silence. The candle's flame goes out. Fade out.

Two Wellman traits are evident here. His allusion to the fight is characteristic, but so is his use of the candlestick as a symbol for Zangiacomo. Wellman preferred to present death indirectly, most often by using a device that has been closely identified with a character. The candle is an early example (not the first) of this trait and, while eloquent, is not quite as well thought out as later epitomizing objects would be. It effectively conveys the violence of Zangiacomo's end, but it doesn't identify him in any other way. In 1929, Wellman had the instinct but was not quite able to use its full potential.

Still, the candlestick looks back to the airplane pro-
pellor that slows to a stop as Richard Arlen dies in Wings
and looks forward to the bathrobe being buffeted by the waves
in A Star Is Born, the trumpet buried by the sand in Beau
Geste, the abandoned artificial leg in the mud in Wild Boys
of the Road, the rocking horse floating briefly, then sinking
in the flood-swollen river in The Great Man's Lady.

Wellman realized that we could be made to feel the
loss of human life more strongly if we can see a possession
that no longer has an owner.   There is something infinitely
more sad and touching in that rocking horse, something more
brutal and horrifying in that candle than the straightforward
documentation of the deaths would be.   In this use of suggestion, Wellman makes the audience participate, imagine, work
and believe.

As though Dangerous Paradise weren't already filled
with a normal quota of villains with Schomberg and Zangiacomo,
the latter's death introduces three more remorseless (if stylish) killers: Mr. Jones (Gustav Von Seyfertitz), Ricardo
(Francis MacDonald), and an ape-like wrestler with a keen
appreciation for brutal murder, Pedro (George Kotsonaros).
As Schomberg sits beside Zangiacomo's body, the three stroll
in.   They calmly survey the scene.   Ricardo smiles and says,
"Sweet job."   Mr. Jones, the leader of the pack replies, "Not
bad" and, laughing, they go to their rooms.

Dangerous Paradise is strongly assisted by the beautiful location photography.   Most of the film was shot on Cata-
lina, which is quite convincing as Heyst's remote island.   As
beautiful as the scenery is the lovely Nancy Carroll.   One of
the biggest stars at Paramount during this period, it is Carroll who receives top billing on Dangerous Paradise though it
had been only two years since Wellman and Arlen had made
the phenomenally successful Wings.   Her performance in this
picture is marvelous.   She was such a sure-footed actress
that she remains natural, compelling, and believable in the
midst of the outrageous hams that surround her.

There is a remarkable scene where Alma and Heyst
stand outside of the hotel and listen to a native love-song
wafting across the bay.   Heyst begins to translate the words
for her.   The look of admiration and interest (concentration,
even) on her face is impossible to describe.   She is so completely listening to what he is saying, that it ceases to be
acting and becomes a convincing reality.   A small detail in
a brief moment in a modest film, it still strikes one as the

very model of screen acting. It brings home what a capable
actress she was and how unjustly neglected she has been and
continues to be.

        Wellman kept up his breakneck pace into 1930. Dan-
gerous Paradise had been complete in late 1929 and was released on February 22, 1930. His next film, Young Eagles,
appeared in theatres less than a month later, on March 21.
The speed with which he worked can be attributed to many
things; foremost was his characteristic hyperactivity. But
there is also reason to believe that he was dissatisfied at
Paramount. Signed in 1928 to a seven-year contract, he
found himself, not two years later, working on material that
he felt was of a programmer-type.

        There is some evidence that his tactics in finishing
Wings made many lasting enemies for him at Paramount.
Too, the subsequent contract bargaining handled for him by
Myron Selznick made him quite wealthy, which was galling
for those enemies. For whatever reason, Wellman did one
more film for Paramount, then terminated his contract to go
to Warner Bros. For his last film, he returned to the scene
of his first glory--the sky.

        In some ways, Young Eagles forms the last chapter
of a World War I trilogy, with Wings and Legion of the Condemned. Since there is no first-hand knowledge of the quality
of Legion of the Condemned, there's no way to be absolutely
certain that Young Eagles is the weakest link, but all the evidence points that way.

        Concerned as it is with the great love of Wellman's
life, flight, it's hard to understand how he could let Young
Eagles turn out to be so lackluster. "Buddy" Rogers made
his second and last appearance with Wellman in Young Eagles
and he speaks ruefully of this experience today.

                We used quite a bit of footage from Wings. The
                film didn't come off well at all. I didn't know why,
                we had a good cast, Paul Lucas and others. I was
                disappointed. The film was a cheater, strictly for
                promotion and cash-value. I was still young and
                didn't know anything then. We wouldn't go anyplace
                on location.

        Paramount had apparently decided to cash in on the
still-potent box-office magic of Wings, but with typical studio

Part of the team that struck gold with Wings tries again with Young Eagles: "Buddy" Rogers, pilot Dick Grace, and their tousle-haired director.

short-sightedness, did not wish to lavish any money or care on the production. Besides, they reasoned, they had so much stock footage left over from Wings that they could make a dozen more films.

In fact, there is little time spent in the air in Young Eagles. The greater part of the film is taken up with a rather contrived spy-vs-spy plot. "Buddy" Rogers' gee-whiz enthusiasm had not quite modulated itself to sound, and co-star Jean Arthur is stiff and awkward without much of the charm that was to make her a favorite just a few years later.

Stock shots or not, the aerial scenes highlight the picture. One can almost feel Wellman's relief at soaring high above the trivial action below. In all of Wellman's films about flying, there is an exhilaration felt by filmmaker and audience that takes the film to a higher level of expression. Wellman's men with planes form a unique coterie in the Amer-

ican film. No other director was so eloquent on the freedom
and beauty of flight. That great love of the sky is very much
in evidence in the brief aerial scenes in Young Eagles and is
what lifts the film out of the mire.

The one other location that Wellman feels comfortable
with in Young Eagles is the barracks. There is a casual,
amiable spirit to the scenes set there. The barracks in this
picture is one of those classic Wellman places, like the gym
in The Man I Love or the back room in The Public Enemy.
It is a room filled with bored men bursting with energy, looking for any excuse to get a sock on the jaw or give somebody
the hotfoot.

The constant horseplay, bickering, and practical joking
in these scenes from Young Eagles invoke the feeling of their
being put on film by someone who knows what barracks life
is like and who knows the nature of fighting men. Even in a
film that ultimately shows little interest from its director,
he can't resist affectionately leaving a little of himself on the
screen.

Though not the last film Wellman directed under his
first contract at Paramount, Woman Trap is perhaps the most
important. Released on August 30, 1929, between The Man
I Love and Dangerous Paradise, the film anticipates 1931's
The Public Enemy in its tale of two brothers on opposite sides
of the law. Woman Trap is one of Wellman's earliest forays
into the world of crime (only Ladies of the Mob and Chinatown
Nights precede it), a theme that he would return to often in
the thirties.

Characteristically, Wellman depicts the lawman versus
criminal struggle through personal terms. In Woman Trap
this tension is worked out through the deteriorating relationship of two brothers, Dan and Ray Malone (Hal Skelly and
Chester Morris), on opposite sides of the law.

Unlike the antagonistic Powers brothers in The Public Enemy, Dan and Ray have an easy, genuine affection for
each other. The film opens on their affable horseplay and
closes on a note of familial sacrifice and the conflict arises,
not out of their diverging views on law, but from their eroding bond of brotherhood.

The relationship of the Malone brothers is the prime
subject of Woman Trap, but the picture is composed of an

"I thought you and my brother would be married by now."

Chester Morris and Evelyn Brent in one of Wellman's early crime films, <u>Woman Trap</u>.

intricate labyrinth of intertwining relationships. Dan is in love with Kitty Evans (Evelyn Brent), but their courtship is a stormy one. He tells his mother (Effie Ellsler), "There's something I'd be asking her if we'd ever stop scrapping long enough for me to get in a word." Kitty's brother Eddie (Leslie Fenton) is Ray's best friend. The two are peripherally involved in bootlegging, which is of great concern to Dan and Kitty.

In essence, each of the four characters is in one way or another accountable to each of the other three. Dan is brother to Ray, lover to Kitty and, being a police officer, an authoritarian figure to Eddie. Kitty is Dan's mirror image (or feminine side) and her relationship to the other three in the quadrant is similar to his.

The link between Dan and Kitty is a sub-theme of the
film. Virtually every change in his character is mirrored
by the same change in hers. They begin the film together,
drift apart, become deadly enemies, and return to each other
in their grief at film's end. Kitty makes their mutual development quite clear in the latter half of the film. Dan has
arrested Eddie for being involved in a dynamiting of the City
Civic League. Everyone else involved escaped and Dan rail-
roads Eddie through a swift trial and succeeds in having him
hanged. At the moment of Eddie's death on the gallows,
Kitty barges in to Dan's office and berates him for what she
considers the cold-blooded murder of her brother. She ends
by snarling, "I'm just as cold and heartless as you, except
colder and harder. And I'm gonna get you ... so that you
cry the way I've been crying. "

As Dan caused the death of Eddie, so Kitty betrays
Ray, an act which ends in his death. Earlier in the film,
Ray and Eddie are on a bootlegging job. Ray is to return
a borrowed car after the delivery and when he does, he is
set upon by government agents. Ray scuffles with one and
in the struggle, the officer is shot. Ray believes that he
is dead and runs. When Dan discovers his brother's responsibility, he is changed from the tolerant, easy-going
officer, to a cruel and ruthless cop. A sign hangs on his
desk: "The Law Lies In The End Of A Policeman's Night
Stick. "

The agent that Ray believes to be dead is, in fact,
only wounded and Ray's desperate flight from a murder
charge is futile. The act changes Ray into an actual criminal. When he sneaks into town to have a last look at his
mother (who has been told by Dan that Ray died in a heroic
act), he trusts Kitty to arrange a rendezvous with Eddie, for
Ray does not know of Eddie's hanging.

Kitty sees this as a perfect opportunity to get back at
Dan, so she arranges for Ray to be ambushed. She thinks
he will merely be sent back to jail on a theft charge. What
she doesn't know is that Ray has met the same government
agent again. They fight and this time the agent is killed.
When the trap is sprung, Ray shoots himself, to avoid having
his mother know the truth about his life. Thus do Dan and
Kitty cause the deaths of their brothers and complete the cir-
cular pattern which they began.

Woman Trap is so fast-moving and so packed with plot

that one is rather taken aback to realize that the entire picture runs its course in just over an hour. Wellman takes great care in every facet of Woman Trap which results in its superiority over its origins as a programmer/melodrama.

Every scene is staged in a unique and provocative manner. Early in the film the Malones' mother is accidentally blinded. They take her to the hospital and, as they await word on her condition, Dan and Ray stand uncomfortably in the hospital corridor, griefstricken, worried and a little embarrassed by their public display of emotion.

There is a long and skillful camera track down the corridor and snatches of conversation are picked up here and there. As the Malones stand morosely by, a couple of orderlies tell a dirty joke. The punchline is obscured when a young nurse noisily drops a tray and is loudly reprimanded by the head nurse. The orderlies roar with laughter.

When they get their mother home, they find the night nurse (Virginia Bruce) to be of little solace. She wonders if there's a good picture playing in the neighborhood and whines for Dan to stop pacing around. There is no sympathy for personal anguish in Woman Trap.

Dan wanders toward Kitty's house for solace and meets her on the street. They step inside a hotel lobby to talk. The scene is played with both principals' backs to the camera and continues to the sound of contrapuntal jocularity. As Dan pours out his feelings to Kitty, a little boy walks by with his mother and asks, "Why is that man crying like that?" Across the room, two secretaries giggle over a recent proposition ("... so I kissed him where it would do the most good: on top of his bald head!"). By playing the sentimental scenes to the accompaniment of everyday sounds, Wellman manages to make the sentiment more recognizable. As a character is later to say in Roxie Hart, "Laugh and the world laughs with you. Cry, and you look like a chump." Dan feels like a chump and this awkwardness makes his sorrow the more genuine. How much more effective this approach is than if Wellman had conventionally staged the conversation backed with tremulous strings.

The strains of contrapuntal laughter continues throughout Woman Trap. When Ray meets Kitty at the beauty shop where she works, his doom is sealed while a woman screams with laughter during an apparently very strenuous massage.

At the bar where Ray meets, fights with, and kills the government agent, a young man and woman emerge laughing from
a side room. They are drunk and the woman's dress is torn.
The man keeps babbling, "I'll buy you a new one" to which
the woman replies, "I'll take the cash!"

Wellman continues his trait of suggesting, rather than
showing, the action in Woman Trap. When Ray has his first
fight with the agent, he tries to escape via a freight elevator.
The agent is able to jump in and stop the ascent, causing the
entire fight to be conveyed by the men's legs. This is not
just a gimmick of Wellman's; he uses it to prolong the suspense. When we hear the gunshot, it is impossible to tell
who has been hit. Only when the agent drops to the floor
and rolls out onto the ground do we know the results.

The film is well thought out and one finds little touches
that seem incidental, until one realizes how much they add to
the fabric of the narrative. When Kitty confronts Dan in his
office as Eddie is being hanged, there is a shadow behind her
head of the windowshade cord. It looks like a little noose.
As she angrily spews forth her hatred and vows revenge, the
little noose-shadow swings slowly back and forth.

Similarly, when Ray shoots himself at the end of the
film, Dan walks toward the room where Ray's body lies and
leans on the door. From our vantage point, we can see his
entire body, but the shot is framed in such a way that his
head is obscured from view. The result is a neat pictoriali-
zation of a man without a head--which is what Dan is looking
at in that room.

Neither of these examples are as overt in the film as
they seem when describing them. Wellman uses them so as
to be subconsciously effective. In fact, they were very probably subconscious to Wellman, as well; he worked as much
from instinct as from any pre-conceived ideas on "art," yet
it is the instinctive that claims our attention and makes an
artist unique.

Another instinctive Wellman touch in Woman Trap is
the way Ray refers to his brother as "Beanpole." Throughout the film, the nickname is used as a kind of litany of
brotherly affection. When they are estranged, Ray always
refers to his brother as Dan, but when he prepares to kill
himself, he calls out "Goodbye ... you Beanpole." The use
of the name brings home the tragedy of their reunion as it
conjures up images of their happier past.

The device is one that Wellman uses often.   It is an
identifying tag on the characters who use it, which helps us
to know them more quickly and thoroughly and informs us of
the changes in their lives with economy.   In Wings ("All
set?"), Beau Geste ("I promise you!"), A Star Is Born ("Do
you mind if I take just one more look?"), Other Men's Women
("Have a chew on me."), Battleground ("That's fer sure, that's
fer dang sure.") and on and on, Wellman supplies his characters with a physical or verbal calling card.   One would be
hard pressed to think of a Wellman film in which this did not
occur.   It supplies a crucial thread throughout each film and,
in a larger sense, the whole of his career.

These first five talkies at Paramount are rarely shown
anymore, but so many of Wellman's traits first appear in
them, that they seem the product of the most crucial time in
his career.   The remarkable personality that would more fully
express itself in the later thirties and forties begins to crys-
tallize in these brief, unpretentious pictures.   These were
the films that saw him change from a promising young director to a superb craftsman and, perhaps, a fine artist.   In
fact, these are films that showed he knew how to combine
artistry and craftsmanship and how he enriched his work by
letting the diverse facets of his personality have equal reign.

CHAPTER SIX

It seems as though Wellman never completed the terms of any contract that he signed. By late 1930, only a little over two years after he signed his generous seven-year contract at Paramount, he had left that studio to go to Warner Bros. As interesting as his films at Paramount had been, he felt that they were little more than "B" material; certainly a man who had brought Paramount the first Academy Award for Best Picture could have been given more important assignments.

No one is sure whether Wellman asked out of his contract or whether he was fired. Screenwriter John Bright claims to know the reason of Wellman's premature departure. "Wild Bill had been fired by Paramount for goosing a girl. She bolted into a twenty-five-thousand-dollar Mitchell camera and smashed it to the floor just as some bankers were walking on the set to inspect the studio for refinancing. Zukor wasn't at all pleased."

That story can pass since there is no more probable one to put in its place. Suffice it to say that March 1930 found Wellman at Warner Bros./First National. On the 24th day of that month, Wellman signed a two-year contract which was every bit as favorable as his late Paramount deal had been: $2,500 per week for the first twenty-two weeks of the period, $2,750 per week for the next forty weeks and $3,000 per week for the remainder. At the end of that two-year period, Wellman signed another contract for the same duration, but, typically, didn't see it through to the end.

Wellman probably moved to Warner Bros. because of

his friendship with Darryl Zanuck. Their fiery relationship
was to intermittently blaze up and cool off for the greater
part of both their careers. John Bright says, "Wellman
fascinated (Zanuck) because he was a big game hunter, because he had so much 'macho.'" Wellman admired Zanuck

> for his guts and the quality he had of grabbing a
> headline and generating the speed and enthusiasm
> all down the line to make a good picture quickly--
> at this, he was a master and the hardest-working
> little guy you have ever seen in all your life. We
> had good moments and bad, but there was one thing
> you could count on: when you wanted an answer,
> you got it right then and there; if he shook hands
> on a deal, it was a deal, period.

Wellman's first picture was to have been called Precious Little Thing later re-titled The Man Who Dared and
still later re-titled The Star Witness. He did eventually get
to the project, but all that name-changing takes time, so
Wellman was put to work on a Joe E. Brown vehicle, Maybe
It's Love.

This football story had been written by Zanuck (he
billed himself as "Mark Canfield" in the credits) and Joseph
Jackson, and starred (in addition to Brown) Joan Bennett and
James Hall. For extra beef-cake appeal, the members of
the 1929 All-American football team appeared as themselves.

Maybe It's Love is not exactly bad, but it could be the
most trivial and inconsequential movie Wellman ever directed.
He might have made worse films in his career (Darby's
Rangers) but Maybe It's Love has the added sin of being in-
stantly forgettable. There is virtually nothing of Wellman or
Zanuck in this little quickie. The film was a fair-sized hit,
but then as now, it rose or fell on the audience's tolerance
for Joe E. Brown.

Having said that, there are one or two moments of interest in the film. The plot is rife with opportunities to fill
another kind of movie: the president of Upton College is
threatened with firing unless their football team can rally
from its recent slump to beat Upton's traditional rival, Parson's University. The football team's only decent player,
Speed (Brown) is talking with the president's daughter, Nan
(Bennett) about the dilemma.

Nan: "We've got to do something. It'll break

his heart if they force him to resign."
      Speed: "It's tough all right, but we'll never
be able to get football players to come here. What
can we do?
      Nan: "Think, Speed, think of some idea. Con-
centrate."
      Speed: "I've got it! You, your eyes. Why,
if you take those cheaters off and just look at them
with your eyes naked--sort of like this [his eyelids
flutter] ... hmmm. You could recruit a squad of
All-Americans."

Which is, of course, what she does. What gives the
film the little edge that it has is the thinly-veiled sexual un-
dertone with which Nan snares her recruits. She goes to as
many good football players as she can find and flirts and offers herself to each of them if they'll only come to her college. Toward the end of the film, when her ruse is dis-
covered, there seems to be a real threat of gang-rape; all
of the football players converge on Nan's bedroom to "collect"
at the same time and their fury on being told the truth really
seems about to erupt into something not suitable for a Joe E.
Brown vehicle. Of course, the moment passes quickly and
everyone forgives Nan and goes on to win the big game, but
it represents an odd quirk of Wellman's, a dark underside to
even the most frivolous material.

The year 1931 was an even more prolific one than 1930
had been. Wellman hit his stride at Warner Bros., working
quickly, seemingly taking on any project that Zanuck deigned
to throw his way. However, 1931 was to contain no such
frivolities as Maybe It's Love; every one of the five features
he completed that year was exceptionally fine and at least two
(The Public Enemy and Night Nurse) were among the best films
he ever directed.

The first film Wellman released that year was Other
Men's Women, starring Grant Withers, Regis Toomey, and
Mary Astor. The picture was based on a story called Steel
Highway by Maude Fulton and some confusion exists yet about
the two titles; several filmographies list both titles as though
they were two different films. In fact, the script retained
the title Steel Highway until the final version, but the picture
was released as Other Men's Women and not, as some have
claimed, with its original title.

Wellman was back in his element here. Again, he re-

turns to the romantic triangle theme of so many of his films,
and again he complicates matters by having the two men involved be close friends.   The attitudes of the protagonists,
the near-documentary look of the railroad sequences, the
snappy, imaginative dialog, and the fact that nearly half the
film takes place in the rain all show Wellman's influence.

Other Men's Women is chiefly notable for the early
appearance of two young actors recently arrived in Hollywood
from the New York stage: Joan Blondell and James Cagney.
Both of their roles are brief but savory.   Blondell plays a
wise-cracking waitress who has perhaps the most memorable
line in the script.

> Yardman: "Gimme a slice of you on toast and
> some french fried potatoes on the side."
> Marie (Blondell):   "Listen, Baby, I'm A. P. O."
> Yardman: "What does she mean, A. P. O. ?"
> Marie: "Ain't puttin' out."

Cagney plays a sort of "best friend to the best friend"
role, though he clearly demonstrates the charm and authority
that was to burst him headlong into stardom just a few months
later.   Much of his dialog is clearly improvised and he even
gets to do a few dance steps.   (Wellman was apparently fond
of Cagney's dancing, for he again has the actor do a brief
routine upon meeting Jean Harlow in The Public Enemy.)

The romantic triangle bent of the script is done in
such a matter-of-fact manner in Other Men's Women that it
seems fresh and, perhaps, "modern."   Bill and Jack (Withers
and Toomey) are such good friends that they naturally assume
a reasonable attitude toward their dilemma (after a brief bitterness) of the sort that a more "sophisticated" film would
spend its entire length trying to justify.   As in Wings and
others, Wellman makes it clear that Bill and Jack's is the
important relationship; their individual love scenes with Mary
Astor, while heartfelt, are somewhat nervous and tentative,
yet they have no compunctions about expressing their deep
affection for one another.

Though they lapse briefly into rivalry, they become
friends again when one is prepared to sacrifice himself for
the other's happiness.

> Jack: "I'm sorry, Bill, oh, that we had to end
> up like this.   We've had scraps--plenty of them,

> ever since we was kids.   But I didn't give you a
> fair shake on the last one.   Doubting you the way
> I did.   I could never get the straight of it, between
> you and Lily, I mean, I guess I was seeing too
> much grub. "
>   Bill: "Shut up; there's no time to talk.   I'm
> the guy that did it.   I don't know how it happened.
> I didn't mean to hurt you, God knows. "

The sacrifice is accomplished through a spectacular
train wreck during a storm and flood.   Wellman externalizes
the emotional anguish that the three characters have gone
through by having them separated, tested and, finally reunited through the torrential rains.   Though one-third of the
triangle is killed, thus leaving the possibilities open for the
other two, the plot is actually resolved earlier through the
reconciliation of Bill and Jack.

A main character also gets a good look at himself in
the rain in Wellman's next film, when James Cagney as Tom
Powers, the Public Enemy, falls face down, riddled with
bullets, in a rain gutter, his blood joining the downward flow
of the water.   He mutters to himself, "I ain't so tough. "

This moment of self-realization, so typical of Wellman, was actually the brain-child of the authors of a multi-
storied gangster novel, Beer and Blood: John Bright and
Kubec Glasmon, who thinly fictionalized the stories of several famous gangsters for their book.   Darryl Zanuck became
interested in the property.   He called the writers in and told
them that he would be willing to make a motion picture of
Beer and Blood if they could find the one most pertinent story
in the book and stick to it; the novel was too rambling to
make a good film--particularly a good Warner Bros. film.

Glasmon and Bright decided on the story of Tom Powers and Matt Doyle, wrote a treatment and submitted it to
Zanuck.   He approved and assigned the film to Archie Mayo,
director of the recent gangster hit Doorway to Hell.   For the
leads, Zanuck chose Edward Woods as Tom Powers and that
promising newcomer James Cagney as his side-kick Matt
Doyle.

Bright recalled, "Zanuck, we knew by this time, was
a terribly imperious man.   A man of considerable talent, a
man of many abilities, but at that time very weak in the casting department.   He just simply couldn't cast things correctly. "

Somehow Wellman got a copy of the script and fell in love with it. He went to Zanuck and pleaded to be allowed to make it. Zanuck replied that the film was to be directed by Mayo, and besides, the gangster film cycle had about run its course. Wellman replied, "Let me make it and I'll make Beer and Blood the toughest goddam one of them all." Zanuck realized that Wellman would bring a vicious edge to the film and so he relieved Mayo. Wellman was given the assignment.

The prolog scenes were shot first. Frank Coghlan, Jr. played Tom Powers as a child and little-Cagney-lookalike Frankie Darro played Matt. Characteristically, Wellman gave the children physical tics and little bits of business that their adult characters would retain (Matt's full-armed wipe of his nose, Tom's cruelty to Matt's sister). The opening scenes of The Public Enemy are masterfully evocative. Cleverly combining new footage with stock shots of early-20th-century Chicago (with none of the sped-up jerkiness that often accompanies such library footage), Wellman creates a complex, believable period atmosphere.

Wellman loved using children to introduce his characters, for it gave his films a wholeness and a unity of purpose that they might otherwise have lacked. In addition to the physical details that the children introduce, Wellman is very scrupulous about introducing details into the early section of the films that are used as comments on the action later. For instance, our first view of Tom and Matt show them carrying a pail of beer, which is to be the cause of their rise and fall. When the two first enter the "club" where Puttynose, a Fagin-like character, presides, to be given their first guns, someone is playing "I'm Forever Blowing Bubbles" on the piano. The song is, of course, the one that Tom's mother puts on the Victrola just as Tom's dead body is being dumped on the doorstep. There are dozens of other little touches that illuminate the characters and the situations, some brought to the film by the actors, others written into the script, still others suggested by Wellman on the set. Combined they make The Public Enemy one of the director's most fully-realized films.

Throughout the shooting of the childhood scenes, Glasmon and Bright had been urging Wellman to switch the actors in the roles of Tom and Matt. It seemed obvious to everyone that Cagney was a natural for the leading part. Wellman agreed that the switch should be made and went to Zanuck about it. "Look there is a horrible mistake," he claims to

Sibling antagonism, a recurring theme in Wellman's work,
forms the heart of the conflict in The Public Enemy.   Left
to right: James Cagney, Beryl Mercer, and Donald Cook.

have said.   "We have the wrong guy in here.   Cagney should
be the lead."   Bright remembered,

> We got an executive summons, the same day, and
> Zanuck said, "I just got a great idea.   I'm changing
> the casting from Woods playing Tom Powers to
> Jimmy Cagney playing Powers."   He didn't give
> Wellman credit and Wellman didn't give us credit.
> But that was all right.   It wasn't all right, how-
> ever, for Zanuck not to credit Wellman.   But he
> gave credit to nobody.

Even Cagney always believed that Wellman had been

solely responsible for the switch. "Fortunately, Bill Wellman, who had seen Doorway to Hell, quickly became aware
of the obvious casting error. He knew at once that I could
project that gutter quality, so Eddie and I switched roles
after Wellman made an issue of it with Darryl Zanuck."

Whoever was responsible, the switch paid off. The
Public Enemy was Wellman's biggest hit since Wings and Cagney was immediately catapulted to stardom. Perhaps its
great success and its lasting importance to film history are
the reasons that so many of the people involved in the making
of The Public Enemy have spent so much time claiming responsibility for various aspects of its success. The other
big argument is, of course, the Grapefruit Scene. Zanuck
later claimed, "It was my idea, the grapefruit. I think I
thought of it in a script conference. When I made The Public Enemy I was way ahead in thinking. No love story but
loaded with sex and violence."

Wellman responded in his second volume of memoirs,
Growing Old Disgracefully,

Getting mad at Zanuck was not unusual. In fact,
it had long been a habit of mine, but this one siz-
zled. A man who had made as many pictures as
he, picking one bit of business to claim as his own
typifies Zanuck, a good picker of other people's
work.
The hell with it--this is the way it was and how
I got the idea of this rather unusual so-called touch.
These acclaimed touches are oftentimes something
the director stole or had happen to him sometime
in his crossword life, and some few times, parti-
cles of a vivid imagination. My so-called touch
came from none of these three, it came from beauty.

At about the time Wellman came over to Warner Bros.
from Paramount, he had made his third plunge into marriage.
It's easy to see how he became attracted to Marjorie Crawford, for she was something of a female Tommy Hitchcock,
she flew a plane and she played polo. Marjorie was "rough
and tough with the face of an angel--a beautiful blonde angel--
and a figure, amen."

"How crazy can you be and not be confined?" he wrote.
"I knew fliers; I was one of them, not too reliable, on the
goofy side, hard to handle, impossible to control, and not too
good to live with day in and day out, so I married one."

Their marriage was stormy from the beginning and it
got worse from there. One morning, after a particularly
bitter argument, Wellman came down for breakfast,

> hungover and sick. No good mornings but the usual
> half grapefruit at my place. She had finished hers
> and was drinking coffee. She looked beautiful, as
> usual, but she was playing the game called silence--
> the only difference was that she looked stony beauti-
> ful and I looked stoned ugly.
>
> I started on my grapefruit and suddenly a fan-
> tastic idea hit me, one that would show how I felt
> about [her]. I looked at her face, breathtaking but
> absolutely expressionless. It was a statue. She
> looked at me but I outlooked her, as she turned
> her head slightly--this is your chance, you silly
> bastard, squash that grapefruit in her lovely face,
> and put some northern lights in it, at least it would
> break the monotony. I didn't do it--there must be
> something chaste about me.

The scene in the script of The Public Enemy ends with
Tom Powers standing up, starting out the door, and then
throwing the grapefruit at Kitty (Mae Clarke). With the
seemingly minor refinement of having the fruit ground into
her face, Wellman added a bit of gratuitous cruelty that
should have made Tom Powers even more despicable. Oddly, the scene seems to have had the opposite effect and it
became stylish for men in the movies to mistreat women.
That this series of contemptible misogynic actions was begun (and continues to be perpetuated) by the film, is the single regrettable aspect of the otherwise brilliant Public Enemy.

Interestingly, Wellman seems to have been conscious
enough of the unsavory aspects of this scene to attempt to
correct his attitudes in later films. Though Wellman men
very often strike Wellman women, after The Public Enemy
he always thought enough of the women to have them fight
back, often to equal or greater effect.

What Wellman had done for Cagney in The Public Enemy, he was to do for Barbara Stanwyck in the three films he
made with her at Warner Bros. Like Frank Capra, Wellman
adored Stanwyck, thought she was tough and talented, a no-
nonsense type of woman who was equally at home in a love
scene or a fist-fight.

Their first film together, Night Nurse, is a delight.
The rather hysterical plot concerns a ruthless doctor who,
with the aid of his brutal chauffeur (Clark Gable) is starving
two little girls to death in order to collect a trust fund.
Stanwyck plays Lora Hart, an idealistic young nurse who un-
covers the plot and spends most of the film trying to get
people to believe her story.

Melodrama aside, Night Nurse is packed with great
dialog, wonderfully morbid moments, and non-stop action.
It has that pre-Code sensuality, a suggestiveness that is
still quite effective. Wellman spends a great deal of time
in Night Nurse having Stanwyck and sidekick Joan Blondell
taking off their clothes and playing long scenes in their frilly
underwear.

Stanwyck's character in Night Nurse most resembles
that of the stripper in Lady of Burlesque of all her roles

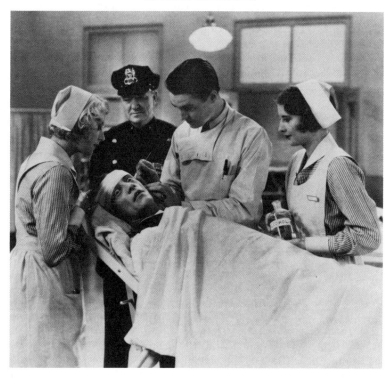

A scene from Night Nurse.

with Wellman. The hard-boiled side of her nature was just in the process of being formed in 1931 and she makes no concession to sentiment as she would in her other work with Wellman, So Big, The Purchase Price, and The Great Man's Lady. She gets slugged by the villainous Clark Gable, flings a bucket at the head of a drunken man who is trying to make a pass at her, and wrestles the starving children's tramp mother to the floor in an attempt to get her to understand the danger her babies are in. When the woman passes out, Stanwyck sneers, "You mother!"

Besides, how can one not like a film that features as the comedy relief a scene featuring the two nurses removing a bullet from a criminal's scalp, or one in which Stanwyck finds a skeleton in her bed or, for the final big laugh, when Gable's murdered body is taken to the morgue in a speeding ambulance.

Gable's performance as Nick the chauffeur is quite unlike anything else he ever did. The character is completely unsympathetic and has no redeeming virtues at all. Wellman wrote,

> [Gable] played a black-clothed chauffeur who punched the doctor [Charles Winninger] in the nose and stole food from two lovely girls. He was trying to kill them through malnutrition. One of the most despicable heavies imaginable, and he did it with such savoir faire that he became a star. The powers-that-be at Warner Brothers liked his performance but decided he was not worth fooling with, not star material: his ears were too big. They forgot to look at his dimples and listen to his voice and see his smile.

A review said that Gable "seems to undertake his role with considerable enthusiasm" and another called the film "lurid, hysterical melodrama, unpleasant in theme, yet well presented." Exactly.

In his next film, The Star Witness, Wellman extended his boundaries by having the heavies beat up not only a pretty girl (Sally Blane) but her father (Grant Mitchell), her grandfather (Chic Sale), and her little brother (George Ernest). In addition, the little boy is kidnapped and held prisoner by the gangsters.

Left to right: Chic Sale, Dickie Moore, and Walter Huston in The Star Witness.

The Star Witness is certainly melodrama, but Wellman directed with such a lightness of touch that it almost seems a comedy. The character of the grandfather, as played by Charles "Chic" Sale is the obvious comedy relief, but his broad, obvious playing is not to everyone's taste. Sale made a career out of playing old geezers and was so convincing that the portrayal seeped into everyday life. Wellman wrote,

> Chic Sale, as old Gramps in The Star Witness [was] tough to handle, late on the set, complaining about everything and everybody. I was so understanding and polite and patient and suddenly realized that he wasn't an old man, he was just acting it. He was my age. No one was ever debearded as quick as he was. I told him that if he didn't behave himself, I would put a little age on him in a very un-

usual way, and it wouldn't be with make-up. He
behaved himself.

Wellman obviously liked Sale enough to play a scene
with him, for the director appears in one of his own movies
for the first time since Wings. Actually, he doesn't quite
appear, only his voice is heard. Sale is out searching the
town for his kidnapped grandson when he hears work from
inside a man-hole. Wellman's is the voice of the lineman.

> Gran'Pa: "What are you doin' down there?"
> Lineman: "Fixing a conduit."
> Gran'Pa: "Huh?"
> Lineman: "Fixing a conduit."
> Gran'Pa: "How long you been down there?"
> Lineman: "Oh, a couple of hours."
> Gran'Pa: "How in Sam Hill do you go about
> getting down in there?"
> Lineman: "Fell in."
> Gran'Pa: "Smart Alec! I reckon anybody as
> dumb as me.... Could you tell me where the
> Adams Exchange district is?"
> Lineman: "Lincoln Avenue to around Venice
> Boulevard. Fourth Street to about Twelfth. Why,
> Dad?"
> Gran'Pa: "Oh, just getting to know my way
> around...."
> Lineman: "Oh, a stranger in the city?"
> Gran'Pa: "Oh yeah, I only got here about sev-
> enty years before you got down there."
> Lineman: "How old are you, Dad?"
> Gran'Pa: "Land of gracious, buddy, I'm just
> older than anybody.... I'm old enough to stay out
> of holes."

Besides Walter Huston's usual fine work in the role of
the District Attorney, The Star Witness is distinguished mainly
by Wellman's imaginative staging of the scenes and the brisk
pace he maintains. The gang's beating of the father is remarkably brutal and the final confrontation with the police is
done with Wellman's characteristic just-off-frame style of
staging; the shoot-out is all smoke and feet seen through ban-
ister rails. At times like these Wellman adopts a nearly expressionistic style since more is alluded to than shown; he
was a master of shadow and suggestion.

From the crime-ridden streets of the Big City, Well-

man took as his next location an unnamed island at the end of
the earth. Safe in Hell concerns a prostitute (Dorothy Mackaill) who believes she has killed one of her clients and who,
with the help of her lover (Donald Cook), escapes to a Carib-
bean Island from which no criminal can be extradited.

Safe in Hell is Wellman at his most unrelievedly dramatic. In its slow pacing, thick atmosphere, and painful
situations, Safe in Hell looks forward to Track of the Cat
and The Ox-Bow Incident. All concern groups of people
thrust together in claustrophobic circumstances in which
their personal guilts and fears are given free reign and resolved only in death.

Gilda (Mackaill) is among the first of Wellman's protagonists to choose death in favor of breaking her moral code.
She has married her sea-faring lover and he has left her on
the island which is the home of a large group of criminals,
there for the same reason she is. When the man that she
thinks she has killed turns up alive, he tries to rape her
and she kills him--for real, this time. She stands trial
and is on the verge of being acquitted on the grounds of
self-defense when Bruno, the "jailor and executioner of the
island," tells her that, as a prisoner of his, she will be expected to make certain "concessions." Rather than break
her vow of faithfulness to her husband, Gilda confesses to
the murder and is sentenced to death.

Bruno, the man who would be her lover, then, ends
the film by throttling her. "My activities are confined to
island crime, my friend," Bruno says. "While we do not
believe in the International Laws of Extradition, our own
laws are very strict. But as long as you behave yourselves
here, you are safe from both jail and gallows--safe in Hell."

One notable item about the film is the presence of two
popular black actors, Nina Mae McKinney and Clarence Muse.
In a period when blacks were so often exploited and stereo-
typed, these two characters are refreshingly positive; they
may, in fact, be the only two reputable people in the film.
Interestingly, the script is filled with a white writer's idea
of "Negro dialect" ("I'se a N'Orleans lady mahself"), but no
such talk reaches the screen. Either McKinney and Muse
had enough clout to demand that they speak in normal language or Wellman just wanted to avoid a convenient cliché.
Subsequently, Safe in Hell provides a rare opportunity to see
these two fine actors in major roles.

In 1932, Wellman kept up his five films per annum
rate, directing The Hatchet Man, So Big, The Purchase
Price, Love Is a Racket, and, for RKO and David Selznick,
The Conquerors. The Hatchet Man starts off with one big
strike against it. This story of the tong wars in San Francisco's Chinatown requires that virtually all of the characters in the story be Chinese. The strike is that all of the
actors are Caucasians. While otherwise quite an interesting
film, many in the audience could not (and still cannot) get
over the first hurdle of pretending that Edward G. Robinson,
Loretta Young, Dudley Digges, J. Carroll Naish, and Leslie
Fenton were Oriental.

Given that incongruity, though, The Hatchet Man is a
film of great beauty and style, lavishly decorated, exquisitely
photographed, and beautifully directed. Robinson plays Wong
Low Get, a hatchet man (executioner) for his tong faction who
is called upon to kill his good friend Sun Yat Sen (Naish).
Before he does the deed, Sen asks him to be the guardian of
his young daughter Toya. Wong agrees, then carries out his
duty.

Years later Wong marries the now-grown Toya (Young),
who has become quite Americanized (our first view of her reveals her to be dancing to the music of a Cuban band and
sighing, "Gee, this is swell. "). When she starts an affair
with a gangster who has been hired as her guard, Harry En
Lai (Fenton), Wong threatens to kill the both of them. Toya
reminds him of his sacred promise to never cause her un-
happiness and he relents. However, he has now lost the respect of the rest of the tong faction and is banished for allow-
ing his wife's seducer to live. Eventually, Harry grows tired
of Toya and sells her into prostitution in an opium den in
China, Wong goes to rescue her, they are reconciled, and
Harry is killed.

The stylized visuals and precise, Hollywood-style Oriental speech inspired Wellman to pull out all the stops and
fill The Hatchet Man with signs and symbols. The death of
Sun Yat Sen is an example of two of Wellman's traits (more
than two, really) showing up in one brief scene.

[Opposite:] Dorothy Mackaill finds that there are advantages
and disadvantages to being the only woman on a remote island
in Safe in Hell.

Though Edward G. Robinson, Loretta Young, and Leslie Fenton make rather unlikely Orientals, The Hatchet Man is one of Wellman's more interesting and atmospheric films.

The tension of the scene derives from the fact that executioner and victim are friends since childhood. When Wong is given the assignment by his tong faction, he protests:

"We were boys together. We came on the same boat from China. This scar is a bond of blood brotherhood. His and mine. Don't you understand? I can't do it. You can't just kill your best friend. You must get someone else to do it."

The tong leader replies: "Someone else to do your sworn duty? Your arm is not your own, but the Tong's and an oath to the Tong is an oath before your honorable ancestors."

As Wong arrives at his friend's house, Sun Yat Sen is preparing his will, naming Wong as the sole beneficiary. In addition, Sun Yat Sen has provided in his will that his daughter, Toya, will enter into the guardianship of Wong and when she comes of age will become his wife.

Wellman thus uses the "romantic triangle" in two different ways in The Hatchet Man: Wong and Sun Yat Sen both love Toya as a daughter and one, in sacrificing his life, entrusts her to the other's care. When Toya is grown, she becomes the fulcrum of another three-way affair, though this time Wong has become her lover and husband. Wong dispatches both of his rivals with his hatchet; he kills Sun Yat Set unwillingly, his duty to the tong winning out over his love for his friend. Harry is also killed by Wong's hatchet in the opposite circumstances--Wong dearly wants to kill him, but does so by accident.

Sun Yat Sen's death is rendered discreetly. Knowing why his friend has come, Sun Yat Sen bows in prayer as the camera tracks toward Wong's shadow which reveals the hatchet emerging from Wong's voluminous sleeve. Wong throws the hatchet and there is a quick cut to young Toya's bedroom. The sleeping child is holding a doll and as she shifts in bed, the doll's head falls off.

Harry's death is one of the grisliest scenes Wellman ever put on film. Wong has burst into the opium den to rescue Toya from the life of prostitution that Harry has sold her into. Since his expulsion from the tong for cowardice, he has become very poor and no one at the opium den will believe that he is an honorable hatchet man. To prove that he is, he points out a spot on the opposite wall and flings his hatchet which hits bull's (uh, dragon's) eye. The "madame" rushes into the next room to berate Harry for selling her a girl that wasn't his to sell and becomes infuriated when he doesn't answer; he simply smiles slightly and nods. Through intercutting, we see someone is trying to pull Wong's hatchet from the wall and each tug makes Harry's head nod: the hatchet has imbedded itself into Harry's skull and he is dead.

After the ritualized world of Chinatown, Wellman was rather relieved to get back to more familiar ground in his next films--the open plains of The Purchase Price and So Big, fast-paced big-city life in Love Is a Racket and the pioneer territory of The Conquerors.

Wellman again worked with Barbara Stanwyck in So Big and The Purchase Price, the last time he would do so in ten years. So Big, based on Edna Ferber's novel, is only

partially successful as a film. For one thing, the running
time (82 minutes) is far too brief to adequately cover sixty
years in Selina Peake's life. For another thing, Wellman
(and Warners, at this period) was not the one to handle a
big, sprawling, sentimental story like this one at least not
during these years. His best work at Warners is characterized by the fast-paced, unpretentious style, clean, propulsive editing and simple, direct photography. So Big
probably would have fared better at a studio like M-G-M at
this time, a studio that wouldn't be ashamed to give it the
style, flourish and finish that would elevate it to superior
soap-opera.

Upon release, So Big was generally ignored critically,
though it did fairly well at the box office. Only Stanwyck
was singled out for praise. William Boehnel in The New
York World Telegram wrote,

> By her performance in So Big Barbara Stanwyck
> definitely establishes herself with this writer as
> being a brilliant emotional actress....
>   No matter what one thinks about the picture,

Barbara Stanwyck and Dickie Moore in So Big.

the final conviction of anyone who sees Miss Stanwyck's Selina Peake will be that she contributes a
fine and stirring performance, making of it a char-
acterization which is direct and eloquent all the way.

No such praise was forthcoming for The Purchase
Price, even though it (unintentionally, perhaps) turned out to
be one of the most bizarre films that Wellman ever directed
or that Stanwyck ever appeared in. Most critics sneered at
it; The New York Times reviewer said,

> If The Purchase Price were simply unintelligent, it
> would be easy to dismiss it in a phrase, or two
> phrases. That it happens to give sanctuary to one
> of the weirdest scenarios within the memory of man
> and that it happens to be totally incomprehensible
> even to its best friends at the Strand, are factors
> that make life difficult.

These very traits that made the reviewer so angry are
exactly the reason that The Purchase Price is worth anything
now. Wellman shows an admirable disregard for plausibility
and motivation and ends up with a film worthy of Luis Buñuel.
Stanwyck plays Joan, a nightclub singer (when first we see
her, she is singing "Take me away, somewhere far from the
crowds we've known, where we can be alone, take me away")
who is fed up with city life. She has a casual boyfriend, a
racketeer played by Lyle Talbot, but she wants to marry a
rich young "college kid" who'll make her respectable. When
the boy's father breaks up the engagement, Joan looks for a
way out of town.

She finds that her maid is about to become a mailorder
bride with a "wheat farmer" and, further, that her maid sent
the man Joan's picture.

> Joan: "Emily, would you like to make a hun-
> dred dollars?"
> Emily: "Oh, who wouldn't?"
> Joan: "You sent him my picture. He's expect-
> ing a woman that looks like me. I've got to get out
> of town quickly."
> Emily: "You ain't committed no crime, have
> you?"
> Joan: "Of course not, but I have to leave town.
> I have to go away some place where somebody can't
> find me. I'll give you a hundred dollars if you'll
> let me bat for you."

Barbara Stanwyck and Lyle Talbot in The Purchase Price.

　　　　Emily decides to take the money and run and before
you can say quick dissolve, Joan is aboard a train heading
for the Canadian wheat fields.   She is seated with three more
mailorder brides who are comparing pictures of their husbands-
to-be.

　　　　　　　Queenie: "Oh, yours has bushy eyebrows. He'll
　　　　tickle you every time he kisses you."
　　　　　　　2nd Girl: "I don't care, as long as he kisses
　　　　me (laughs)."
　　　　　　　Queenie: "You know what they say about men
　　　　with bushy eyebrows and a long nose!" (With this,
　　　　she takes a big bite out of a banana!)
　　　　　　　2nd Girl: "Queenie, I can tell you've been mar-
　　　　ried before!"

　　　　Upon arrival, Joan meets her taciturn fiancé who takes
her straight to the justice of the peace to be married.   The

wedding is witnessed by the Justice's wife (who is mixing a
bowl of cake batter through the ceremony) and their half-wit
hired man who is distracted midway through the wedding by
a dogfight. This obviously leaves an impression on him, for
everytime he sees Joan thereafter, he barks and howls.

The bulk of the film is taken up in Joan's trying to
win the affection of her new husband after she has alienated
him on their wedding night by refusing to sleep with him.

Of course the film cannot be resolved (at least, in
Wellman's terms) until Joan has learned to exist in her new
environment, a state of mind which comes only after a shiva-
ree, a blizzard, the birth of a baby (a neighbor's, but Joan
delivers), a foreclosed mortgage, a saloon fight, and wheat-
fire. Things are quite packed in for a 68-minute movie and
Wellman seems to have run into something of a brick wall
trying to resolve all the plot's loose ends. He finally decides to not even try; the film doesn't end, it simply stops.

Love Is a Racket is Wellman on firmer footing. There
is nothing particularly bizarre about this picture, but it is
also quite enjoyable, containing a witty, fast-paced script and
bright performances by Douglas Fairbanks, Jr., Frances Dee,
Ann Dvorak, Lee Tracy, and Lyle Talbot.

Fairbanks plays Jimmy Russell, a Walter Winchell-
type gossip-monger, who becomes involved in murder and
scandal. In its light-hearted portrayal of black-hearted
newspapermen, Love Is a Racket looks forward to Wellman's
other two comedies of cynicism (did he ever make any other
kind?): Nothing Sacred and Roxie Hart. Russell is as much
a faker as all of Wellman's newspapermen are, but he has
certain standards that he holds to. However, he's not above
changing the news a little in order to get it into print. The
film's climax comes when he throws a notorious gangster's
body from an eighteenth-story penthouse in order to disguise
the fact that he was murdered by their mutual girlfriend.

In the midst of Wellman's new contract at Warner
Bros., Zanuck loaned him out twice to other studios. Wellman was throwing himself headlong into his work churning out
a new film every two months or so (in 1933, more often than
that). Niven Busch has said, "Wellman would take on any assignment at that time ... a contract director had to do as he
was told." Perhaps, but Wellman took on more projects than
he normally would have been assigned. When he had reached

his quota, he would ask Zanuck for another picture to do, which probably explains projects like Maybe It's Love or College Coach.

His intense activity took another toll; in mid-1932 Wellman divorced for the third time. His marriage to Marjorie Crawford had always been a rocky one since they seem to have had little in common and she wasn't very interested in bearing Wellman any children--something that he passionately wanted. "Two married screwballs can murder each other," he wrote. "It didn't quite come to that but got awful close, so she crossed her beautiful legs and I paid through the nose once more, only she didn't get so much--there wasn't much left."

So, free again, Wellman plunged back into his work. His first loan-out was to RKO where his friend David O. Selznick was trying to come up with a follow-up film for the enormously successful Cimarron, which had won the Academy Award for best picture in 1931. What resulted was one of Wellman's best though least-known films, The Conquerors.

The Conquerors is a multi-generational story of a family of bankers which uses a historical metaphor of the contrasting periods of depression from the 1870's (when the film opens) to the present (1932). Special effects genius Slavko Vorkapich almost deserves co-director status, for his evocative montages crop up at each period of history that experienced a depression; he uses toppling stacks of coins, mountains of money, melting silver and every other trick he can come up with to metaphorically describe the economic situations.

Richard Dix and Ann Harding head the cast which also includes such stalwarts as Edna Mae Oliver, Guy Kibbee, Donald Cook, Skeets Gallagher, and J. Carroll Naish. Though the film is obviously meant just to cash in on Cimarron's success, it is a far finer film in and of itself.

Dix, so stiff and stodgy in Cimarron (and, indeed, in most of his films) is warm, natural and charming in The Conquerors (The New York Times calls him "alert and vigorous"); he's versatile as well, for his is a multiple role.

There is much of Wellman's style in The Conquerors: in a riverboat scene in which Dix and Harding are attacked by river pirates who come floating, magically almost, from

In this unusual photograph, Richard Dix is shown playing two roles in The Conquerors.

the trees onto the craft (it recalls the scene in Beggars of Life when the bums suddenly enter a box-car from every available orifice. "It's raining hoboes, that's what it's doing," exclaims a tramp already in the car); in the mass hanging of an outlaw gang which is remarkably bold and brutal even for a pre-Code film; in the birth of a baby at the exact moment of his father's suicide.

Wellman makes himself felt in the film in a more personal way, as well: at the outbreak of World War I, Dix goes off to France to join the Norton-Harjes Ambulance Corps and later transfers to the Lafayette Flying Corps, which is, of course, identical to Wellman's own wartime experience.

Though The Conquerors was a failure at the box-office, it remains one of Wellman's most intriguing films, not for the rah-rah You Can't Lick America theme, but for the boldness of his images and the sincere, unpretentious approach to what is, after all, a simple love story.

Back at Warner Bros., Wellman was assigned to two films with Ruth Chatterton, Frisco Jenny and Lilly Turner. Wellman was skeptical about the star.

> Ruth Chatterton! Directors wouldn't direct her. Zanuck called me in to give me an assignment. He said, "I've got a wonderful story written by Bill Mizner, your best friend [Wilson Mizner]: Frisco Jenny." I said, "I know all about the story. It's great. Is that all you're gonna tell me?" He said, "No, the star's coming in," and he pressed a button and in came Miss Chatterton. Now I didn't say one word but she interrupted him when he started telling us about the production. She said, "I wouldn't work with him." (She never even said "Mr. Wellman") and Zanuck started to panic and I said, "Mr. Zanuck, I wouldn't work with her!" He said, "I've got news for you. You're both gonna work together or you can look for another job. And it isn't gonna be easy to find, when I get through."
> So she looked at me and I looked at Zanuck and I said, "Are we excused?" So I got the script and we got started and I never said a word to her. She got her script and the time came for her to get some fittings--I had my assistant call her up. She was on time but I never saw her, never said a word to her until the first day of shooting. I was very polite to her, and she was a magnificent actress.
> At the end of three days, she said, "Truce?" I said, "Yep. Truce." She said, "These have been the most enjoyable three days I've ever spent." I said, "It's gonna be enjoyable every time, because you're a great artist and you're a lot of fun to work with and you're in love with a guy I'm crazy about-- George Brent." And from that moment we became nothing but pals. We made a hell of a picture together.

Frisco Jenny is cut from the same cloth as Madame X. It's the story of a prostitute whose illegitimate son grows up to be a District Attorney and when she kills a man to keep her son from learning his (and her) true identity, he prosecutes her and sends her to the gallows.

Ruth Chatterton and Donald Cook in the closing scenes of
Frisco Jenny.

The film begins at the time of the San Francisco earthquake, a sequence that is handled with far greater style and impact than one would have looked for in a rather routine programmer like this one.   Some of the earthquake footage is stock footage from In Old San Francisco, but a great deal of the sequence was shot directly for the film.   But, as The New York Times review noted, "the pity is that the rest of the film does not live up to these scenes of destruction, terror and death."

In fact, the plot from here on is strictly predictable, yet Wellman directed with his usual rather baroque sense of style.   He shows a marked propensity for coming up with unusual dissolve devices in this film and his tendency to shoot with "odd angles" was now at its peak.   There seems hardly a scene in Frisco Jenny that isn't shot through the legs of a chair or over someone's elbow or from overhead or any other of the least-likely viewpoints.

The passage of time is handled in a rather novel way. When Jenny gives up her son, she always tries to keep track of his life and so she keeps a scrapbook.   He is hardly shown in the interim between his baby- and adult-hood except in the newspaper articles (items from gossip columns and sports pages and, later, genuine news articles about his promising political career).

Otherwise the story is formulaic melodrama, though pretty interesting, even compelling, for all that.   In addition to Chatterton, whose favorite film role this was, the cast includes the too-seldom seen James Murray and, in a cameo as a newspaper reporter, Wild Bill Wellman.

Lilly Turner lacked the style that Wellman and Chatterton gave Frisco Jenny and its story (again, a triangle) was not fresh enough to hold things up on its own.   There are good scenes (a seduction in a truck stuck in the mud during a rainstorm, Chatterton being exhibited in a medicine show as a Perfect Body) but the main interest in Lilly Turner is in seeing the various Warner Bros. stock people who play the minor roles: Frank McHugh, Guy Kibbee, Grant Mitchell, Mae Busch, and others.

Coincidentally, it was during the filming of Lilly Turner that Wellman first got bit by the golf bug, a passion that was to remain with him throughout his life.   A newspaper article read,

Mr. Wellman, at work on Stage 3, is acutely conscious that on Stage 10, just across the way, is
Bobby Jones, attired in a sort of Pierrot-and-
Columbine costume of black and white, and analyz-
ing before the slow motion camera, the correct
golfing swing separated into its fundamental details
by a new idea in photography.

Thus we have Mr. Wellman, a golf enthusiast
of the purest ray serene, suffering more than anybody else on the lot. For Mr. Wellman, who one
year ago cared less than nothing about golf, now
would exchange a guarantee of permanent happiness
in the world for anything like a decent assurance
that he would be able to direct a golf ball through
the temporary Elysian fields of this world in something like 80.

Wellman was delighted when Jones visited the Lilly Turner
set and gave him a few pointers, with the cast and crew
cheering him on.

It's hard to imagine how Wellman had time to even
think of golf at this time, for he was churning out movies
at an alarming rate. By April 1933, he released his third
picture for the year, Central Airport (incidentally, one of
the shorts that appeared with Central Airport in its Warner
theatre engagements was Bobby Jones's series "How to Break
Ninety").

Central Airport stars Richard Barthelmess as a pilot
who loses his professional reputation when he is forced to
crash-land a passenger plane. He tells his parents:

When a commercial flier cracks up, he's through;
that's all. So from now on I'm a Jonah pilot. The
officials said it was carelessness. Can you picture
it? Passengers climbing aboard and asking who the
pilot it? "Oh, he's the fellow who cracked up last
year." No, I couldn't get another passenger run
right now if I was the last pilot in the world.

He solves his dilemma by joining a carnival as a stunt
pilot and does an act with a pretty parachutist, Jill (Sally
Eilers). They fall in love, but Jim is reluctant to be married; he has known of too many pilots who crashed, leaving
grieving families behind. "Anybody who makes a living in
the air can't afford the responsibilities that go with a wife

and family, " he says.   "People like ourselves have got to
find our happiness where we can find it. "

        "But, " Jill asks, "what if you're a flyer and you're
in love?"

        "Well, just because you're hungry, you don't have to
buy a restaurant, " he answers, sensibly enough.

        When Jim's younger brother, also a pilot, enters the
picture, Central Airport begins to look like an inverted Men
with Wings.   Jill marries Neil when she realizes that Jim
will never settle down; she is drawn to stability and respecta-
bility as much as her counterpart in Men with Wings unaccountably chooses the shiftless, ambitionless (if more romantic) gypsy pilot.

        Though Wellman was often drawn to triangles in which
two of the parties were close friends, this is a rare instance
when he experiments with the unique tensions that arise when
two brothers love the same girl.   The theme of brothers in
rivalry is, of course, a hallmark of many of his pictures
(notably The Public Enemy and Woman Trap) but the point of
rupture is generally one of power, not of sex.   In Jim Blaine's
case, once he has lost his heart to the marriage of the two
people he loves most, Wellman employs a graphic metaphor
of the painful separation: Jim quite literally begins to lose
other parts of himself: "an eye in Nicaragua, a heel in China,
a couple of ribs in Chile.   It's been a habit wherever I go.
I leave 'em something to remember me by. "

        In a Wellman film, it's not enough for the loser in a
triangle to accept his loss, he is often called upon to go out
and save the life (or reputation, or both) of his rival in love.
When a Wellman protagonist is faced with the prospect of having his rival wiped out, character is measured by how long
it takes him to make the rescue.   This situation crops up
most often in the aerial films: Men with Wings, Thunder-
birds, and here in Central Airport when Neil's plane goes
down in the ocean and Jim realizes that he could have Jill
back again in a flash if only he ignored the call.

        Central Airport was one of Wellman's more minor fly-

[Opposite:]   Richard Barthelmess as a pilot who leaves various
parts of his anatomy wherever he goes in Central Airport.

ing films, but it still benefits from his characteristic terse-
ness. The aerial scenes (the head stunt pilot was Paul Mantz)
are well done but routine alongside Wings. However, Central
Airport, better than Wings, perhaps, caught the spirit of the
flying man with accuracy. Though the character of Jim Blaine
is wrapped in a couple of layers of noble self-sacrifice, he
has a quiet dignity, a dedication to duty, and an unswerving
allegiance to those whom he cares about that makes him a
typical, even exemplary, Wellman citizen.

As an aside, John Wayne, who was under contract to
Warners at this time, appears as an extra in the scene where
Neil's plane is foundering in the ocean. Why Warner Bros.
chose to put Wayne (who was currently starring in "B" westerns) in a role that any Central Casting name could have filled
is a mystery. He also appeared in College Coach in a not-
much-larger role, but at least in that film he is recognizable
and even says a couple of words. Humphrey Bogart, despite
Wellman's many claims to the contrary, does not appear in
Central Airport; even the closest scrutiny of the crowd scenes
does not turn up anyone remotely resembling him.

Despite Warner Bros.' reputation for making "social
conscience" pictures, Wellman had steered clear of stuffing
his movies full of messages. The Public Enemy had hit the
screens as a scathing indictment of a social problem that
"we, the public, must solve" only as an afterthought, as a
way of skirting the censors and Wellman's only film to directly comment on the Depression was The Conquerors, which
he made at RKO.

Zanuck, who was respected by Wellman for his talent
for "grabbing a headline," felt that Wellman had the fire and
fervor necessary to make films that could follow in the footsteps of I Am a Fugitive from a Chain Gang, a motion picture
that not only described a particular problem, but went a long
way toward eliciting changes that improved the situations depicted in the film.

Wellman's two "topical films" for Zanuck were Heroes
for Sale and Wild Boys of the Road. Both dealt with the Depression and its effect on people's lives. Each tends to be
grim and depressing but there is an optimism inherent in each
that owes much to the current New Deal of Franklin D. Roosevelt. Heroes for Sale is about a man who struggles through
drug addiction, the loss of his job, the death of his wife, and
harassment by "Red squads" when he is thought to be a Com-

Edwin Philips (center) is flanked by his co-stars Rochelle
Hudson and Dorothy Coonan in Wild Boys of the Road.

munist. The "wild boys" are ordinary, middle-class kids
who have the symbols and dreams of their Andy Hardy-world
stripped away from them one by one by the worsening economic conditions until they are forced to live on the run,
stealing or begging to provide themselves with food and shel-
ter.

Yet both end with optimistic statements. Heroes for
Sale's Tom Holmes sits in a freightyard, dejected, homeless
and being soaked by a traditional Wellman rain. Someone
says to him, "What do you think of all this? The country
can't go on this way ... it's the end of America."

Tom replies, "No. Maybe it's the end of us, but it's
not the end of America. In a few years it'll go on bigger
and stronger than ever. That's not optimism--just common
horse sense. Did you read President Roosevelt's inaugural
address? He's right. You know, it takes more than one sock
on the jaw to lick a hundred and twenty million people."

And when Eddie, Tommy, and Sally (in Wild Boys) appear before a judge on the charge of vagrancy and armed
robbery, the magistrate comforts them. "Things are going
to get better now, not only in New York, but all over the
country. Eddie, I know your father will return to work
shortly."

Both films have been criticized for the alleged artificiality of the endings, but they are so much a part of the
fabric of the rhetoric that the films set up that one can't
imagine the films leading to any other conclusions.

Certainly, the bleak ending of a film like I Am a Fugitive from a Chain Gang is appropriate to a piece that demands
changes in a corrupt system, but Heroes for Sale and Wild
Boys of the Road are not pointing out institutional flaws; they
are dealing with an environment--the Depression--and are
acknowledging that "prosperity is right around the corner."
Heroes for Sale has, in fact, been called "the first topical
film released in New Deal America" by writer Andrew Bergman; there's no doubt that both films' writers bought Roosevelt's line and swallowed it whole. In retrospect, this seems
the greatest fault of both films--this unquestioning, nearly
naive belief that the Depression was ending and that Americans,
standing shoulder to shoulder, could weather the last bleak
days and emerge triumphant.

It was during the filming of Heroes for Sale that Wellman first met the woman who was to become his fourth and
final wife, Dorothy Coonan. Dottie had been born on Thanksgiving Day, 1914 in Minneapolis, Minnesota. From early
childhood she had had an interest in entertaining, found that
she had a talent for dancing and, in 1930, came to Hollywood
to take the movies by storm. Her dancing was good enough
to get her a job with choreographer Busby Berkeley. Though
Dottie herself is not quite sure how many films she appeared
in under Berkeley's direction, she showed up in some of the
landmark musicals of the early 1930's: 42nd Street, Golddiggers of 1933 and Footlight Parade at Warners and Kid from
Spain (in which she had a featured solo dance number) among
others for Goldwyn.

Wellman wrote of her, "She was nineteen, supporting
her family, as pretty as a picture--a freckled picture--and
the only one of the so-called leading dancers that was not under contract." He happened to see her one afternoon when
the dancers were breaking for lunch and, in a romantic con-

Wellman and his fourth (and final) bride, Dorothy Coonan,
on their honeymoon at Arrowhead Springs Hotel in April 1934.

vention that he would have dismissed from one of his movies
with a sneer, fell in love at first sight.

After talking the matter over with himself, Wellman
decided to follow in the footsteps of so many other men on
the Warners lot: he went to Berkeley and asked to be introduced to one of his dancers.

Berkeley was working on the "Shadow Waltz" number
from Golddiggers of 1933 when Wellman approached him.
"He introduced me to Dottie," Wellman recalled, "and I said,
'I'd like to take you to dinner, how do I ask you?' She said,
'You just did ask me.' 'Well, will you go?' She said, 'No,
you're married.'"

"I said, 'Now, wait a minute, I'm going through that horrible year period that you have to wait for before you can get the final decree.' She said, 'Well, when you get it, you come and talk to me.' She wasn't kidding."

Eventually, Dottie softened and she and Wellman began seeing each other on a regular basis. When Wellman was assigned Wild Boys of the Road, he felt that Dottie would be perfect for the role of Sally, a young girl who has left her struggling family and started riding the rails. But, "she didn't want to act," Wellman wrote, "she hated it." Dancing was one thing, but Dottie had no desire to take on the busy, public life of an actress. Wellman pleaded with her. "Look, I've looked at all the girls that they've got," he said, "and I couldn't find the girl I wanted."

The girl he needed for the role had to have "beauty and boyishness ... an athletic something and ... a softness about her. A tough thing to get."

"You've got it," Wellman told Dottie. "You're not as pretty as these other girls, but you're prettier to me." Finally, this dubious appeal to her vanity worked and Dottie agreed to act in Wild Boys of the Road. Almost immediately, the Warners star machinery was put into motion. On August 25, 1933, The New York Sun carried this burning scoop:

> GIRL TAKES OUT $100,000 FRECKLE INSURANCE.
> Dorothy Coonan has many freckles--182 in fact.
> Now in her teens, Dorothy earns her living by facing the cameras and exposing her good-looking but freckled countenance to the public gaze on movie screens. Her contract provides that she's out of a job if she loses her freckles. So yesterday she applied for $100,000 worth of freckle insurance.

Her co-stars in Wild Boys were equally unknown. Of the young actors, only Frankie Darro and Rochelle Hudson had appeared in enough films to be recognized by the public and virtually none of the kids went on to bigger things. This serves to accentuate the documentary-like quality of the second half of the film, for we more closely identify the actors with the roles they are playing.

Wild Boys of the Road emerged as one of Wellman's finest films and the last few years has seen a re-emergence of its popularity in college courses. Though tripped up by

the script here and there, Wellman seems to have been very
involved in the making of Wild Boys, emotionally involved to a
far greater extent than was usual for him during this period.

One telling point that indicates how much care Wellman lavished on Wild Boys of the Road is the fact that his
production costs ran $29,000 over budget; the film eventually
cost $203,000. Compare this to The Public Enemy, which
was shot in twenty-six days for $151,000. (In fact, for The
Public Enemy, Wellman only shot 360 feet of film that didn't
make it into the final cut!)

Despite the extra care lavished on Wild Boys of the
Road and Wellman's passion for the film, it did not do well
at the box-office. Oddly, the "happy ending" seems to have
hurt the film commercially; at least most critics objected
strongly to it. The New York Times's reviewer said,

> By endowing [the film] with a happy ending, the
> producers have robbed it of its value as a social
> challenge. The responsibility for its weakness
> must be laid at the door of the director, William
> A. Wellman. He has taken a theme with broad so-
> cial implications and has converted it into a rather
> pointless yarn about three wandering youngsters.

Stung by the failure of a film he believed in (which
was to be a recurring motif throughout Wellman's career),
he ended his contract with Warners in the same manner in
which he started it, with a comedy about football.

At least College Coach turned out far better than did
Maybe It's Love and in many ways it's indicative of Wellman's
growing professionalism. Where he could hardly invest the
trivial Maybe It's Love with any fire or spirit, he had become adept enough with the conventions of the Popular Movie
to make College Coach (a similar premise as the earlier film
and with no more potential) a fine, cynical comedy, briskly
directed and well-acted, in a matter-of-fact sort of way.

Along the way there are some "in-jokes" (one of the
football games involves a "Wellman University") and a surprisingly brutal fight between rivals Dick Powell and Lyle Talbot;
one is a bit startled to find such a knock-down-drag-out in
what, up to this point, had been a relatively innocuous comedy, and when people fight in a Wellman film, they bleed.

By the time <u>College Coach</u> was released in October
1933, Wellman had already flown the Warners coop, with
several months left to go on his contract. Darryl Zanuck
had also left just prior to this to form his own company,
Twentieth Century Productions and it's quite possible that he
invited Wellman along on the new venture. At any rate,
Wellman's next film, <u>Looking for Trouble</u>, was produced by
Zanuck and released through United Artists. Later in 1934,
Zanuck's young company merged with William Fox to form
Twentieth Century-Fox, a company that was to release sev-
eral of Wellman's finest films.

CHAPTER SEVEN

The formation of Twentieth Century Productions was a rather odd affair. When Joe Schenck, president of United Artists, approached Zanuck to head up the new producing company, Zanuck found that Twentieth Century was being partially financed by Louis B. Mayer, vice-president in charge of production at M-G-M. Why would Mayer deliberately help a rival company to get off the ground? Mayer invested the money with Zanuck and Schenck on the condition that Mayer's son-in-law, William Goetz (who was an assistant director at RKO), be taken on as Zanuck's assistant.

In addition to the financial assistance, Mayer also made sure that Twentieth Century, in its early days, would receive the benefit of being loaned some of M-G-M's top talent.

Wellman was already known around the M-G-M lot. Since his rather embarrassing exit from his Metro Contract in 1926, he had built up his reputation to the degree that Zanuck had been asked to loan Wellman to M-G-M for a film in the summer of 1933. Apparently, his handling of the project, Midnight Mary, reflected the speed and professionalism which had become his trademark while at Warners, for upon its release, Wellman was again (if temporarily) in M-G-M's good graces.

Midnight Mary was a gangster story written by Anita Loos. Wellman's star was again Loretta Young, who had already appeared with him twice (The Hatchet Man and Heroes for Sale) and was still to make a fourth film with him (The

143

Franchot Tone and Loretta Young in <u>Midnight Mary</u>.

<u>Call of the Wild</u>).   Only Stanwyck starred in more of Well-
man's films.   Young commented,

> I felt very secure when I was working with Well-
> man.   There was nothing phony or artificial about
> him.   He was also very attractive, in every way.
> He liked to shoot fast, in one take, and his energy
> went right through him and into the actors.   A di-
> rector is boss for a reason, and Bill was good.

    <u>Midnight Mary</u> used a complex flash-back technique to
tell its story; flash-backs are devices that Wellman never
cared much for and critical reaction to <u>Midnight Mary</u> was
split pretty evenly on the technique's effectiveness here.

    "William Wellman directed, using the flashback technique to develop the story to its fullest," wrote the New York Telegraph's Al Sherman, "but the tale is told coherently and intelligently, even its few implausibilities are presented in a most convincing manner." Thornton Delehanty, of the Post, sniffed,

> It is an old, old story and, consequently, a trite one. So trite that even the pornographic touches which attempt to enliven it are woefully flat. Someone must have told the authors that they had a sure-fire box-office success on their hands if only they would pep it up with a dash or two of sex.

One of the flashbacks took Young and sidekick Una Merkel clear back to the age of nine. As fond as Wellman was of the device of showing his protagonists as children, Midnight Mary presents the only case where he actually let his adult stars revert to such an early age. By shooting them without makeup and slightly elevating the camera's gaze to look down on them, the effect was quite convincing.

Though Wellman was known throughout the industry for his explosive personality, quick temper, and dynamic activity, he had always worked in a professional manner and had made himself get along with antagonistic actors, technicians, and so on for the good of the picture. All this changed on the set of Looking for Trouble.

Looking for Trouble is a comedy/melodrama about, of all things, telephone repairmen. As befits its subject, the film is brief and unpretentious and overcomes the obvious shortcomings, from a plot point of view, by introducing a gangster (and romantic triangle) sub-plot. Since there is nothing inherently dramatic about repairing downed telephone lines, scenarists Leonard Praskins and Elmer Harris shifted the emphasis to wire-tapping which causes the plot complications (a lineman plans a robbery through tapping the phone lines of a broker) and resolves them at the end of the film (after an earthquake has knocked out the lines, the protagonists rig up a portable line to the police station on which a dying gun-moll phones in her confession).

The stars of the picture were Spencer Tracy, Constance Cummings, Jack Oakie, and Morgan Conway, and there is nothing about the good-natured if somewhat ordinary Looking for Trouble that betrays its director's constant battling with his cast and crew.

Wellman took an immediate dislike to Spencer Tracy
and on two occasions the pair had to be forcibly separated,
while brawling, by members of the crew. In addition, on
October 30, 1933, as shooting for Trouble Shooter (Looking
for Trouble's working title) was nearing completion, Wellman
was involved in another well-publicized fight, this time with
former assistant director Mike Lally. Lally had worked with
Wellman on Midnight Mary and the two had argued bitterly
throughout the filming. Popular legend has it that Wellman
even leveled a pistol at Lally and fired it, nearly missing
him--allegedly because Lally wasn't working fast enough.

On this occasion Lally came by the set of Trouble
Shooter and his presence antagonized Wellman. Wellman
told a reporter,

> There has been feeling between us for quite some
> time and I ordered him off the set. He had no
> business on the set and I'd like to know how he
> got on the lot. Lally refused to leave and we
> started fighting. His friend [described as a
> "former Chicago policeman"] innocently got mixed
> up in it. Lally also exchanged blows with [Dolphe]
> Zimmer [Wellman's assistant on the current film].

Zimmer was treated for a cut beneath the eye and
Wellman's hand was thought to have been broken in the fray.
Two weeks later, Wellman and Tracy met in a bar, started
fighting again, and were finally removed by the police. The
nickname "Wild Bill" was starting to become widely known.
Whether his growing reputation as a hell-raiser had anything
to do with it or not, Wellman was not put under contract to
a studio for nearly two years.

Looking for Trouble was released in April 1934, nearly
six months after completion. By the time it went into the
theaters, Wellman was at RKO working on an Irene Dunne
vehicle, Stingaree, produced by Pandro Berman and also
starring Richard Dix. Stingaree, the title character, is
something of an Australian Robin Hood: a rogue, and a
charming one, substantially wittier, more learned and cul-
tured than any of the outback rubes he robs. (After all,
how serious a bandit would have Andy Devine as a sidekick?)

[Opposite:] Jack Oakie and Spencer Tracey ponder a little
pre-Code decoration in Looking for Trouble.

When Stingaree (Dix) meets aspiring singer Hilda Bouverie (Irene Dunne), he utilizes his own peculiar talents to
further her career: he kidnaps a famous music critic and
forces him to listen to Hilda sing (a recital at which he himself accompanies her at the piano) and uses his ill-gotten gains
to send her to Europe to receive the proper training. She
becomes a major opera star but finally gives up her career
in order to live the free, unencumbered life with Stingaree.

Dix, here as in The Conquerors, gives a relaxed,
charming performance of the type that few other directors
could ever get out of him. His Stingaree is good-humored,
can whistle all of the latest arias from the operas he heard
in Europe and is capable of quite operatic gestures himself;
at Hilda's Melbourne concert, Stingaree appears in the audience in uniform, having held up the governor's wagon and
taken his impressive clothes. Once there, Stingaree sits in
the Governor's Box and acknowledges the cheers of the crowd
who think that he is the representative of the crown.

Immediately after shooting was completed in Stingaree,
on March 22, 1934, Wellman married Dorothy Rae Coonan.
The newlyweds had a long honeymoon at Arrowhead Springs
Hotel. Wellman said,

> She was only nineteen years old when I married
> her, and that [Walter] Winchell, great pal, took a
> picture of each one of my wives and over their
> heads he put the amount of money that I had paid
> --for our divorce settlements. And they earned
> every dime they got, I'm being very honest with
> you. And over Dottie's head, nineteen years old,
> they put a question mark.

As he was fond of saying, the "question mark" stayed over
her head for the next forty-one years.

After their honeymoon, Wellman began to look around
for a job. Walter Wanger offered him a topical melodrama, The
President Vanishes, and Wellman agreed to undertake the project.
However, just as he was about to start work, Wellman received
word that his father had died and he and Dottie flew to Massachusetts for the funeral and cremation to comfort his mother.

Arthur Wellman died at his home at 22 Davis Avenue
in West Newton on August 31, 1934, at the age of 75. He
and Celia had lived there since 1927 and Celia would stay on in
the modest, comfortable house until her death on June 11, 1967.

Irene Dunne and Richard Dix in Stingaree.

        Returning to Hollywood in early September, Wellman
started filming The President Vanishes. A cautionary tale,
one that many critics have compared with MGM's Gabriel
over the White House (1933, Gregory La Cava), The President Vanishes was based on a story that mystery writer Rex
Stout had published anonymously. It concerned a Roosevelt-
ish president (in Wellman's films, are there any other kind?)
who fakes his own kidnapping in order to jolt the country out
of its growing War Hysteria. He engineers his disappearance
to look like the work of a Fascist organization, the Gray
Shirts, led by a madman named Lincoln Lee. His subter-
fuge has the dual effect of re-channeling public thinking on
the erupting European situation and turning the country's
anger on the Gray Shirts. That the ruse also ends in Lee's
murder is rather glossed over; the end, apparently, justifies
the means.

The President Vanishes was launched just two weeks
after Smedley Darlington Butler had startled a Con-
gressional committee and amused the nation with an
old wives' tale about a Fascist putsch to replace the
president with a military dictator ... the consequent
uproar gave producer Wanger, who believes that
Hollywood is terrified by new ideas and hampered
by stupid censorship, a convenient chance to state
some of his notions on cinemafacture.

Wanger was quoted as saying, "The public is interested in
politics, eager for themes that dare to grapple with real
problems. I would rather film a new idea fairly well than
an old idea very well."

Perhaps the most prescient notion in The President
Vanishes is that war is actively promoted by Big Business.
Lincoln Lee's Gray Shirts are revealed to be subsidized by
leaders in publishing, oil, and steel who constantly compute
the anticipated number of people killed in the impending war
against the profit that can be had ... and find that it's worth
it.

Paramount, who was to release the picture, suddenly
got cold feet about the subject matter and considered shelving
the project, but at the last minute they decided to go ahead.
Many critics predicted that the film would herald riots and
protest, but after the initial hoopla it became apparent that
the public watched The President Vanishes and saw only a
good, excitingly made melodrama with a political setting.
The film was quite successful. There were no riots.

After The President Vanishes was released in December 1934, Wellman spent a few more months "at liberty" until Darryl Zanuck contacted him about directing the movie
version of Jack London's Call of the Wild. Virtually the entire film was to be shot on location at Mount Baker in Washington and at the RKO ranch in the San Fernando Valley.
Probably Wellman was more enthusiastic about the location
work than the literary property, for he dearly loved the outdoor life. He gladly accepted the project.

From the beginning, Wellman enjoyed working on The
Call of the Wild. The screenplay was being written by one
of his closest friends, Gene Fowler, and the cast included
Clark Gable, Loretta Young, and Jack Oakie, all of whom
had worked well with the director in the past.

Loretta Young, Jack Oakie, and Wellman (right) on the train
bound for Mount Baker National Park, the location for <u>Call</u>
<u>of the Wild</u>.

Very little of Jack London made it onto the screen.
The emphasis was shifted from Buck, the St. Bernard who,
in London's novel progresses from pampered pet in California
to abused sled dog in the Yukon and finally to noble beast
living among the wolves. In the final script, the story of
The Call of the Wild focused mainly on the gold-hunting activities of Jack Thornton (Gable), Shorty Hoolihan (Oakie),
and Claire Blake (Young) and the romance between Thornton
and Blake. Buck was relegated to sub-plot status, though
Gable's scenes with the dog are natural and affectionate and
come to be the emotional center of the film.

Simple and direct, The Call of the Wild has a gleam-
ing, open quality to its photography and an admirably under-
stated, unpretentious attitude in its direction and playing.
The emotional layers, though, are surprisingly dense.

Jack Thornton is the central character, in that everyone else in the film is defined by his or her relation to him.
He "tames" two of his closest companions: Buck is a "bad
dog," vicious and untrained until Thornton, with patience and
skill, learns how to get along with him; similarly Shorty is a
jailbird, possibly a drunk, who has just emerged from prison
after serving a sentence for stealing mail and reading it.
Thornton's trust in Shorty, his willingness to become equal
partners with him, give Shorty the impetus to go for the gold
with him.

By the same token, Thornton is "tamed" by Claire
Blake. At first wary of her, he eventually comes to respect
her determination and resolve ("I'll cross the river as you
men do") and finally falls in love with her.

The "call of the wild" in the film refers more to the
law-of-the-Yukon possessiveness that Thornton feels for Claire
than to Buck's eventual reversion back to his "savage" self.
Thornton and Claire's relationship is mirrored by Buck's
"memories of a time when there was only one law"; as Buck
sheds his affections for Thornton to mate with a wolf and
father her pups, so do Claire and Thornton shed society's
strictures by "taking what they want" in their wilderness
home.

Interestingly, there is only the touch of the savage before unions are consummated. Claire and Thornton sniff each
other warily in the human counterpart to Buck's actions with
his wolf-mate, but both couples become quite domestic after

sex. Buck and his mate are shown contentedly gazing upon
their young; Claire and Thornton set up housekeeping (our
first view of them after the suggestive fade-out is of Claire
at the fireplace cooking supper while Thornton repairs the
roof) and act "married" even though, by law, they are not.

The romantic triangle here is unspoken throughout
most of the film. Claire believes her husband to be dead
and so do we. We learn that he is alive just when the three
are setting off on their search for the gold. Our knowledge
of the inevitable moment when the couple is confronted by
Claire's husband, colors our perception of their budding romance. Typically, there is no enmity in the triangle.
Claire's husband turns out to be a kind, decent man whom
neither Claire nor Thornton can bring themselves to hurt.
One law yields to another law. Both Thornton and Claire
have their codes.

Atmospherically, The Call of the Wild is prime Wellman. There are evocative, convincing shots of gold-rush
towns and the chaotic (and expensive) offerings therein. The
opening saloon scene is particularly successful in conveying
a genuine 1890's feel right down to the plump dancing girls
and Alfred Newman's accurate period music.

Other highlights of the film include Buck's pulling a
thousand-pound sled, the villainous Smith's (Reginald Owen)
portable bathtub and a striking subjective view of the three
drowning thieves which shows them struggling to unload the
heavy gold from their clothes even as its weight pulls them
to the river bottom.

The film was released in a 91-minute version, but for
a major re-release several years later, it was trimmed down
to 77 minutes. This is the only version currently available.
Originally, Shorty was to have been killed by Smith and his
thugs and apparently the film was shown with that ending in
preview only. When it brought on the disapproval of the audience, Zanuck asked Wellman to shoot one scene where Shorty
turns up at the cabin, having filed the claim that will make
them rich and bearing an Indian squaw, whom he introduces
as his "cook." With this new ending, The Call of the Wild
went on to become a hit and got Wellman an invitation to sign
a contract with Metro-Goldwyn-Mayer.

CHAPTER EIGHT

Wellman had gone over to M-G-M in late 1934 in the hopes of working with his friend David O. Selznick. As it turned out, however, their time at M-G-M overlapped by only a few weeks, for no sooner had Wellman signed his contract, than Selznick left the company to form his own production company, Selznick International, which was to release through United Artists.

Wellman often claimed to have done some work on Selznick's last film at M-G-M, Viva Villa, with Wallace Beery and Fay Wray. Though several directors did work on the picture, including Howard Hawks, Jack Conway (who eventually signed the film), and Richard Rosson, it's very unlikely that Wellman did any work at all on it.

He was chagrined to find that, again, he had been signed on at M-G-M without any picture to work on and he spent several months doing additional shooting on films like Tay Garnet's China Seas. Finally, he was given a film to direct. He hadn't worked on Viva Villa, but he was assigned to M-G-M's attempt to follow up on that film's success, The Robin Hood of El Dorado.

The film was based on Walter Noble Burns's glossy biography of the famous Mexican bandit Joaquin Murrieta, I Am Joaquin! Wellman himself worked on the screenplay with actor/writer Joseph Calleia and Melvin Levy. The result was an odd but effective mixture of the angry films of social concern of Wellman's Warner Bros.' days and the slick well-produced entertainment movies of 1936 M-G-M.

The Robin Hood of El Dorado softens Murrieta's character a great deal and he is played by Warner Baxter as a
kind, gentle man driven to violence.   In fact, the real Murrieta was a sadistic man who gleefully murdered anyone who
crossed him.   Baxter's Murrieta dies on his wife's grave,
murmuring her own dying words; the real Murrieta was shot
in the back by one of his own men, decapitated and the head
placed in a jar and carried about the territory that he had
terrorized, a sight that met with rejoicing at every stop.

Though the film dispensed with the facts, Wellman was
able to make a hard-hitting film about racial prejudice and
the violence that breeds violence.   Within this limited frame-
work, Wellman made a stronger statement on the subject of
racism than a whole spate of later films (like Gentlemen's
Agreement) were to do.

What is admirable about the film is Wellman's unwill-
ingness to place the blame on either party, the Mexican natives or the white settlers.   The film's sympathies are definitely with Murrieta and his Mexican band, but even they are
shown to possess an irrational racism.   When Murrieta joins
the bandit gang of Three-Fingered Jack (J. Carroll Naish) he
spies a string hanging from a tree and asks Jack what the
objects are that are hanging on it.   "Oh, those are Chinamen's ears.   I don't know why, but every time I see a China-
man, I want to slit his throat and cut off his ears.   I love
Chinamen!"   So the roundelay of racial hatred goes on, in-
fecting everyone.   Though occasional alliances may be formed,
when the film's final conflict comes, each man sides with his
own race.

The Robin Hood of El Dorado anticipates the "revision-
ist" western of the 1960's in its blurring of "good guy/bad
guy" distinctions, in its violence, and in the questions it
raises about the nature of such generic western themes as
"settling" and "homesteading."   Specifically, The Robin Hood
of El Dorado prefigures Sam Peckinpah's The Wild Bunch
(1969) in its mixture of sentimentality and violence and in the
strong undercurrent of nostalgia and regret for a way of life
that is in the process of vanishing.

Certainly the massive battle at the end of The Robin
Hood of El Dorado anticipates the appalling massacre that
climaxes The Wild Bunch, but there are other, stronger,
links as well.   The Mexican folk song "La Golondrina" fig-
ures in both and serves much the same purpose in each film.

Wellman talks over a scene with Warner Baxter and J. Carroll Naish on the set of The Robin Hood of El Dorado.

Joaquin's people sing it as a farewell to him when he an-
nounces his plan to leave his band and return to Mexico. As
the song ends, the posse attacks the camp, killing the entire
band. Similarly, the villagers sing the song as a farewell
to the wild bunch as they ride out to go on to the large for-
tress/city where they will eventually lose their lives.

This sentimentality as a prelude to violence is striking
and poignant. It is interesting to find the same song being used to
similar effect in two films that seem so different on the surface.

Most of the location work was done in the Strawberry
Flats in the Sierras. The location seems to have been typical of a Wellman company: brawling, drinking, endless poker
games. Wellman, however, never spoke much about the film
one way or the other. In his autobiography, A Short Time
for Insanity, he recalls,

> J. Carroll Naish as Three-Fingered Jack in Joaquin
> Murrieta, misnamed The Robin Hood of Eldorado,
> pulling a gun loaded with blanks in a scene with
> Warner Baxter and catching the hammer in his belt,
> and it goes off just before he gets it out of the hol-
> ster. It dug into him in the upper side of the thigh,
> bad, and he wouldn't look down because he wasn't sure
> of the location, just gazed at me with a stricken, plead-
> ing face, "Bill, Bill, tell me it isn't so.

When Wellman received the assignment to do the film,
he asked for Robert Taylor to play the title role. He was
turned down and informed that Warner Baxter was going to
do it. Wellman later complained,

> Baxter was old enough to play Murrieta's father. I
> liked him, but I couldn't make a picture with him.
> I knew all the tricks. I had dancers around the fire,
> and all kinds of fights, and everything else you can
> imagine, but the minute you got with Baxter and his
> girl, in the love stories, it was really embarrassing.

In fact, there is no love story to speak of. Murrieta's
wife is killed in the first reel and he never forms another romantic union, though Juanita de la Cuesta (Ann Loring) falls
in love with him. For the rest, the film is as action-packed
as a serial and succeeds on virtually every other level. Bleak
and hard-hitting (The Ox-Bow Incident notwithstanding), The
Robin Hood of El Dorado is the best western Wellman ever made.

Wellman brought to the location a young writer, Robert
Carson, who had been assigned to the director when Wellman
requested a writing partner from M-G-M. Carson had written a few short stories, but was inexperienced in the movie
business. He was put under contract to M-G-M in 1935, but
did nothing of any note until he was informed that Wellman
needed a writer to help him work out story ideas. Wellman
was no writer and what he probably wanted was someone to
listen to his ideas and to do the actual labor. Carson said,

> Our method of work was very simple. We dis-
> cussed the project in detail, and then I wrote it.
> Wellman read it--when he got around to it, because
> he didn't like to read anything--but he read it, and
> we'd discuss it again. That was it. He didn't do
> any of the actual writing. He was engaged socially,
> emotionally and alcoholicly in many other endeavors,
> and he had, in addition, his directing chores.

Wellman and Carson were to work together on every
one of Wellman's films from The Robin Hood of El Dorado
until The Light That Failed (1939) and the partnership was
to be fruitful for both.

In their spare time, Wellman and Carson came up
with a story called The Longest Night. It was to have been
Wellman's next film after The Robin Hood of El Dorado, but
he and Carson argued with producer Larry Weingarten and
were removed from the project. Later, "quickie-director"
Errol Taggart directed The Longest Night, but Carson's
script had been jettisoned and only the title remained. Taggart's film is interesting for one reason: it was the shortest
feature--50 minutes--that M-G-M ever released.

Meanwhile, producer Hunt Stromberg was busy arrang-
ing to transfer Ben Ames Williams' novel, Small Town Girl,
to the screen. M-G-M announced that Jean Harlow would
play the title role, but an eleventh hour switch put the gentler
Janet Gaynor into the part. The project was giving the studio
a little trouble in other ways, too, and by the time Wellman
was signed on as director, at least four screenwriters--John
Lee Mahin, Edith Fitzgerald, Frances Goodrich, Albert

[Opposite:] The appalling massacre scene that ends The Robin
Hood of El Dorado.

Hackett--had had a hand in the script.   Even at that, Wellman brought Carson along with him for "additional dialog."

The story is rather like The Miracle of Morgan's
Creek as written by Fanny Hurst.   Bored, small town girl
Gaynor is picked up by a dashing Robert Taylor on the night
of the Yale-Harvard game.   After an evening of drunken
roistering, the two are married and awake the next morning
wondering how to get out of this predicament.   Frank Nugent,
in The New York Times wrote, "For appearance's sake, (Taylor) decides to let the marriage stand for six months until a
quiet divorce can be arranged.   It takes Miss Gaynor, we regret to say, almost the full period to show Mr. Taylor the
error of his ways.   Miss Harlow, we are quite sure, could
have done the job over the weekend."

Wellman feuded throughout filming with Janet Gaynor
and asked to be let out of the picture.   His request was denied, but not forgotten and after Small Town Girl was finished,
Wellman had a hard time getting assigned to any other films.

At this time, M-G-M was having a hard time itself.   The

Janet Gaynor in Small Town Girl.

problem was the next entry in the popular Tarzan series, The Capture of Tarzan. The picture had been shot in early 1936 by director James McCay. After a preview had terrified a theatre-full of children, the decision was made to reshoot some of the more objectionable material. This started a series of reshooting and rewriting that lasted nearly the entire year. At one point, Wellman was called in to redo McCay's picture, Wellman was succeeded by writer John Farrow, who was making his unofficial directoral debut. Finally, Richard Thorpe came in and reshot everybody else's material.

At last, the film was given a new title, Tarzan Escapes (it was a different picture, why not give it a different title?), and released to great success. It's quite tantalizing to wonder what the film was like originally, for the film today is still horrifying--particularly a ghastly scene that shows natives being torn apart when they are tied to two trees that are bent to the ground and released to spring to their full height in two different directions. Wellman later said that he loved the experience of working on the Tarzan picture.

> I never had so much fun in my life. It was absolutely fantastic. The little chimpanzee [Cheetah] was taught to spit at people if Johnny [Weismuller] didn't like them. I fell in love with the whole thing, and when it was over, I went in to Mayer and I said, 'I want to do the next Tarzan.' I begged him to let me do another Tarzan and he wouldn't let me do it. I never had so much fun making a picture. God, swinging across the thing on vines and doing all these silly things. I did all of them. Had more fun than I've ever had in my whole life and they wouldn't let me do another one.

Robert Carson, however, has said that Wellman was "disgusted with the project" and thereafter started looking for a way out of his M-G-M contract. This version could have some truth to it, for Wellman soon left M-G-M and was hired by his good friend David O. Selznick.

CHAPTER NINE

Wellman brought Robert Carson over to Selznick International and the pair presented Selznick with two stories. One was envisioned as a sequel to The Public Enemy, called, appropriately, Another Public Enemy; the other was a behind-the-scenes look at the people who made movies called, It Happened in Hollywood. "The whole story [of It Happened in Hollywood] is of remembering things," Wellman said. "Everything in it happened to somebody that I knew very well, sometimes a little too well."

Wellman and Carson's original story was about a young Canadian girl, Esther Victoria Blodgett who comes to Hollywood to break into pictures. Once in California, she meets her cinematic idol, actor Norman Maine, with whom she becomes involved and, eventually marries. Maine is already in decline when Esther meets him and his career sinks lower and lower as his wife becomes more and more successful as an actress. Maine's drunkenness causes his wife great humiliation when he disrupts her acceptance speech at the Academy Awards ceremony by berating the audience for their hypocrisy. Later, he is arrested for drunkenness and Esther vows to give up her career in order to care for him. Maine overhears this and walks into the ocean and drowns himself, in order to save her career. At his funeral, Esther is mobbed by fans, who see the event as not much different from any other "movie-star event." Disgusted with life in Hollywood, Esther returns to Canada. Selznick later claimed

A Star Is Born is much more my story than Well-

man's or Carson's. I refused to take credit on it
simply as a matter of policy. Certainly Wellman
contributed a great deal, but then any director does
that on any story. The actual original idea, the
story line, and the vast majority of the story ideas
of the scenes themselves are my own.

However, the finished film differs from the original story that
Wellman and Carson submitted in minor ways only. Esther's
stage name in the original outline is "Mona Lester"; in the
finished film it is "Vicki Lester." At the end of the film,
she opts to remain in Hollywood, mostly through the urging
of her grandmother, instead of returning to Canada as the
Wellman/Carson story prescribed. Further, the producer
in the original story, Joseph Grantham, was a "comic-relief"
character; in the final version, his name has been changed to
Oliver Niles and his character has become kind and sympathetic.

Too, Selznick had rejected the story when Wellman
presented it to him. "David said he was sorry, but he didn't
like it," Wellman said. "I thought it was a hell of a good
story and I told it to his wife, Irene, just before they went
off on their Hawaiian vacation, and she went crazy over it.
When they came back, David called me and said he had decided that he wanted to do the story." This was one occasion, apparently, that "pillow talk" did no harm to a project.

Selznick had originally felt that the script was too sa-
tiric, but he came to see that the outline was basic enough
to make simple, powerful drama and complex enough to em-
brace many of the great, true, Hollywood tragedies. Thus,
as the script began to take shape, Norman Maine took on
characteristics of John Bowers, John Gilbert (whose career
was ending, even as his young wife, Virginia Bruce's, was
just taking off), John Barrymore (who was even then being
destroyed by alcohol), and even B. P. Schulberg, whose career had been ruined by his drunkenness.

Also, Selznick's good friend Irving Thalberg died un-
expectedly at about this time and his funeral was a disturbing, almost uncanny realization of the Maine funeral in the
script. Thalberg's widow, Norma Shearer was set upon by
hordes of fans waiting outside the church and the whole affair
resembled a grotesque Hollywood premiere. The incident
strengthened Selznick's resolve to make the film, though It
Happened in Hollywood became a darker, more tragic tale as
a result.

Wellman and Carson had already developed two more drafts of the script and, unknown to them, Selznick turned their work over to Dorothy Parker and Alan Campbell for "punching up."

Because Technicolor cameras were at a premium in 1936, the equipment had to be reserved far in advance. This meant that It Happened in Hollywood would have to start shooting on October 31, 1936, at the very latest. As the deadline approached, Selznick worried about the film's title. He wired his secretary Katherine Brown:

> About to break some important publicity stories on the Hollywood picture and don't want to waste them on a temporary title.... Our feeling is that Holly-wood has become identified with cheap titles of cheap pictures, and this is more true today than ever because of Hollywood Boulevard which has been an outstanding failure as Paramount quickie, and also because of Hollywood Hotel which Warners are making as a musical and which will probably be released before our picture.

Selznick suggested The Stars Below as an appropriate title. John Hay (Jock) Whitney, Selznick International's Chairman of the Board, countered with A Star Is Born. Selznick agreed and the film was so named.

In September, one final scene was inserted into the script before shooting began; it took place in a sanatorium where Norman Maine had gone to dry out. The idea came from director George Cukor (who was to direct the re-make of A Star Is Born in 1954). Cukor said,

> When I was going to direct Camille, I went to see Jack Barrymore about playing De Varville, the part that Henry Daniell finally played. Jack had put himself into some kind of home in Culver City to stop drinking. It was an old frame house that called itself a rest home. I went into some dreary, de-pressing room. Back of it was the dining room, and I noticed something that always strikes me as very shabby and sad: they hadn't taken away the tablecloths, and you knew that they never changed them. Then Jack came in, with a sort of aide called Kelly. He took us into a gloomy sitting room and said, "Can we sit here, Kelly? No-

A promotional pose for A Star Is Born, with co-stars Janet
Gaynor and Fredric March on the left.

body's going to come through and disturb us by pretending he's Napoleon?" I reported this episode to
David Selznick [and] William Wellman. They liked
the scene so much they included it in the picture.
Then, years later, I found myself re-doing it.

Wellman and Selznick now began to devote their energies to casting A Star Is Born. The part of Norman Maine,
though based on several people, was so much like John Barrymore that he would have been ideal for the role, if he were
not living out the details of the script so explicitly in his
private life. So, Selznick turned to an actor who had made
his first big splash in the movies by playing a Barrymore-ish
character in The Royal Family, Fredric March. March was
given a script by Myron Selznick, who was his agent, and
after reading it, accepted the part.

The part of Vicki Lester was accepted even more immediately by Janet Gaynor. Gaynor had just worked with

Wellman on Small Town Girl and the two had clashed on the
set. However, Wellman agreed with Selznick that she would
be perfect in the part and so offered her the role.

The rest of the film was cast, as was Wellman's wont,
with some of the finest character actors working in Hollywood:
Adolphe Menjou as producer Oliver Niles, Lionel Stander as
the Russell Birdwell-esque publicity agent Matt Libby and such
stalwarts as May Robson, Clara Blandick, Andy Devine,
George Chandler, Edgar Kennedy, J. C. Nugent, Guinn (Big
Boy) Williams, and Franklin Pangborn.

Wellman also indulged in some rather eerie casting.
Owen Moore, Mary Pickford's first husband was cast as director Casey Burke. Moore was a former star of the silent
screen, but alcoholism had ruined his career. Marshall
(Mickey) Neilan, a fine director whose career had been similarly halted was given a brief cameo as one of three people
who encounter Norman Maine, during his decline, at Santa
Anita. "These has-beens give me the creeps," says one of
the trio. "He was great while he had it," says Neilan, "and
he had it for quite a while." Other "has-beens" who were
given roles in A Star Is Born include Charles King, a star
of early musicals; Vera Stedman, a former leading lady reduced to doing extra work; and, incredibly, Helene Chadwick!
What Wellman felt about giving Chadwick a bit in A Star Is
Born has never been recorded, but he was certainly aware
of the irony of "throwing a bone" to the ex-wife whose mail
he once delivered. Chadwick, incidentally, never made the
come-back that she was trying for. In June 1940, she slipped
on the stairs in her home and tumbled to the bottom, sustain-
ing extensive injuries. On September 4, 1940, she died at
the age of 42.

Filming began on Saturday, October 31, 1936, and was
completed less than two months later. Wellman was not hampered by the use of Technicolor; his pace, in fact, was just
as frenzied on A Star Is Born as on any modest, black-and-
white feature. He said,

> Everybody around the studio seemed to think we had
> worked something of a miracle, running a few days
> ahead of schedule. As a matter of fact, there's no
> reason why a color picture can't be turned out as
> quickly as the ordinary black-and-white film. I
> think the chief trouble is that everyone is so over-
> awed at the very thought of a new development that

> they just kind of sit around and look impressed.
> I insist on working at top speed for the obvious
> reason that I believe it produces better results.
> A performer gives a better show when he's all
> keyed up. So do I.

Wellman was very concerned that the film's color not be
garish and obvious.

> Color should be used to set a mood, speed up or
> slow down action and artificially stimulate pace.
> It's not a static thing. Already we have achieved
> effects with the chromatic lens which were never
> dreamed of ten years ago.

The first preview of the film made him think that he
had muted the color a bit too much. Selznick had decided to
preview the film in Pomona, a small town set in the midst
of the orange groves that were its main industry. As the
film started, Wellman noticed sinkingly, that the picture was
extremely dark. He was confused; the rushes had seemed
all right. Several times, he sent Carson into the projection
booth to tell the projectionist to make the lamps brighter.
Finally, Wellman went up himself. "Look," the projectionist replied, "I'll put more light in if you want me to, but
it's going to burn your film. That's all the light there is!"
Finally, it was brought to Wellman's attention that the orange
groves were being smudged and smoke was entering the theatre. This barely perceptible haze was what was darkening the
screen.

"When [the preview] was all over," Wellman said,
"the cards they got were complimentary, [the audience] applauded and applauded. But despite that, David said, 'Look,
it's all wrong. The first half is comedy and the second half
is tragedy.'" Wellman argued that he liked it the way it was,
but Selznick thought the transition was too abrupt between the
often-amusing first half and the sad ending. He approached
two young contract writers, Ring Lardner, Jr. and Budd
Schulberg (B. P.'s son) to work on some transitional scenes.
They didn't last long, however, and none of their material
was ever filmed. M-G-M's John Lee Mahin was brought in.
"David wasn't sure about the balance of the comedy and the
build-up to the tragedy," Mahin said. "It wasn't coming together. After I looked at the picture I told him he shouldn't
think about making it more of a comedy. The handwriting is
on the wall when the girl first sees him drunk at the Hollywood Bowl. It had to be a tragedy."

Mahin wrote some additional material, but perhaps his most significant contribution to A Star Is Born was his rewriting of the final scene. The picture had ended with Vicki entering Grauman's Chinese Theatre after seeing her dead husband's footprints in the cement. There was no lift to the scene, nothing memorable. Mahin's version brings Vicki up to the radio microphone to speak to the "world-wide hook-up." With tears glistening in her eyes, she says, "Hello everybody, this is Mrs. Norman Maine."

A Star Is Born was a smash. It opened at Radio City Music Hall in New York and Grauman's Chinese in Los Angeles. On February 6, 1938, when the Academy Award nominations were announced, A Star Is Born was nominated for Best Picture, Best Director, Best Actor and Actress, Best Assistant Director (Eric Stacey), Best Original Story (the only award it won), Best Screenplay (Carson, Parker and Campbell). W. Howard Greene was given a special Oscar for his color photography. Wellman, upon receiving his Oscar for the original story, allegedly took it to Selznick's table and said, "Here, you deserve this. You wrote more of it than I did."

Perhaps, as Wellman suggested, A Star Is Born is, in spirit, more Selznick's than Wellman's. The script had gone through so many permutations that it could really be claimed by no one, in the end, and the care, detail and taste lavished on the film is very much a part of the Selznick legacy. Where Wellman really comes through in the film is in the individualistic style of his direction; had another of Selznick's favorite directors--like John Cromwell--done the picture, the only major difference would have been in that elusive, almost indefinable visual style that marks every Wellman production.

If anything, A Star Is Born (like Nothing Sacred, which followed it) is more boldly and imaginatively framed and paced than most of Wellman's films. Unlike the stark, bas-relief clarity of the images in Beau Geste, for instance, A Star Is Born is filled with half-concealed faces and large, murky dark patches of screen. Wellman used "over-shoulder" shots in a unique way; much more shoulder is exposed to our view than face, and often that face is underlit, so that details are softened and only certain parts (like the eyes) stand out with startling strength.

This suggestiveness is representative of Wellman's

style throughout his career, but before A Star Is Born, it usually took the form of actions taking place off-screen; here he sculpts shadow and light to conceal pieces of visual information, to make his scenes part-literal and part-suggestive.

This tendency was carried over into his next project for Selznick, Nothing Sacred, though, due to its subject matter, the picture is rather more direct and unadorned visually than is A Star Is Born.

Nothing Sacred was almost not Wellman's follow-up to A Star Is Born. He was first assigned to Selznick's Technicolor production of The Adventures of Tom Sawyer*, then considered filming Dark Victory. Carson was really pushing Dark Victory, but Wellman, after some initial enthusiasm, decided not to do another tragedy right away. Carson insisted and went to Selznick about it. He later remarked,

> I was in the wrong place at the wrong time. Selznick was lying on a massage table, groaning, and a man was massaging him. He said he thought he had appendicitis, but he didn't know for sure. He was distracted by this terrible pain, which was a terrible attack of gas, and I told him the story.

While Carson recited the tragic tale of a woman who is dying of a brain tumor, Selznick lay on the table groaning. At the end of the story, Selznick said, "It's a good story and I feel much better. I'll let you know what I decide."

The next day, Selznick announced that their next project would be Ben Hecht's comedy, Nothing Sacred. The story was about a young woman, Hazel Flagg (Carole Lombard), who is believed to be dying of radium poisoning. An unscrupulous newspaper reporter arranges to bring her to New York for the time of her life. Hazel agrees to come to New York for the all-expenses-paid trip, even though she has found out that the diagnoses was wrong; she is not dying. Eventually, she falls in love with the reporter (Fredric March) and they must find a way out of the predicament: all of New York is waiting--impatiently--for her to die.

---

*After Wellman was withdrawn from the project, it was assigned to William Wyler, then to H. C. Potter, and finally to Norman Taurog.

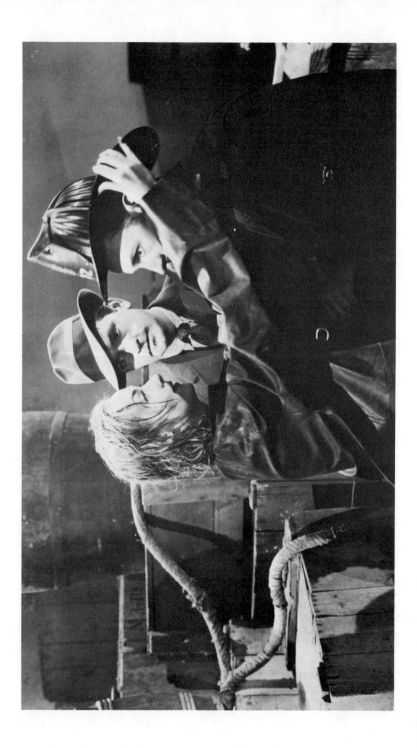

Both Wellman and Selznick were enamored with Technicolor, so it was decided to film <u>Nothing Sacred</u> in that
process.   Wellman went so far as to say that he would never
make another black-and-white film.

> I would no more think of making a picture without
> color than I would of doing one without a musical
> score.   I honestly believe that the black and white
> film is as obsolete--or will be in a few seasons--
> as the silent screen.   But more important to me
> is the fact that color gives a director what might
> be called new tools.

As on <u>A Star Is Born</u>, Wellman worked on <u>Nothing</u>
<u>Sacred</u> at breakneck speed, bringing the picture in five days
under schedule.   Ben Hecht's script was written in much the
same way: "<u>Nothing Sacred</u>," Hecht wrote, "done for Selznick in two weeks, had to be written on trains between New
York and Los Angeles."   The script was, for the most part,
brilliant, but it had several glaring flaws in Selznick's estimation.   For one thing, Selznick didn't quite like the idea
of the newspaper editor and publisher being portrayed as such
an opportunistic fraud--Selznick had too many friends in publishing.   When asked to change the script, Hecht angrily refused and walked off the project, leaving Selznick with the
better part of a good script.

Selznick sent the script through much the same course
as the <u>A Star Is Born</u> scenario had traversed.   Dorothy
Parker worked on the dialog, along with Robert Carson.
And, though they had not come through with a similar challenge on the previous film, Ring Lardner, Jr. and Budd
Schulberg were handed the script of <u>Nothing Sacred</u> and told
to come up with an ending.   They came up with a rather
weak one: Hazel and reporter Wally slip out of town and
the newspaper holds a fake funeral for the benefit of its
readers.

The final moments of the picture are a let-down, but
they don't erase the wit and sparkle of the rest of the film.
Ben Hecht's notorious (but peculiarly unspontaneous) cynicism
is given free rein.   From the opening titles ("This is New
York, skyscraper champion of the world, where the Slickers

[Opposite:]   Carole Lombard, Fredric March, and John Qualen in <u>Nothing Sacred</u>.

and Know-it-alls peddle gold bricks to each other, and where
Truth, crushed to earth, rises again more phony than a glass
eye"), <u>Nothing Sacred</u> is concerned only with casting asper-
sions at everyone and everything in its path.

    Every single character in the film is a fraud. Hazel
and her doctor take the newspaper for all it's worth, knowing
full well that she's not going to die. The newspaper pretends
to lavish love and affection on Hazel, but only as a means to
sell papers. (When she faints in a nightclub--from drunken-
ness--the editor thinks the end has finally come. "Don't
spare our feelings," he tells the doctor. "We go to press
in fifteen minutes.") The public laps it all up, all the while
weeping crocodile tears and congratulating itself on its good-
heartedness.

    As in Wellman's only other comedy, <u>Roxie Hart</u>, the
newspaper reporters come in for especially vicious attacks;
they are shown to be unprincipled, venal opportunists who
will go to literally any length to get a story. Hecht pro-
nounces his curse on his own profession: The doctor (Charles
Winninger) says, "I'll tell you what I think of newspapermen.
The hand of God, reaching down into the mire, couldn't elevate one of them to the depths of degradation!"

    <u>Nothing Sacred</u> has been seen as an epitome of screw-
ball comedy, but at its heart, it is closer to "black comedy";
the film is concerned with death, deceit, greed, and betrayal.

    Despite the dark undertones, Selznick believed the film
would establish him as a top comedy producer. He wired
Jock Whitney on June 12, 1937: "<u>Nothing Sacred</u> started
shooting this morning. You wanted comedy--boy, you're going to get it, and be it on your own head. After this one,
I'm either the new Mack Sennett or I return to Dr. Eliot."*

    For Wellman, the greatest delight of working on <u>Noth-
ing Sacred</u> was Carole Lombard. He observed,

        She was the only beautiful woman who was also a
        comedienne. Most women who are funny are not

---

*Dr. Charles William Eliot was the editor of the Harvard
Classics. Apparently, Selznick didn't feel like the "new Mack
Sennett," for after <u>Nothing Sacred</u>'s release, he "returned to
Dr. Eliot" by filming <u>The Adventures of Tom Sawyer</u>.

so pretty, but she was exquisite. We were close
friends. She loved my kids and my wife, Dottie.
We went out together. That was the one time I
knew Clark Gable well, because they were married.

The set of Nothing Sacred was constant pandemonium,
for Lombard had every bit the talent and enthusiasm for
pranks and mischief as Wellman. Lunch hours were spent
driving a fire engine around the lot at top speed, siren blar-
ing and the set was a place of never-ending practical jokes,
good-natured rough-housing, and continuous uproar. That
energy and enthusiasm somehow got onto the screen; it is
what gives Nothing Sacred a rather hysterical edge over many
other comedies. It is a frenzied film made by frenzied people. Hilarious and disturbing, Nothing Sacred is unique.

The two films that Wellman made for Selznick represent the peak of his career. Not necessarily his best films
(though they are both certainly among his best), Nothing Sacred and A Star Is Born are summits; on the one hand they
are superb examples of studio craftsmanship--on the other,
biting, eccentric, personal films.

The reason A Star Is Born and Nothing Sacred are un-
matchable is that Wellman never again worked with a producer of the caliber of David O. Selznick or with a producer
who commanded as much of Wellman's personal and artistic
respect. Wellman wrote that Selznick made "one great hit
after another. All done with great feeling, great understanding, great imagination, and great taste. David had courage,
and courage can see a long way. I didn't make pictures for
him. I made them with him."

CHAPTER TEN

After the success of Nothing Sacred, Wellman and Carson assumed that they would be signed on for another Selznick
film with little delay.   As it turned out, delay was all they
got.   From time to time a project for Wellman would be announced to the trades, but nothing ever materialized.   As this
inactivity went on week after week, Wellman began to feel as
though his M-G-M experience was being re-lived.   Selznick
was paying his salary, but he wasn't providing any work.
For a man of Wellman's restlessness and volcanic energy,
the situation was intolerable.

At about this time Wellman and Carson were approached
by Paramount with a script called Men with Wings.   The story
attempted a scope no less extensive than the entire history of
aviation, from the Wright Brothers to the present.   Carson
felt the script had promise and Wellman, who had not done a
film about his pet subject since 1933's Central Airport, was
anxious to get back into the air.

Carson began revising the script immediately, while
the pair of them started talking with Paramount about a contract.   When that contract was signed, Wellman began a five-
year association with Paramount as producer and director.
At first he was delighted about being a producer, for it meant
one less person breathing down his neck.   By the time the
contract was over, however, he was more than willing to
leave the producing to someone else.

Men with Wings was cast with Paramount's most promising young stars.   The leads were to be played by Fred Mac-

Producer-Director Wellman in his Paramount office in 1939.

Murray and Ray Milland, as Patrick Falconer and Scott
Barnes, two pioneering aviators. The woman who is torn
between them (and who is an expert on the air herself) is
Peggy Ranson, played by Louise Campbell. Others signed
to the cast included Wellman's close friend Andy Devine
(making his sixth appearance out of seven in a Wellman motion picture), Walter Abel, Porter Hall, James Burke, and
Lynne Overman. Wellman told a reporter,

> We wanted to get that feeling that every man has
> who flew in the war. That restlessness. Hard to
> describe. Well, I tried to get it into Fred and I
> think finally he caught the idea. Anyone who flew
> back in 1917 would know that feeling. They keep
> on feeling it afterwards, too. You must have no-
> ticed how it marks them.

In his review of the film, Graham Greene called it
"one of those clean stories which call for Freudian analysis.
It is about two men who have loved one woman from childhood. One marries her and is always leaving her; the other
stays around, doglike."

The triangle sub-plot is finally the un-doing of Men
with Wings, not because it's handled poorly, but simply because it dominates the film at the expense of the air story.
This is equally true of virtually every other aviation picture
directed by Wellman. He seemed unable to keep the soap-
opera out of the way of the flying machines.

In some of the films (Wings, Central Airport, Gallant
Journey) this is quite palatable, even helpful. The personal
stories in these films gives the flying scenes a tension which
separates them from the purely documentary. In such films,
however, as Men with Wings, The High and the Mighty and
Lafayette Escadrille, the aviation is strictly of the backdrop
variety. As stunning are the flying scenes in Men with Wings
(and they were stunning enough to be used again in the black
and white Lafayette Escadrille), we are again and again
brought to earth to suffer through the Sirk-type angst that
Wellman puts his characters through.

A great deal more care went into the technical aspects of Men with Wings than the slight story might have
called for. So much care, in fact, that the film was Wellman's only release for the year 1938. From the beginning
of the shooting to the end of editing took nine months, with
four months allotted for the flying scenes alone.

Wellman (right) discusses a stunt with pilot Frank Clarke on the set of <u>Men with Wings</u>. The apprehensive looking man with the glasses is Robert Carson.

The first major problem that faced the filmmakers was locating the planes appropriate to represent the period from 1903 to 1938. The search began in mid-1937. One plane was found in Bermuda, another in the basement of a hotel in Imperial, California. Assistant director Joseph Youngerman found a Fokker in a barn in El Centro, California. The oldest airplane actually used in the production was a Bleriot built in 1905.

In the instances when it proved impossible to locate the correct planes, mechanics at Metropolitan Airport in Van Nuys (where most of the location footage was shot) built facsimiles or reconditioned newer planes to appear to be earlier models. Among the extremely rare planes that were found and used in the film were a Savoia-Marchetti amphibian plane and a duplicate of Lindbergh's "Spirit of St. Louis."

Using Technicolor caused some problems. The first

was the easily-overlooked fact that close attention had to be
paid to the colors of the various buildings, uniforms, and insignia used in the film. Wellman and Zoila Conan, his secretary, set up a special research library to collect information on this aspect.

The other problem caused by shooting the film in
Technicolor was the weight of the cameras. All of the aerial
photography was directed by Wilfrid Cline, who had special
camera mounts built onto the planes so that the actors could
be photographed in flight, the technique that Wellman had used
in Wings and Young Eagles.

New and improved camera mounts had been designed
to handle the heavy Technicolor equipment, which made
Cline's job easier. Their swivel design allowed the camera
to move straight up or down as well as a lateral movement
in a 180-degree circle. Cline wrote,

> We shot most of our air scenes from 2,000 to
> 13,000 feet above sea level and it was plenty cold.
> The high altitude demands a lot of warm clothes.
> After donning leather jacket, flying suit, overshoes,
> fleece-lined gloves and the twenty-pound parachute
> that is an absolute "must" under present regulations,
> one feels as though working in a straitjacket and
> it's no cinch to handle that camera standing up in
> a 180-mile-per-hour "breeze."

This was not Cline's first brush with shooting aerial
scenes in Technicolor. He was responsible for the panoramic
views of New York in Nothing Sacred and the aerial scenes in
William Keighley's God's Country and the Woman (1936). "It
was a relief," he wrote, "to get back on the ground for the
comparative ease of a regulation Technicolor production,
Hearts of the North at Warners."

For four months, Cline photographed the work of twenty
pilots, including Paul Mantz, Frank Clarke, Tex Rankin, Dick

[Opposite:] Cast and crew of Men with Wings gather for a
group portrait as filming nears completion. Wellman and
Andy Devine lean on the nose of the plane. Louise Campbell
and Ray Milland are at Wellman's right, Fred MacMurray is
at Devine's left, and assistant director Joe Youngerman sits
at Wellman's feet.

Rinaldi, Dick Grace, and Garland Lincoln. During February
and March 1938, according to Cline, "we got some of our
best stuff, " though it took a tragedy to provide some of the
background they needed. For some of the dog-fight scenes,
Wellman wanted the right kinds of clouds and was prepared
to sit it out and wait for them, as he had done for three
months during the filming of Wings. "And what happened?"
he told a reporter. "We needed clouds for backgrounds.
So God sent us that terrible, tragic flood out in California,
and we had clouds such as never before. " He called this
"luck--pure luck. "

        In May 1938, as the dramatic scenes were beginning
to be filmed, trouble came from an unexpected quarter.
Wellman and Carson were ordered by Paramount to change
the last twenty pages of the script, to eliminate any "pacifist
preachment. " The film was to end at a banquet honoring Pat
Falconer and the new bomber that Scott has designed and
which has been accepted by the U.S. Government for use in
the up-coming war. Just as the banquet is about to begin,
Peggy hears that Pat has been killed doing mercenary piloting in China. This causes her, in her grief, to launch a
tirade against war and the development of bombers and the
banquet which seeks to honor these dealers in death.

        Both Paramount and the U.S. Government denied that
any pressure had been placed on Wellman and Carson to
change the script. Luigi Laraschi, head of censorship at
Paramount claimed, "no government representation has been
made through this office. " A New York Times article claimed,

> It was asserted by a highly reliable source that "the
> army, The State Department and The Executive Divi-
> sion" had protested the pacifist quality of the film
> and that, because the studio had a number of films
> that depend on Washington's cooperation, it was de-
> cided to eliminate the offending sequence rather than
> raise an issue.

        The previous year, Paramount had requested Govern-
ment assistance on Men with Wings, but none was ever
granted. Eighteen planes had been requested to represent
insurgent combat planes during the Spanish Civil War. The
request was denied because "it is against the policy of the
War Department to furnish personnel and equipment to represent foreign military forces. " The Times article quoted a
government statement: "Neither side in the Spanish War could

be equipped with new American planes except in violation of the neutrality act.   It would be inappropriate for the United States Army to cooperate in making a picture that would indicate that this law was being openly violated."

Whether the edict finally came from Washington or from Paramount, the offending twenty pages were changed. Wellman never commented on the episode, though a newspaper report mentions that Wellman "and his writer Robert Carson were highly exercised over the incident."

Wellman had originally planned a quite different ending for Men with Wings. Joseph Youngerman remembers,

> Wellman went up to the front office and said, "I'd like to build a little set, which is a ramp that goes up to a big airplane. And all you see is the ramp and people going up to the plane and you hear a voice saying 'All aboard for China, England, places all over the world.' " The studio thought he was out of his mind. But that's exactly what's happening today. You can fly anywhere. He wanted to establish that the plane started from nothing and was gonna get to the point where it would fly all over the world.

This futuristic scene was never filmed and Men with Wings ends at the banquet honoring Pat Falconer. There is no "pacifist preachment" to keep the country from going to war with a good conscience.

*   *   *

Upon completion of Men with Wings, Wellman and Carson started in immediately on their next project, a remake of Herbert Brenon's 1926 classic of the French Foreign Legion, Beau Geste. The Foreign Legion had been a popular setting of films in the 1920's, due entirely to the immense popularity of Brenon's film, but the unending rash of poor imitations soon soured the public on desert melodramas. Therefore, Wellman had been somewhat surprised when Eddie LeBaron asked him to do a new version of Beau Geste.

Of course, he had very nearly directed the sequel to the 1926 version--Beau Sabreur (John Waters, 1928)--and, ironically, had he done so, he would have directed the star of his new version, Gary Cooper. As it was, Cooper was

in the unique position of appearing in a film thirteen years
after he had appeared in its sequel ... sort of.

Beau Geste had been announced in 1938 as Wellman's
next film and Paramount released publicity stating that it
would be a Technicolor production, starring Fred MacMurray.
When the time came, however, it was decided that black and
white photography would better serve the subject--Paramount
wanted it to be an exact replica of the original--and it was
decided that Gary Cooper was more suited to the part than
MacMurray. This was true, of course, though neither actor
is exactly an ideal choice for a part that calls for a genteel
Englishman.

Also cast in the film were Ray Milland, Robert Preston, Susan Hayward, Brian Donlevy, J. Carroll Naish, Broderick Crawford, Albert Dekker, and Charles Barton. Barton
was perhaps the least likely member of the cast. Having
started in movies as a child actor with Broncho Billy Anderson, Barton soon opted to try his luck on the other side of
the camera. He worked with Wellman as propman and assistant director on all of Wellman's Paramount films from
1926 to 1930. In 1934, Barton became a director at Paramount himself, but was mostly assigned routine, "B" pictures.
His friend Wellman thought of him when the script called for
a very short, very tough little cowboy. At 5 feet 2 inches
Barton was the right size for the role and his countless
brawls in Wellman's company attested to his stamina. Barton recalled,

> Wellman wanted me to be in Beau Geste and hell
> wouldn't stop him. He came over to the house and
> said, "I want you to be an actor. There's a hell
> of a part for you in Beau Geste." I said, "Bill,
> I'm making good money as a director." He said,
> "Don't worry about the money. You tell them what
> you want and you'll get it, 'cause I won't do it with-
> out you."

Barton signed on and joined the company of a thousand
men--cast and crew--at Buttercup Valley, in the desert near

[Opposite:] Wellman poses with the stuntmen and film crew
of Beau Geste. To the director's left, with diamond-shaped
viewfinder, is photographer Theodor Sparkuhl. At Wellman's
feet, in white shirt, is assistant director Joseph Youngerman.

Yuma, Arizona. This was the same location that the first
Beau Geste had been filmed in April and May 1926 and,
though the old fort was still standing, it was in such dis-
repair that a new one was erected.

About a mile and a half from the fort, the company
made camp, which was comprised of 136 tents, a post-office,
a movie theatre, a recreation tent and other modern con-
veniences. Entertainers from Yuma were regularly brought
in to put on shows for the company. Other forms of entertainment were arranged as well. Wellman remarked,

> At the beginning, I ran a bus to the local house of
> ill-fame in Yuma, and the first couple of weeks it
> was packed. They were riding on top of it. But
> after they had been there for two or three weeks,
> there was only one guy who would go there, an old
> stunt man. He was the only one, and he ended up
> burning it down.
>   That was a rugged picture. You had to be
> tough.

Assistant director Joe Youngerman agreed:

> Yeah, it was a very rough location. One night we
> got blown out of our suppers, sand storm came up.
> [The company] didn't say anything about not getting
> any supper. There was sand in everything, in all
> the food. It was tough.

Barton, always the maverick, said,

> Oh no, it wasn't strenuous. It was beautiful. The
> camp they had down there was wonderful. I mean
> to say, you had a shower in your tent, [there was
> a] mess hall, a playroom. Beautiful.

The location proved tough enough to many men there.
By the end of the four-week location schedule, over twenty
men had been admitted to the hospital because of the heat.
Robert Carson left the camp in despair more than once, finally checking into a hotel in Yuma for the duration.

Tempers began to flare as well, and star Brian Donlevy quickly became one of the most unpopular men in camp.
Wellman recalled,

Everybody hated Donlevy because he lorded it over
everybody. Everybody moved out of his tent. De-
spised him. I've never seen a guy that could get
everybody to dislike him as he did. Yet, he was
good in the picture, so I kept him right in.

Youngerman added,

Brian Donlevy messed around somewhat; he was
kind of a pain. Wouldn't learn his lines. One day
Wellman asked him, "How come you don't know
your lines?" and Donlevy said, "Nobody told me
what to do." That was a lie, 'cause I used to get
four or five scripts and cut out [the actors'] parts
and give it to them the night before, to give them
sort of a new look on it. Wellman said, "Don't
hand me that baloney. I know Joe gave you your
lines."

Youngerman continued,

Also, did you know that Donlevy got jammed with
a bayonet? Well, he did. I don't know if he was
clowning around. I didn't see it.

Wellman saw it, though, and the incident became one
of his favorite anecdotes:

Milland hated [Donlevy's] guts and Milland is one
of the toughest guys I've ever known in my life,
believe it or not. Now, there's a scene in which
[they] fenced with a bayonet. We had [Donlevy's]
whole chest covered with this thick [pad] so if Milland stuck the bayonet into him [Donlevy] wouldn't
be hurt. But Milland found out that Donlevy's arm
and both sides were not padded. They went into
this scene and when they got to the end of it, Milland went through there [and nicked Donlevy in the
side of his chest] and Donlevy saw the blood and he
fainted.

Countered Youngerman,

No, I don't believe that. I don't believe that Ray
Milland would ever do anything like that. Donlevy
got it, though, right through the shoulder. That's
not the scene that's in the picture, though.

Left to right: Ray Milland, Gary Cooper, and Robert Preston
strike heroic poses in <u>Beau Geste</u>.

There is, in fact, no fencing scene in the film, though the incident could have happened during the climactic scene where the evil sergeant Markoff (Donlevy) is stabbed with a bayonet by John Geste (Milland). Or, more likely, it was just an accident that Wellman built up into one of his patented tall tales.

At the end of the four weeks, most of the company returned to Hollywood to complete shooting the interiors at Paramount and the flashback scenes of Brandon Abbas, the Gestes' childhood home at Busch Gardens in Pasadena (where parts of Wings were shot).

The second-unit crew and stunt corps stayed behind at the fort with second-unit director Richard Talmadge to film miscellaneous stunts and action footage. It was during this time when one of the film's most memorable stunts was shot: the fall from the look-out tower by the treacherous Rasinoff (J. Carroll Naish).

Though Wellman and Carson stuck eerily close to Brenon's film, Beau Geste benefited from Wellman's bold composition and fluid camerawork. The battle scenes are so rhythmically exciting, the propulsive tracks along the wall of dead faces so gripping that scene after scene is easily Brenon's better. As fine as the silent film is, the 1939 Beau Geste is finer, though critics at the time went to great lengths to state the opposite.

Paramount, in fact, invited comparison between the two versions. In a press screening designed to demonstrate the superiority of sound pictures to silent ones, Wellman's Beau Geste was preceded by the first reel of Brenon's. Paramount's plan did not work exactly as they had thought it might. The critics, to a man, preferred the earlier version.

Otis Ferguson wrote in The New Republic,

> Paramount's 1939 Beau Geste is like meeting up with an old schoolmate who has become the town idiot. The weakness here has something to do with the heart's having gone out of a thing--characters being booted around like old tomato cans, every dramatic effect being thrown bodily into your face, and no time or concern left for such minor things as plausible motives or reason.

Graham Greene cried,

> Alas! we have not yet reached the end of Beau
> Geste; Technicolor and stereoscopy wait another
> decade. There is something in the brazen tale
> which appeals to the worst in human nature--the
> cowardly will always find satisfaction in the im-
> possible heroisms they will never have to imitate
> and the weak in the disgusting and irrational bru-
> talities of Sgt. Markoff.

Brian Donlevy's portrayal of Markoff dominates the
film and won him an Academy Award nomination for best
supporting actor. Beau Geste's only other nomination in that
Gone with the Wind-dominated Oscar year was for the art
direction of Hans Dreier and Robert Odell.

Graham Greene's prediction proved accurate in a way.
Beau Geste was remade in Technicolor and widescreen in
1966, but it was a dull TV-movie-like affair, which made
not the feeblest attempt to incorporate P. C. Wren's story.
There were only two brothers, not three, and they were
Americans. There was no theft of the Blue Water, the
world's most fabulous diamond--instead there was some em-
bezzled cash. Gene Kelly had been offered the project, but
when he found that it was to be a low-budget picture, utilizing
out-takes from Bengal Brigade, he wisely took a raincheck.

In 1977, Marty Feldman directed a spoof called The
Last Re-Make of Beau Geste, which utilized some cleverly
incorporated footage from Wellman's version. Feldman neglected, however, to incorporate any clever footage in the rest
of the picture.

Wellman's Beau Geste still finds itself compared un-
favorably to Herbert Brenon's version occasionally, but it
remains one of Wellman's most popular films, through frequent revival on television. Though it reflects a very ques-
tionable political perspective and is drenched in values--
bravery, chivalry and honor--that have deflated somehow,
Beau Geste remains the epitome of the adventure film: exciting, involving, amusing, and a little fantastic. Logic is
thrown out the window in reel one and the viewer is asked to
live for two hours in a world with laws of its own; which is,
of course, what the movies are all about.

*   *   *

There was trouble brewing on The Light That Failed
before the cameras even rolled. "Ronald Colman and Wellman. An odd combination, to say the least," Wellman wrote.
"He didn't like me; I didn't like him--the only two things we
fully agreed upon."

Rudyard Kipling's romantic novel of a painter, struggling to finish his masterpiece before he goes blind, had been
filmed twice before. The first version, a Pathe release from
1916, starred Robert Edeson as Richard Heldar and Jose Collins as the unfortunate model, Bessie Broke. Paramount ac-
quired the property in 1922 and entrusted it to director George
Melford. Heldar, in this version, was played by Percy Mar-
mont, Bessie by Jacqueline Logan, Maisie by Sigrid Holm-
quist, and Torpenhow by David Torrence.

Both silent editions of The Light That Failed ended
happily. Heldar does go blind, but is reunited at film's end
with his childhood sweetheart, Maisie, who dedicates the rest
of her life to his care. In fact, Rudyard Kipling had engaged
in an argument of some years' standing with the publisher of
The Light That Failed over how it should end. Kipling wanted
Heldar to go back to the Sudan after his painting is destroyed
by the spiteful Bessie, to die at the hands of the Fuzzie-
Wuzzies. The novel was printed with both endings and the
public, at first, favored the happy one. Eventually, Kipling
won out, and his tragic ending became the official edition.

When Wellman was asked to direct the sound remake
in 1939, he agreed on the condition that he and Robert Carson be allowed to follow the book faithfully. The studio
agreed, and Carson began to work on the script.

The property seemed to have everything that Wellman
required in a motion picture: there was humor, tragedy, battle scenes, a cute dog, a rain scene, and lots of opportunity
for odd angles, clever lighting effects, and other tricks that
he loved. His enthusiasm was dampened, though, when he
was informed that the picture was to star Ronald Colman.

The casting came as an unpleasant surprise to Wellman since the project had been widely announced as a Technicolor feature to star Ray Milland, whom Wellman liked very
much. Colman, on the other hand, didn't seem like the kind
of actor that Wellman could get along with. He said,

I was a crazy guy, and he was very much the gen-

Ida Lupino and Ronald Colman in The Light That Failed.

tleman. He was a funny guy and he proved very
hard to know. He was accustomed to someone who
took great pains; I took great pains, but I probably
printed more first takes than anyone in the business;
if I had to rehearse over and over I'd say, "Oh, to
hell with it!" and go out and get drunk or something.

Besides their differences in working methods, Wellman
and Colman soon had a falling out over casting.

He didn't like Ida Lupino. That's who I wanted for
the picture. This crazy little dame who stormed
into my office one day--I'd never even seen her!--
she went by my secretary and everyone and said to
me, "You're doing Kipling's The Light That Failed,
and this is my part. You have got to give me a
chance. I know it right now. I know the whole
script, because I stole it!" I said, "I can't let
you read for the part, I haven't got Colman here."

She said, "You'll be Colman." I played the scene
with her--I was lousy as Colman--and she was fantastic! I said, "You stay there!" and I went right
into Schulberg's office and I said, "Look, we don't
have to look anymore. We've got the girl; Ida Lupino. You want to see something screwy?" And I
brought her down and we played the scene for him.
He was fascinated. So was I. And she got the
part.

Colman had as much as promised the part to his friend
Vivien Leigh and he was infuriated when informed that "bit-
player" Ida Lupino was to be given the role. He stormed into
Schulberg's office and demanded that the role be given to
Leigh. Schulberg agreed to talk with Wellman, but the director was adamant. "No," he replied, "you get yourself
another director. The hell with Colman. If he is going to
cast the picture for me, then you don't need a director, you
need a messenger boy!" Schulberg agreed to keep Lupino in
the part.

As in Beau Geste, the initial shooting on The Light
That Failed was done on location, this time near Santa Fe,
New Mexico. Wellman's assistant director on Men with Wings
and Beau Geste, Joseph Youngerman, ended up doubling as
second-unit director on The Light That Failed. Youngerman
was sent ahead of the company to scout for locations around
New Mexico. When he had found a spot that contained desert,
a river and various kinds of landscape, he made arrangements
to bring the company there. He then returned to Los Angeles
to find the stuntmen to fill the roles of the Fuzzie-Wuzzies.
According to Youngerman,

I took some black cowboys out to Griffith Park, to
see how they rode and hired about thirty of them
to play the Fuzzie-Wuzzies. I also hired about
thirty white cowboys to be British riders. We
picked up about two hundred black extras in Albu-
querque, and we used the New Mexico National
Guard as the British soldiers.

The location shooting was to take about four weeks,
but on the first day, Wellman and Colman began to argue.
That night Wellman came into Youngerman's tent. "Joe,"
he said, "I'm going back to the studio. You're going to stay
here and finish this." Youngerman was aghast. He had been
in Hollywood since 1926, but he was a little disturbed to find

one of the major productions of Paramount's schedule so suddenly thrust into his hands.

Wellman, true to his word, returned immediately to Los Angeles and began shooting what interiors he could. Youngerman recalled that the crew was sympathetic to his predicament and many went out of their way to help him out.

> I did all the fight stuff; the British square, the Running W's, the attack of the Fuzzie-Wuzzies on the railroad. In one shot I had the soldiers form a British square: three deep; the guy who lays on his stomach, the guy on his knee, the guy who stands upright. They fire on order only. There was a cannon in each of the four corners of the square and we had [stuntman] Yakima Canutt and two other [stuntmen] who were going to jump over the cannon as it went off.
>
> The stunt, as it was laid out, cost $600, (funny the things you remember) and as we did it, the smoke from the cannon blocked out the shot. You couldn't see anything.
>
> So I was in the hotel that night, moping around about the shot I didn't get. Yakima Canutt came in and said, "Joe, if you want to do the shot over again, the three of us have decided to do it for nothing, if you have some way of licking the problem."
>
> The unit manager went down to Albuquerque and got the body of an old airplane, not the wings, just the motor and fuselage, and we set up the motor to blow the smoke away. And we got the shot. I've been so grateful to this Yakima Canutt to this day.

The location shooting had the same problems that Beau Geste had: the oppressive heat, the frequent sandstorms. One such "dust devil" nearly caused serious injury to Walter Huston and Dudley Digges when the wind picked up the portable dressing room that they were sitting in, carried it nearly forty feet, and then dropped it, smashing the dressing room to pieces, but leaving Huston and Digges unharmed.

Another windstorm occurred during the shooting of a battle scene. The wind pulled the bushy wigs off the extras playing the Fuzzie-Wuzzies and a day was lost while the wigs were gathered from all parts of the desert.

Later, reviewers would say that Wellman was at his best in the fine battle scenes of The Light That Failed. Ironically, he never shot a foot of them. Back in the studio, there were battle scenes of even greater ferocity. Wellman described a major conflict between star and director:

> Ida Lupino had this one scene where she really went hysterical. Now Colman is an actor like Stanwyck--now, she's great, I love Stanwyck. Stanwyck memorizes a complete script. She knows every part in the thing. So does Colman. Colman never misses a comma, he's as smart as a whip. So we started and it was a tough scene for Ida--it was the big scene of the picture--and right in the middle of it he missed his line. Now I'm a rugged sort of a guy, but I said to myself, "Hold it down" 'cause it was so impressive that I would have missed a line, too, so I didn't say anything. Well, I said, "I want to go right off the bat, Ida, so you don't lose it"--I didn't want her to go down again. So we did the scene again and when it got to that point, he missed again. Then I knew that there was a little larceny in Mr. Colman. So I said, "Cut!" and I walked over to him and I said, "Let's you and I take a little walk." So we walked behind the set and I said, "Look, Mr. Colman, once more and I will make a character man out of you. I will kick the hell out of you"--which I would and could--"I'm not kidding. Once more and that pretty face of yours is going to look awful funny."
> So we got right back to the set and as soon as she was ready, poor kid, we did the take again. They played it beautifully. Colman was wonderful. But he didn't talk to me again during the picture, except when necessary, and then it was "Mr. Wellman" and "Mr. Colman."
> Years later when he did The Halls of Ivy, that was the television show he did, the heavy was named Wellman.

The Light That Failed turned out to be a textbook example of great pain and stress producing great art, for it is arguably Colman's finest performance, Robert Carson's best script, and among Wellman's best directoral efforts. The film was released just before Christmas, 1939. It proved popular, which gratified Wellman who had been warned that

the tragic ending would hurt at the box-office. Frank Nugent
of The New York Times, in a curiously misogynic review,
lauded the film's "fine tweedy, tobacco-ey, stout-booted air"
and praised the film for its "directness of approach and clarity of thought."

In 1951, The Light That Failed's composer Victor
Young told columnist Erskine Johnson that Wellman had asked
Young for some "authentic Hindu music" for the film.

> I knew Wellman wouldn't like authentic Hindu music
> even if I gave it to him. I got a crazy idea to play
> "Yankee Doodle Dandy" backwards. I tried it out
> on the piano. It sounded good. Then I arranged it
> with cymbals and played it for Wellman, claiming
> it was old Hindu music which I had found in a li-
> brary book.
>   Wellman listened to it and said, "Terrific. Just
> the kind of Hindu music I wanted." I played it as
> part of the musical score for the picture. The pic-
> ture was released and no one ever discovered what
> I had done.

Wellman and Carson's fruitful partnership came to an
end over Reaching for the Sun. Carson had sensed a certain
distance in Wellman's attitude during the filming of The Light
That Failed. The success of that film caused Carson to urge
Wellman to follow it up with another Kipling adaptation, The
Man Who Would Be King.

Though it is possible that Wellman would have otherwise been attracted to such a project, his changing feelings
about working with Carson led him to refuse the property.
Understanding Wellman's attitude of this time is difficult, but
it reveals a recurring behavior pattern. Always one to es-
pouse teamwork and to take pride in being a company man,
in reality, Wellman possessed an enormous ego. Very possibly, he began to feel that Carson was claiming too much of
the credit for the string of hits they had done together and
felt that the only way to re-establish his reputation as the
maverick director was to cut off the partnership. During the
filming of The Light That Failed Carson was

> no longer in on the cutting. Wellman didn't want
> me there. We used to have models made before
> we began a picture. We had a model of Fort Zin-
> derneuf, and we had little figures that we'd move

around. It was the same with The Light That
Failed. We'd try the dialogue, and sometimes
we'd act it out to each other. He'd play the hero
and I'd play the heroine and the rest of the cast.
We'd see how it was going to play. Well, this
was beginning to disappear. I think it was really
the beginning of the end.

Reaching for the Sun caused the final break in Wellman
and Carson's relationship. Carson didn't like the property
and didn't like working with Wessel Smitter, the author of the
novel that the film was based on. When he approached Wellman and demanded some changes in things, the two began to
argue and Wellman fired Carson from the project. Eventually,
Smitter, too, was released and W. L. River was called in to
complete the screenplay.

Wellman soon realized that there were controversial
elements to Smitter's novel F. O. B. Detroit. The film's production notes explain, "The book was a novel of social sig-
nificance--a story of man against machine, and an indictment
of the motor magnates for their alleged exploitation of the
workers; the picture, on the other hand, is a romantic comedy quite devoid of social significance."

Second-unit director Joseph Youngerman adds, "The
story had a little bit of a Communist slant. Maybe. Wellman wanted to make the story, but it really became not too
good because they went way off the track." As enjoyable as
Reaching for the Sun is, it remains a disappointment for the
missed chances it contains. The result is tantamount to making Upton Sinclair's The Jungle into a light-hearted romp
through the meat-packing industry. It's possible that Wellman himself supported the changes in the script, for he was
rabidly anti-Communist and would take care to expunge anything that could be construed as Communist sympathies from
the script altogether.

On the other hand, he had an unquenchable, career-
long desire to stir up controversy, to "shoot off his gun in
all directions" which makes his reticence to film F. O. B. Detroit as it should have been done all the more puzzling.

For whatever reason, it is quite obvious that he lost
interest in the project very quickly. As he had done on The
Light That Failed, Wellman sent Joe Youngerman to do all of
the second-unit work and even had him work with the actors

In this scene from <u>Reaching for the Sun</u>, the back gate of the Paramount lot doubled as an automobile factory.   At center is star Joel McCrea and to his right is George Chandler.

on location.   The second-unit work was done on location in Detroit at the Packard Motor Car Company.   Some additional scenes (transparencies for the big fight scene) were shot by A. Finkl and Sons Company in Chicago.   Said Youngerman,

> Wellman never saw the location, never knew what
> I was doing.   We went to Chicago to film a fight
> between an overhead crane and a manipulator.   Now,
> a manipulator is a tool, a big machine that runs on
> tracks that will pick up seventy tons of steel and
> shove it into a furnace.   Picks it up like you'd pick
> up a pencil.   It takes about sixty hours to get the
> steel red-hot and then the manipulator will pick it
> up and take it over to a hammer to pound it into
> shape.

The fight scene is the highlight of the film, though not as much for its execution as for the novelty of seeing the tra-

ditional good guy/bad guy (Joel McCrea/Albert Dekker) conflict resolved in such gargantuan terms. The fight ends with
McCrea's manipulator being turned over, an accident which
costs him a leg. Youngerman had some difficulty getting the
factory bosses to let him turn over their expensive, vital
equipment. Youngerman explained,

> The guy who ran the forge became a very good
> friend of mine and he finally let me turn the ma-
> nipulator half-way over. The war came along while
> we were shooting and factory production was stepped
> up so we had to get out of there. We got all of
> our shots, but we didn't get the sound. The govern-
> ment stepped in and said, "We can't let the company
> come back into the factory." The foreman said,
> "If you don't let the company come back in here,
> I'm gonna close the shop. I made a promise that
> they could come back and finish their work. Have
> everybody investigated that you want, have a thou-
> sand people patrolling the place, but they're gonna
> come back in here."

Back in Hollywood, Wellman was working on the dramatic scenes with McCrea, Eddie Bracken, Ellen Drew, Dekker, Billy Gilbert, and several Wellman regulars like George
Chandler and James Burke. The exteriors of the factory
scenes were shot at the Paramount studio gates; the gateway
and stub end of Lemon Grove Avenue were closed to public
traffic for more than a week.

Wellman worked at his characteristic breakneck speed.
He shot so fast, in fact that he found himself weeks ahead of
schedule. Youngerman recalls, "He closed down the picture
waiting for the stuff I was shooting. I was making transparencies for the backgrounds and he couldn't go on until I was
through."

Youngerman was proud of the fact that his shooting in
the Packard plant did not slow down production as had been
predicted. Paramount publicity claimed that the "pace for
the assembly line was increased by several units over the
normal 50-units-per-hour tempo."

For the wilderness location that frames the film, Wellman took the crew to Lake Arrowhead, a resort community
in the San Bernardino Mountains, six thousand feet above sea
level. The location was a crucial one and difficult to find,

for there were so many qualifications demanded of it by the
script and by the logistics of filmmaking. It had to be easily
accessible by car and truck and had to be within a reasonable
distance from the areas where the cast and crew were housed
for the week's shooting.

In addition, as a Paramount publicity release put it,
"this lake, in order to fit story requirements for a secluded
spot in the forests of Northern Michigan, had to have a sandy
beach with pine woods close to the water's edge, lofty hills
in the background, a level cabin site, a paved road close by,
water shallow enough for wading and clear enough for the
camera to see through, with trees and foliage duplicating
those of the Michigan Peninsula in the summer, and the fore-
shore free enough of rocks so that deer might come down to
drink."

In fact, a scene which shows McCrea and Drew wading
across a stream was filmed at the Arturo Ranch near Malibu
Lake. In an incident rather reminiscent of the Grapefruit
Scene in The Public Enemy (in which Wellman assured Mae
Clarke that Cagney really wouldn't hit her), Ellen Drew was
deliberately led into a deep hole in the floor of the stream
so that she would plunge in over her head. Wellman told her
that the scene would be done with a stand-in. He was after
spontaneity and he got it. The unsuspecting Drew walked
right into the hole, plunged in over her head and swallowed
a lungful of water. She had to receive medical treatment,
but the shot was fine.

As he frequently did, Wellman inserted a little piece
of his own life into Reaching for the Sun. When the script
called for McCrea to attend a course for expectant fathers,
he brings home several pamphlets. On the covers of the
pamphlets are photographs of Wellman's three children, Patricia, Bill, Jr., and Kathleen.

Reaching for the Sun was released in May 1941, seventeen months after the release of Wellman's last film, The
Light That Failed. This uncharacteristic break in filming was
due to a worsening of Wellman's arthritis, which, by now,
was assaulting Wellman's back in crippling blows. He had
directed and produced the first three pictures under his Paramount contract in frequent pain and finally, upon completion
of The Light That Failed, had collapsed. He spent several
months virtually confined to his home. This arthritic flare-
up resulted in 1940 being the first year since 1923 to have no

new release from Wellman and 1941 had only <u>Reaching for</u>
<u>the Sun</u>.

The pain and discomfort that his back caused him, as
well as the changing nature of the movie business, slowed
down Wellman's amazing productivity. He would never have
another year such as 1933, when he directed no fewer than
seven features. From this point on, he would average a picture a year.

<u>Reaching for the Sun</u> was successful at the box-office,
though several critics questioned the radical changes made in
the transition from book to screen. Bosley Crowther wrote,

> By the familiar device of shifting emphasis and
> omitting the grimmer details, Mr. Wellman and
> his facile scriptwriter have managed to smear a
> thick coat of goo over what was originally a harsh
> and decidedly unsweetened industrial story. All
> suggestion of labor conflict has been carefully left
> out; the attitude of the workers toward their bosses
> and the effect which this has upon their lives have
> been gingerly overlooked.

The audience, however, was attracted to the gentle
comedy and seemingly ignored the fact that Ellen Drew played
as unsympathetic a role as was possible in what pretended to
be a romance and that McCrea and Bracken, while good in
their roles, didn't have that spark under Wellman's direction
that Preston Sturges lent them. The whole project, in fact,
might have made a better Sturges picture than it does a Wellman, for Sturges' inventive approach to humor and the way
that it illuminates the dramatic situations inherent in his
scripts, could have fleshed out the actions of the characters
here; Sturges would have taken the time to bring out the hidden worth in such a story, while Wellman was obviously just
trying to get the thing done.

Before Wellman completed his contract with Paramount,
he went over to Twentieth Century-Fox to direct <u>Roxie Hart</u>.
Upon completion of that raucous comedy, he started work on
<u>The Great Man's Lady</u> with his favorite actress, Barbara
Stanwyck. Wellman was satisfied enough with W. L. River's
script for <u>Reaching for the Sun</u> to retain his services on this
picture. The original was a magazine story by Vina Delmar
which had been adapted by Adela Rogers St. John and Seena
Owen.

After a session with make-up artist Wally Westmore, Barbara Stanwyck appears as a 100-year-old woman in The Great Man's Lady.

The Great Man's Lady spans nearly a century in time
as it traces the life of Hannah Semplar (Stanwyck) and her
marriage to pioneer Ethan Hoyt (Joel McCrea). The film
casts a jaundiced eye on the "pioneer spirit" that built America and reveals the sense of personal loss that accompanies
the forging of new trails. The film is instilled with a knowledge of the price, in human lives, of progress and growth.
Hannah helps Ethan to build an empire, but loses him, her
children, and finally her own identity in the process. The
film is framed by an unveiling of a statue of "The Great
Man--Ethan Hoyt" and 108-year-old Hannah's recollections
of her long and eventful life with him. Her story questions
the entire motive behind American empiricism and frontier-
forging.

Contemporary reviews were somewhat taken aback by
the angry tone of the film. The New York Times' reviewer
sniffed,

It is less the record of the boisterous and often
reckless energies that built an empire than the
story of the rather grubby ambition of two persons
who had a vision of "a mountain of gold with a
white light in the sky." Our pioneer heroes, we
suspect, were fascinated by something larger and
more breathtaking than the gold in them thar hills.

Today, we can find it a lot easier to believe that the
pioneers were often "grubby" and "ambitious" and The Great
Man's Lady seems a more canny picture of the young days of
the West now than it did in its original release.

Hannah Semplar is the very epitome of the Wellman
heroine: strong, intelligent, loyal, witty, and resourceful.
She can cook, hunt, ride, fight, out-gamble a professional
gambler, and out-think anybody else in the film. Hannah is
the emotional and moral center of the film; each man she
comes in contact with is fatally flawed and it is she who
must make the decisions and live with the consequences.

The role of Hannah Semplar was an especially demand-
ing one for Stanwyck, for she had to age from a girl of 16
to an old woman of 108. Make-up artist Wally Westmore created the various faces for her. Stanwyck, Westmore, and
assistant director Joe Youngerman visited the Masonic Old
Ladies' Home in Santa Monica so that Stanwyck could get a
feel as to how a woman of a hundred years would move, walk,

sit, talk. She studied the old women she met there and
brought a unique understanding to the role as a result. In
addition, Westmore developed leg straps which hooked up to
a leather girdle around her waist, which kept her from being
able to straighten her legs.

Make-up aside, Stanwyck's performance is skilled,
varied, and intelligent. The aged woman has the same verve
and spirit that the teen-aged girl exhibits and both show wit,
courage, and a defiance for the conventions of the narrow-
minded society that surrounds them (her). Young Hannah
slides down the banisters in the house of her stuffy father;
Old Hannah, upon struggling up a similar flight of stairs,
turns at the top to spit on them.

The Great Man's Lady was not particularly successful,
a fact which saddened both Wellman and Stanwyck; both regarded it as their best effort together. "I loved that film,"
Stanwyck said, "I was just crazy about it! It was an interesting role to play and I loved the challenge. But it was
never very successful, and that kind of broke my heart. I
thought it was going to be ... but it wasn't."

CHAPTER ELEVEN

Wellman had looked forward to his last picture as a producer/director, The Great Man's Lady, with dread. He had had enough of the dual capacity. He remarked,

> Too many jobs. It's tough enough just to direct a picture. I found (and this is only my opinion) that I didn't have enough brains to handle two jobs.
> And the one thing I really hated was that I began to talk money. I didn't want to be in that class of people--money. That's one of the things that's wrong with the industry.

Even before he completed his five-year contract with Paramount, Wellman had started looking around for another studio. In late 1941, writer/producer Nunnally Johnson asked Wellman to direct Johnson's remake of the popular stage play (and 1927 film) Chicago, now titled Roxie Hart.

Despite the glowing success of Nothing Sacred, Wellman was not really a comedy director; his best films, in fact, are almost devoid of humor. As Raoul Walsh rather dubiously quotes W. C. Fields, "(Wellman's) idea of humor would be watching a parachute fail to open." Still, Nothing Sacred had given him the widespread, if inaccurate, reputation of being a "top comedy director" and he had enormous confidence in his own versatility. He took a leave of absence from Paramount to bring Roxie Hart to the screen.

Roxie Hart is a very funny film, well-paced and bright with, as William K. Everson wrote, "a zest, crackle and

brevity that has quite vanished today." It is, however, a
good example of the traits that kept Wellman from being in
the forefront of comedy directors.   Unlike the subtle under-
playing and the ironic wit of Nothing Sacred, Roxie Hart hammers away after laughs with the relentless urgency of a burlesque skit.   Wellman was so concerned with making Roxie
Hart the most hilarious picture ever made that he leaves no
room for the nuance and shading of character that makes
Preston Sturges' and Ernst Lubitsch's films of the same
period so lastingly delightful.

Too, as in Nothing Sacred, Wellman seems to have
visually planned Roxie Hart without consulting the script.   It
looks like a classic film noir, with most scenes played in
confining quarters (the Harts's small apartment, the court-
room, the jail cell) and all exteriors shot at night, in the
rain.   For the most part, Roxie Hart looks as though it
might have been directed by Fritz Lang or Edward Dmytryk.

Left to right: Lynne Overman, Adolphe Menjou, Ginger Rogers, and George Montgomery in Roxie Hart.

Though <u>Roxie Hart</u> is not the subtlest film in the world, it is thoroughly entertaining. One of the major delights of the film is the cast, made up almost entirely of some of the best character actors in Hollywood at the time: Adolphe Menjou, Sara Allgood, Phil Silvers, William Frawley, Spring Byington, Lynne Overman, Nigel Bruce, Milton Parsons, and Iris Adrian as Two-Gun Gertie ("Got a butt, buddy?"). The film is particularly notable for the relatively large role (that of Roxie's husband, Amos) given to Wellman favorite, George Chandler, who came in for one cameo in <u>A Star Is Born</u> and hit it off so well with the director that Wellman promised him a job in his next picture. In fact, Wellman went Chandler one better than that: he gave the actor a part in every one of his films until the late 1950's.

George Chandler appeared in over thirty of Wellman's films, but <u>Roxie Hart</u> represents a rare major role for him. Wellman claimed that Chandler would "give me, literally, the shirt off his back," and, in addition, Chandler helped give Wellman the reputation of always knowing what he wanted. Wellman wrote,

> George developed a second sight of my moments of uncertainty. If he happened to be in the scene that was bothering me, he would find some way of buggering it up, forgetting his lines, sneezing--not once or twice; a seizure--or whispering while I was talking. Then the roof blew off, and believe me I could blow it a mile. When I had put George and all his relatives and ancestors where they belonged, I called off work for ten minutes, stormed into my dressing-room office, slammed the door shut and sat down quietly and always worked out my problem. It was like magic.

His problems with comedy aside, Wellman was always at his best with the kinds of characters that people <u>Roxie Hart</u>. He had a particular affection for low-lifes, frauds, criminals and sensation seekers. What the picture loses in the ham-fisted laugh-getting, and outsized takes of actors enjoying their roles a bit too fiercely for their own good, it gains in the cartoonish vividness of the action and brash audacity of a film that really believes itself to be the last word in humor. Ginger Rogers is not quite the right choice for Roxie, the "prettiest woman ever tried for murder in Cook County," but she manages to make up in enthusiasm what she lacks in conviction. George Montgomery saunters through the

picture pretending he's Clark Gable (and doing pretty well at
it), but Roxie Hart belongs hands-down to Adolphe Menjou as
Billy Flynn, Roxie's "simple, bare-foot mouthpiece." Not
only does he have the best lines in Johnson's script ("When
you came in here, I didn't ask you is she guilty or is she
innocent. No, I said nothing like that. I simply said, 'Have
you got $5,000?'") but he plays the role with a scenery-
chewing vivacity that is a ham actor's delight.

Lady of Burlesque, made the next year for independent
producer Hunt Stromberg, has a similar feel to Roxie Hart,
though it is not strictly a comedy. In fact, it's a little difficult to describe what Lady of Burlesque is: a comedy-
musical-drama-murder mystery. Based on Gypsy Rose
Lee's autobiographical novel, The G-String Murders, the
film takes place, appropriately, in a Burlesque theatre that
had once been a respectable Opera House. The film looks
very much like one of Wellman's men-in-groups films, except that the majority of leading characters are women. A
Wellman group is a Wellman group, though, and the Burlesque troupe exhibits the same loyalties and conflicts, bonds
and frictions that characterize the garrison at Fort Zinder-
neuf or the Battered Bastards of Bastogne.

Most Wellman groups gain solidarity through a banding
together against a common enemy--the men in Beau Geste
may be preparing to kill their commanding officer, but when
the Arabs attack, they quickly revert to their proper working
relationships--but in Lady of Burlesque, the enemy comes
from within. Someone is murdering members of the troupe
and the group's bonds are strained through wariness and sus-
picion. In this respect, Lady of Burlesque resembles The
Ox-Bow Incident, which was made the same year, in repre-
senting a group dividing against itself and the unexpected alliances and rivalries that result.

The characters in Lady of Burlesque are professionals,
as are most typical Wellman people, and even the tensest
moment in the murder mystery does not keep them from going to work. From a commercial point of view, it's quite
obvious why Wellman spends so much time showing the bad
burlesque comedy skits, dance numbers, and pseudo-Ziegfeld
productions: it gives the picture some songs, some laughs,
and a lot of beautiful girls with not much to wear. There's
a practical side at play here, too, for Wellman can only
really understand characters when he shows them at their
jobs; each bump and grind adds a little bit of biography.

Lady of Burlesque was Barbara Stanwyck's last film
with Wellman and it seems to have represented to both a
chance to let their hair down and work on something frivolous and unpretentious. Stanwyck, who got her professional
start in an atmosphere similar to the one depicted in this
film, reveals herself to be a surprisingly good dancer and
a singer of unconventional yet distinctive style.

There was a little trouble from the Hays office regarding the costumes and the actual "girlie" numbers suf-
fered as a result. Stripteasing, of course, was strictly for-
bidden and the majority of the bumps and grinds are conveyed
through audience reaction shots. One has to take the fact
that daring stuff is happening purely on faith. Stanwyck has
a curious trait, at the climax of her numbers, of whipping
the curtain back and forth, which brings forth wild approval
from the eager men in the audience. For the most part,
we must trust the dialog to sketch in what really brings those
wolf-whistlers back. As Gee Gee (Iris Adrian) says, "Right
at the big moment, I dropped my spangles. And it was embarrassing, believe me. But effective."

Lady of Burlesque followed hot on the heels of a film
that eventually became one of Wellman's most highly praised
and remembered, The Ox-Bow Incident. In fact, the two
films, which seem at first glance to be totally opposite in
tone and intent, were released the same week, but The Ox-
Bow Incident had actually been filmed over a year before.
According to Wellman,

> I bought the property from Harold Hurley, a pro-
> ducer at Paramount studios after he had gotten into
> some sort of beef with the big boys and was re-
> lieved of his job. Things had apparently collapsed
> all around him, and I offered him five hundred
> bucks more than he had paid for the book. This
> he gladly accepted, and then I went to all the pro-
> ducers for whom I had worked and got turned down.
> Zanuck was the only one with guts to do an out-of-
> the-ordinary story for the prestige, rather than the
> dough.

The various producers whom Wellman approached can
be somewhat forgiven for their reaction to Walter Van Tilburg Clark's sombre novel about the lynching of three innocent men. It is a depressing story with little action, no romance or any other ingredient which might pull in an audience.

In The Ox-Bow Incident, the artificiality of the sets somehow
intensifies the claustrophobic intensity of the drama and this
sombre anti-lynching tale retains its power to shock and involve an audience as much today as when it was made nearly
forty years ago.

Wellman, though, was strongly affected by it and for once
trusted his own feelings about a project over its commercial
possibilities. He never felt that the cinema was a "personal"
medium; to him, a film was successful only when it had been
watched and enjoyed by the maximum number of people. But
this sort of feeling went out the window as regards The Ox-
Bow Incident. When he read the book he

> went absolutely crazy about it. I came home with
> my wife, made her sit down, I read her the whole
> goddam book. Right through from the beginning to
> the end. It took me almost all night long. I was

so crazy about it. I said, "Mommy, this can be
the best that I've ever done. " It wasn't, but it
could have been.

Zanuck was similarly impressed with Clark's book and
he agreed to let Wellman make the film, despite pressure
from Bill Goetz, Bill Koenig (Fox's production head), and
Lew Schieber. Zanuck told Wellman, "You can do it, but it
won't make a cent. It's something I want my studio to have.
I want my name on it and I think it'll be good for you. "

There was, of course, a catch. Wellman was asked
to sign a five-year contract with Twentieth Century-Fox, to
make one film a year, with at least two of those films to be
directed sight unseen by Wellman. In other words, Zanuck
would hand Wellman two scripts and Wellman would make them
with no changes or protests. "I said okay, " Wellman recalled. "I'd do anything for [The Ox-Bow Incident]. "

Due partially to this trade-off agreement, Wellman's
new association with Zanuck resulted in the most diverse period, both artistically and qualitatively, of his career. From
1943 to 1948, Wellman would release films of varied ranges
and themes and would have varied success with them. Perhaps these five years represent the model period for looking
at Wellman's strengths and weaknesses, not because any of
his best work (except The Story of G.I. Joe) was accomplished
then, but because nearly every facet of his filmic personality
becomes most evident in these films.

The Ox-Bow Incident has been among Wellman's most
honored films and it is an exceptionally fine and important
western, but it looks less like a Wellman film than any of the
rest of his better work. This is a result of the director's
willfully receding his own personality into the background, in
order to faithfully and simply execute the grim, powerful
story. "I wanted the picture to be the book, " he said. "I
think that is a hell of a talent. " And it is a hell of a talent,
one which Wellman could exercise too infrequently. The Ox-
Bow Incident, as a book, was so good, so direct and so "cinematic" that Wellman could spend his energies on simply getting it onto the screen. What this reveals, paradoxically, is
that Wellman was really at his best (or at least at his most
prominent, personally) when his material was at its least
promising. When the material needed him, he could com-
pensate for its deficiencies with his powerful fund of imagination and skill; when it didn't, he surrendered himself to it
and made the material of uppermost importance.

Lamar Trotti's script for The Ox-Bow Incident is remarkably faithful to Clark's book, but there is one jarring
difference. Much is made, in both film and book, of a letter that one of the three doomed men passes to Mr. Davies
to be forwarded to the man's wife. Davies used the letter
to elicit sympathy for the man, but in the book, its contents
are never revealed. Trotti composed the letter for the finale
of the film and Wellman completely supported the decision to
make its contents explicit. He commented,

> I think the letter scene is beautiful. There's all
> these guys--they're depressed as hell, sitting
> around in the saloon, knowing they've murdered
> these three guys, and Fonda reads this letter from
> the one man to his wife. I think it's very moving.

Though the letter scene has been criticized for simply
tagging on a point that the film had made long before, Wellman always stood by it. Perhaps he was less interested in
what the letter said than in solving the problem of how to
convey the complex feelings of the scene without lapsing into
bathos. His solution almost makes the scene worthwhile.
The director explained,

> I wanted Henry Morgan's profile in the foreground.
> We had it lit so that Fonda's hat covered his eyes,
> and all you saw of him was his mouth. That's all.
> An ordinary actor would have fought like hell about
> that [but] we did it that way and it was fascinating.
> Everybody followed the simple way he read that
> tragic letter.

When The Ox-Bow Incident was released, it was, as
everyone had feared, a box-office failure.

> They sort of pushed it out, [Wellman said]; it didn't
> do much. Then they put it out abroad and it was a
> hit. Then they brought it back. I still don't think
> I could retire on the money it made, but at least it
> was reasonably successful. It's a hell of a story.

The film remains powerful today, for the simple blunt-
ness of the script, the excellent ensemble performances, and
the nightmarish artificiality of the sets and atmosphere. Shooting the film on a sound stage was obviously a financial decision primarily (Fox didn't want to make the film and so ap-
propriated a very low budget in order to cut the risk), but it

makes the film effective in a way it would not otherwise have
been.   The visual style of The Ox-Bow Incident is as right
for its content as that of The Cabinet of Dr. Caligari and
much of the tense, claustrophobic atmosphere would have dis-
sipated on location.

In fact, both of Wellman's "contractual obligation"
films, Thunder Birds and Buffalo Bill were shot primarily
on location in beautiful Technicolor, but neither, of course
is the artistic equivalent of The Ox-Bow Incident.   "They
just gave me the scripts, " Wellman said, "and I made them.
I made them the best I could. "

Thunder Birds, which was released in September 1942,
would seem to have been a perfect story for Wellman.   It
was based at the Thunderbird Airfield in Arizona and concerned the training of British, Chinese, and American flyers
preparing to go overseas for combat.   Frustratingly, the
aerial aspect of the story is given the short shrift almost
immediately, and the bulk of the film is taken up with another romantic triangle, this time involving Preston Foster,
Gene Tierney, and John Sutton.   The Technicolor flying
scenes are stunning, but the film is forgettable in every
other way except for one little autobiographical touch.

Britt (Preston Foster) is a middle-aged flight instructor whose most troublesome pupil is the British rookie, Peter
Stackhouse (John Sutton).   Stackhouse is deathly afraid of flying; every flight makes him nauseous and he is in danger of
being booted out of the school.   Britt appears at Stackhouse's
barracks one night to give him a pep talk.   He tells the young
man that he had known his father in the First World War and
has carried a picture of him around ever since.   He shows
the picture to Stackhouse; it is a snapshot of young Bill Wellman in a heavy fur coat posing in front of one of his planes
in Luneville.

Later on, Stackhouse is shown at his home, visiting
his grandmother (Dame May Whitty) and, on the wall there,
is a large painting of Wellman in his blue French uniform.
This little cameo is just a bit of whimsy on Wellman's part,
for there is obviously little else that he wished to identify
with his own experiences in this tepid film.

This frustrating tendency for coming up with promising
ideas for films and then letting them slip through his fingers
is evidenced again in 1945 in the Wallace Beery vehicle This

Man's Navy. Again, Wellman would seem to be in his element; the picture is set in the Navy's blimp service, which
should provide an interesting sidebar to his other flying films.
Again, though, the aerial aspects are almost totally ignored
except for a few lovely shots of the dirigibles in flight and an
exciting battle between a blimp and a Japanese submarine.

Wellman, apparently, had nothing else to say about
flight. These films, made at a time when he had sufficient
clout to get things done to his satisfaction, have not a tenth
of the exhilaration of flight nor the understanding of men who
pilot planes found in such modest films as Central Airport or
The Conquerors, much less Wings or Legion of the Condemned.

Ironically, in 1945, the year that saw the release of
the flying film This Man's Navy, Wellman made one of the
best films of his career about, of all things, the infantry:
Ernie Pyle's The Story of G.I. Joe. Wellman said,

> I had made flying pictures, you see, and one day
> a little guy appeared at my door, Lester Cowan.
> He said, "I'm producing Ernie Pyle's G.I. Joe"
> and he wanted me to do it. And I said, "Look, I
> am an old broken-down flyer. I hate the God-
> damned infantry. I'm not interested." Well, he
> came back time after time. Once I threw him out.
> The phone rang a couple of days later and it
> was Ernie. He said, "Look, Bill, please come
> down and be my guest at Albuquerque." I said,
> "Ernie, I'll come, but I'm not going to do [the pic-
> ture]. I'll come to see you because I want to see
> you. I'd like to talk to you. I don't like your god-
> damned infantry, but I want to meet you."

Wellman visited Pyle at his New Mexico home and the
two became very close. At the end of the visit, Pyle had
persuaded Wellman to make the film.

Actually, Wellman had not been Cowan's first choice
to direct The Story of G.I. Joe. Because Cowan felt the picture was a "rare opportunity to make Hollywood's first honest
and authentic picture about the infantry soldier," he wanted to
work "with people who know from actual first-hand experience." So he approached John Huston, who was, at the time,
completing his documentary The Battle of San Pietro. Huston
liked the script and worked with Cowan for a while on honing
it, but eventually turned the project down.

Robert Mitchum was catapulted to stardom as the tragic Lt. Walker in The Story of G.I. Joe.

Once Wellman had accepted the picture, he started to show his characteristic enthusiasm. Shooting began in November 1944. Wellman cast a minimal number of actors for the roles, preferring to use actual G.I.'s. The War Department assigned to the film 150 veterans of the Italian campaign who were about to be shipped out to the Pacific. The soldiers were on a six-week "working leave" to do the film. They were given frequent periods of liberty, and some extra spending money, but, in effect, they were in regular training throughout the duration of the shooting schedule. Columnist Hedda Hopper wrote,

> Actors in G.I. Joe were pleading to be shipped to a real combat zone before Wellman finished with them. His set was filled with four feet of ice-cold mud and every night he had the special effects department soup it up.
> When the actors arrived at 8 am and donned their full packs--80 pounds of equipment--they were

ordered to fall in, in the mud. "That's how the
real soldiers live," howled Wellman, "so get in
there." As a result, the actors looked like combat soldiers on the screen. They knew what slog-
ging through mud meant.

Pyle himself had chosen Burgess Meredith to portray
him in the film, and Wellman virtually created a star over-
night by casting young Robert Mitchum in the role of Lt.
Walker. According to the director,

I very foolishly made the test of one of the most
important scenes in the picture, the one where he
was the tired officer writing letters to the mothers
of kids who'd been killed. It was my big mistake.
Really, for I saw something so wonderful, so completely compelling, that I was mad at myself for
not having built the set before so that I could have
made the test the actual scene that came out in the
picture.

The Story of G.I. Joe was the real starting point in
Mitchum's career, though he had been making pictures for
over two years. The role of the doomed lieutenant won him
international acclaim and an Academy Award nomination as
best supporting actor (he lost to James Dunn for A Tree
Grows in Brooklyn).

The film was not released until September 1945; by
that time, Ernie Pyle had been dead for five months. He
had been killed in April 1945 by a Japanese sniper on a Pacific island. Wellman said regretfully,

Ernie never saw it, never knew anything about it,
but he would have loved it. Every one who was in
that picture went into that last battle they had--
Okinawa--and most of them never came back.
I feel lousy. I couldn't have stopped it, but
at least we had some fun together. We were shooting, but they were blanks, and nobody was getting
hurt. We had a lot of laughs together, a lot of
work, a lot of drinks, and I got them a little extra
dough. It all seems so futile now.

The film was universally praised. General Eisenhower
called it "the greatest war picture I've ever seen" and even
the soldiers who had fought in the Italian campaign (including

battles depicted in the film) were enthusiastic.   The general
consensus was, "This is it!" a war film that accurately portrayed their experiences and feelings.

Of all American critics, the one who wrote most perceptively of the film was James Agee:

> Coming as it does out of a world in which even the
> best work is nearly always compromised, and into
> a world which is generally assumed to dread honesty
> and courage and to despise artistic integrity, it is
> an act of heroism, and I cannot suggest my regard
> for it without using such words as veneration and
> love ... it seems to me a tragic and eternal work
> of art.

The Story of G.I. Joe is Wellman's masterpiece; it is
everything that has been attributed to Wings or The Public
Enemy or The Ox-Bow Incident in terms of quality, meaning,
and beauty.   It shares that elusive trait with the world's
greatest art of making enormous complexities of the spirit
seem as clear and simple as a raindrop.   Wellman's grousing
about not knowing "anything about the goddamned infantry"
was only so much smokescreen; he knew men and he understood the quiet dignity and sense of purpose that is often
called bravery.   More important, he understood the camaraderie and love that exist between people under duress, the
loyalty laced with fatalism that accepts the death of a friend
with a stoic shrug and a lifetime of memories.   He knew, as
Agee wrote, "that in war many men go well beyond anything
which any sort of peace we have known, or are likely to know,
makes possible for them."   And he knew what he had accomplished on that "little stage over at the Selznick studio."
The Story of G.I. Joe, he said, "is the best picture I ever
made in my whole life."

                    *   *   *

Not the best picture he ever made in his whole life
was 1944's Buffalo Bill.   This was the second of Wellman's
"contractual obligation pictures," a big, splashy, Technicolor
adventure story about William Cody, buffalo hunter, Indian
scout, and showman.   Wellman claimed to have started working on a script with his good friend Gene Fowler in 1940 about
"the fakiest guy that ever lived, Buffalo Bill."   After some
weeks of collaborating on a script, Wellman said, Fowler
abruptly burned it, saying, "You can't kill any of these won-

derful heroes that my kids and your kids worship.   Buffalo
Bill is a great figure and we cannot do it. "

        This story must be taken with a grain of salt.   Well-
man had a strong sentimental streak, but there's not much
evidence that Fowler did.   If they started a script and later
burned it, there was probably some less noble reason.

        The Buffalo Bill of the film is everything his legends
would have him be.   Chiefly through Joel McCrea's playing
of the character, he comes across as somewhat boyish and
naive and not overly intelligent.   This is one of the film's
points--the comparison of Bill's simple life and innocent
character with the disease-ridden constrictions of civiliza-
tion that his wife (Maureen O'Hara) comes to represent.
This very real conflict gives the film what genuine emotion
it carries and goes far toward enobling the cruder excesses
of the plot.

        The film makes its points through humor or action.
When Bill is invited to a fancy-dress ball, the invitation
reads "r.s.v.p. "   Puzzled, he goes to the Indian schoolteacher, Dawn Starlight (Linda Darnell) for an explanation.
She translates the initials and helps him compose a reply
by writing a note on the blackboard while he laboriously
copies the words onto a piece of paper.   Several times
Dawn thinks of better ways to phrase the note, erases and
begins again.   Bill, writing in ink, must be content to simply scratch out the previous words and fill in the new version; his note ends a total mess.

        The scene is funny and charming, but also telling.
In one stroke it shows us many things: Bill's respect for
the Indian as teacher, his innocent earnestness to do the
right thing (emphasized by his sitting in a ridiculously small
child's desk), and his child-like ignorance of the ways of the
civilized world.   Too, it foreshadows the difficulties that
Louisa (O'Hara) will have in adjusting to Bill's world, for
what use is an "r.s.v.p. " in the midst of the wilderness?

        The most striking scene in the film is the Battle of
War Bonnet Gorge.   Wellman had a particular talent for filming action in a way that the impact is felt rather than seen.
Here, the Indian versus cavalry battle takes place in the midst
of a river and Wellman allows the camera lens to be caked
with mud and splashing water.

This scene was used in its entirety in at least two later films: Pony Soldier and Siege At Red River. William K. Everson wrote,

> Critics with short memories were easily fooled. To a man they praised the battle scene that was over a decade old, and pointed out how much better wide-screen films could present this sort of mass action than the "old-fashioned" small screens!

As a prelude to the battle, Buffalo Bill engages in hand to hand combat with his friend-turned-enemy Yellow Hand (Anthony Quinn) to buy time for more soldiers to arrive on the scene. This fight scene is another prime example of Wellman's penchant for the provocative suggestion. The two men fall from their horses into the river. The camera tracks slowly down the river bank and all we see of the fight is an occasional splash of water, a hand bursting to the surface, an upraised knife. When at last the camera comes to a halt and rests its gaze on the river's surface for a moment, Bill rises from the water to a standing position, while Yellow Hand's body slowly floats to the top.

The rest of the film did not live up to this bravura sequence, though it is certainly not as bad as Wellman liked to claim. He said,

> I should be ashamed of myself, but I didn't like the picture. Having been through this thing with Fowler, [I thought] it was fakey. I tried to do the best I could with it, but when that poor little crippled kid at the end stands up and says, "God Bless you, too, Buffalo Bill" [in fact, the film's closing line], I turned around and damn near vomited. And then Zanuck later on told me it was the second-biggest money-maker we've ever made.

Wellman's contract with Fox was not exclusive, and in 1946 he went to Columbia to produce and direct a film about John Montgomery, the man who is credited with having made the first successful flight in a glider in the United States in 1883. Gallant Journey, as it was called, "was a picture I thought would be wonderful," Wellman remembered, "but it was awful!"

Gallant Journey, like most of Wellman's flying films,

Wellman relaxes with a newspaper between takes on the set of Gallant Journey with Janet Blair, Glenn Ford, and technical adviser Col. C. A. Shoop.

has feet of lead when it comes to the personal stories involved, but it is more beautiful than most when in the air. Perhaps due to the motorless craft featured in the film, the flying scenes have a grace and lyricism that are quite unmatched in the majority of his films on aerial subjects. The gliders were photographed in flight by Elmer Dyer (dramatic scenes were shot by Burnett Guffey) and the footage is majestic. Even the non-flying portions of the film seem devoted to the sky, with typical scenes being staged in panoramic composition, close to the earth, the sky filling 75 percent of the frame.

Wellman, who hadn't piloted a plane since his days at Rockwell Field, flew one of the gliders for a scene in the film--at least he claimed to; it is impossible to recognize him in any of the craft.

Gallant Journey is not "awful," but it did seem further

proof that Wellman no longer possessed any major talent regarding aviation themes.

Wellman's next film was the Capra-esque Magic Town
with James Stewart, Jane Wyman, Ned Sparks, Kent Smith,
and, in his last role (he died during filming), Donald Meek.
The reason Magic Town must be regarded as "Capra-esque"
is that the picture was a result of the imagination of Capra's
favorite writer, Robert Riskin.   Capra said,

> Don't blame it on Wellman.   That was Bob Riskin,
> who I thought was just wonderful and who wrote a lot
> of scripts with me.   We worked together on this script.
> He had a brother who was egging him on to make his
> own pictures and I did, too.   "Bob, " I told him, "I'm
> not going to share credit with you for collaborating on
> this thing.   This is a director's medium, you want
> credit on these films, you go write them and make
> them. "   So he did.   And they were both just stinkers.

Riskin's first directorial effort was When You're in
Love (1937) with Grace Moore.   It had been a failure and Riskin didn't try again until Magic Town.

> But it was sort of a one-note story, [Capra said]
> so in the middle of it--while he was directing it--
> there started to be some concern about how it was
> going along; the actors were doing a little belly-
> aching.   So they came to me and asked if I could
> help out some.   I said, "Not me.   I can't, but
> I'll see if I can find somebody else. "   So I went
> to Bill and I said, "These guys are in trouble.
> What they need is a director to finish it for them. "
> So he went in on the middle of the film.

Focus on Film's John F. Mariani asked Wellman about Capra's
version of the events.   Wellman replied,

> Frank's just being kind about it.   I was in on that
> thing from the beginning, and I wish I had never
> started it.   It stunk!   Frank and Bob had a big
> argument about the picture and Riskin asked me to
> do it.   I told him that this is the kind of picture
> only Capra could do.   It's not my kind of film.   In
> my book, Capra's the greatest, and if you think
> Magic Town has anything good about it at all, there's
> something wrong with you.

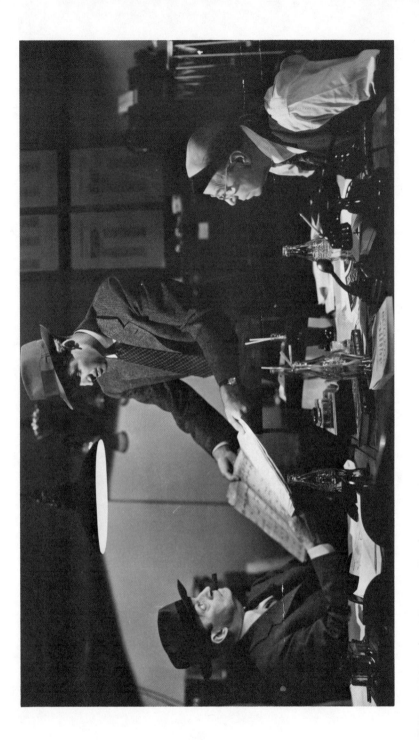

Magic Town had been filmed for RKO and in late 1947
Wellman returned to Twentieth Century-Fox to complete the
terms of his contract.   His first release of 1948 was The Iron
Curtain, a thriller starring Dana Andrews and Gene Tierney.
The melodrama concerns a Canadian cipher clerk at the Rus-
sian embassy in Ottawa who provides the West with details of
Soviet espionage activities.

Though Wellman was rabidly anti-Communist (when he
could work up any political feelings at all), he admirably
down-played the obvious "Red-scare" aspects of the story
and filmed it as a tense spy versus spy tale, photographed
in dark, moody shades of grey and acted in an intent, humor-
less fashion.

The Iron Curtain was based on a book by Soviet defec-
tor Igor Gouzenko, whose work describing the extent of the
Soviet spy network greatly encouraged anti-Russian sentiment
in the U.S. after World War II.   The film version of his
book appeared almost concurrently with the start of the House
Un-American Activities Committee hearings, which ushered
in the "McCarthy Era."   It was a time when Hollywood was
becoming concerned with proving to the world that it wasn't
full of Communist sympathizers; The Iron Curtain was Fox's
(and Wellman's) initial statement of loyalty.   James Agee
didn't take the whole thing too seriously:

> If it could be proved that there is any nation on
> earth which does not employ spies, that would be
> news.   This is just the same old toothless dog
> biting the same old legless man.   However, it is
> efficient melodrama, and fairly constrained in de-
> livering its world-shaking message.

The Iron Curtain, it turned out, was about as political
as Wellman was going to get.   Blood Alley (1955) was also
about Communism, but it, too, was treated simply as an action story, the Communists nothing more than up-dated Indians
from a western.   "Hell, I don't make political films," Wellman claimed.   "After The Ox-Bow Incident and Wild Boys of
the Road, I was accused of being a liberal.   After The Iron
Curtain, I was a leftist.   I mean, I'm a Republican, but I
loathe all politicians."

[Opposite:]   Left to right: Ned Sparks, James Stewart, and
Donald Meek in Magic Town.

And there was nothing political about Wellman's last film with Zanuck. The Ox-Bow Incident, after a successful European release, had been brought out in the United States in late 1946, at which time it garnered the good reviews and respectable box-office that it missed in 1943. Zanuck, Wellman, and Lamar Trotti were beginning to receive acclaim for the film, and naturally they began to look around for a way of duplicating The Ox-Bow Incident's success.

The result was Yellow Sky, based on a novel by W. R. Burnett. Yellow Sky was not particularly subtle in its "references" to The Ox-Bow Incident. Some scenes, like that of the men eyeing the suggestive painting over the bar, are repeated almost word for word and there is a similar grim atmosphere. Yet, in its way, Yellow Sky is as good as The Ox-Bow Incident, though in a more conventional respect. It has no big moral points to make and the trappings are fairly standard; still, it is gripping, exciting, well-written and well-played in a snarling way.

Romance, which did not rear its ugly head in The Ox-

Left to right: John Russell, Gregory Peck, Harry Morgan, Robert Arthur, and Charles Kemper in Yellow Sky.

Bow Incident, snakes its way into <u>Yellow Sky</u>, but, one suspects, only as a vehicle for another rough and ready Wellman
woman. Mike (Anne Baxter) is handy with her fists and accurate with a rifle. When Stretch (Gregory Peck) tries to
get friendly, Mike slugs him, kicks him and grazes his scalp
with a rifle bullet. Wellman warned Peck, "Anne Baxter will
kick the hell out of you. And when you start that fight, you
better look out for yourself and wear something over your
balls, because she'll destroy you."

    Wellman had no trouble getting Anne Baxter to act
tough in the film. "She was a wonderful gal," he said,
"kicked the hell out of him in that scene. She didn't like
him [Peck] and that was her one chance of getting even with
him."

    Gregory Peck gave him some trouble in the toughness
department, though. Wellman said to him, "Well, you can't
fight. Can you kick a football?" Peck said that he could.
Wellman replied, "Well, you're going to have a fight with
John Russell, knock him into the water and when his head
comes up, kick it like a football."

    <u>Yellow Sky</u> turned out fine but the actor who stole the
show was Richard Widmark; <u>Yellow Sky</u> was only his fourth
film. It now seems a much more accurate precurser to the
"adult western" of the fifties than does <u>The Ox-Bow Incident</u>,
though the latter film has been more influential in other ways.
It was remade in 1967 by director Robert Webb as <u>The Jack-
als</u>.

CHAPTER TWELVE

Dore Schary had been working on the project that would become Battleground as early as 1947 when he was head of production at RKO. Writer/producer Robert Pirosh had come up with the idea of making a film about the battle of Bastogne in World War II and the heroic stand of the 101st Airborne Division, known as the "Screaming Eagles." Pirosh had, according to Schary, "been making notes for years" on such a story and when Schary and story editor Bill Fadiman told him they were seeking a war picture, Pirosh leaped at the chance.

Since they were nervous about another studio's "scooping" the project, Schary, Pirosh, and Fadiman began developing the project under the name Prelude to Love.

Abruptly, as the script was nearing completion, Howard Hughes bought RKO and, after a clash over control, Schary resigned. He was able to take the script of Battleground with him to his new position as vice-president in charge of production at M-G-M. Being at Metro was agreeable with Schary, for several of the male stars he envisioned for the picture-- Ricardo Montalban, Van Johnson, George Murphy--were under contract there.

Wellman was offered the film and because he "thought it was a hell of a script" he accepted. He knew that the script was not capable of becoming another Story of G. I. Joe but, he told Schary, "I'll just make a picture about a very tired group of guys."

Battleground was cast with virtually every male star at

224

Van Johnson, Richard Jaeckel, Douglas Fowley, George Murphy, and Bruce Cowling in Battleground.

M-G-M except Tom and Jerry: Van Johnson, John Hodiak,
Ricardo Montalban, George Murphy, Marshall Thompson, James
Whitmore, Leon Ames, Scotty Beckett, Douglas Fowley, Jerome Courtland. The sole female role was played by a French
actress, a Schary discovery, Denise Darcel.

Battleground was known around the studio as "Schary's
folly" for no one believed that the public wanted a war picture.
Louis B. Mayer only agreed to let Schary do the film because
he felt that if Battleground failed, Schary would be easier to
keep in line. Schary, however, felt that

> Battleground had success written on it from the first
> dailies. Wellman zinged into the filming with the
> joy and enthusiasm of a young man. We had pruned,
> polished and timed the script, and Bob Pirosh's ex-
> periences at Bastogne had given the scenario the
> ring of truth.
>   There were no delays in shooting. Bill came
> in twenty days under schedule and about a hundred

thousand under budget--but what was important, he came in with a powerful, well-paced picture full of humor and action.

Wellman had helped to keep the costs down on the film by shooting practically the entire picture on a sound stage. In this controlled environment, Wellman was a master. He knew better than to try to make the stage look real; he used it to create an atmosphere--stylized, artificial, and eloquent. He so often took his companies on arduous location treks that his decision to shoot in the studio must be regarded as an artistic decision and the films he made under those circumstances (The Ox-Bow Incident, Darby's Rangers) are among his most visually striking, whatever their deficiencies in other areas.

When the film was released, Schary was more than vindicated on his choice in properties: the public flocked to the picture and the film was critically acclaimed. When the Academy Award nominations were announced on February 14, 1950, Battleground was nominated in the following categories: Best Picture, Best Director, Supporting Actor (James Whitmore), Story and Screenplay (Pirosh), Black-and-White Cinematography (Paul C. Vogel), Film Editing (John Dunning). Vogel and Pirosh won Oscars for their efforts.

Wellman enjoyed working with Schary at this stage of their association.

> Dore Schary, until he let politics screw him up, was a magnificent producer. Battleground worked out fine, but [our association] didn't end well. He'd say, "We're gonna make pictures that we want to make." I'd say, "What are you talking about 'pictures that we want to make'? You make pictures to amuse the public, not yourself."

But Wellman's next picture after Battleground never got much of a chance to please either the public or Wellman. The Happy Years, however, is one of Wellman's best films. It was based on the popular series of "Lawrenceville School Stories" by Owen Johnson and Wellman had been enthusiastic about the stories and the characters--such as the Tennessee Shad, Tough McCarty and Dink Stover--for some years. He chose to film the stories as a switch from the heavy drama of Battleground.

Dean Stockwell and Darryl Hickman (right) in one of Wellman's most delightful pictures, The Happy Years.

Filming on The Happy Years (also known throughout
filming by various other names including Varmint, You're
Only Young Twice, and The Adventures of Young Dink Stover)
was begun in September 1949 with a formidable cast of juven-
iles including Dean Stockwell, Darryl and Dwayne Hickman,
Scotty Beckett, and Donn Gift. The cast almost drove Wellman crazy. "I get home at night," he said, "and I snap at
my own kids. What kind of life is that? Besides, I'm getting too old for this stuff."

If he encountered trouble in the filming of The Happy
Years, it doesn't show on the screen, for it's among the
gentlest of films. It is not hard to imagine a great deal of
young Billy Wellman in the character of Dink Stover and the
setting of the film at the turn of the century--the time of
Wellman's childhood-strengthens his identification with Dink.

The boys of Lawrenceville form an ideal Wellman
group, their codes of behavior and loyalty are strict and the
firmest friendships have their beginnings in enmity. Dink
and Tough are as thoroughly antagonistic as Powell and Armstrong in Wings; there is even a reprise of the "Gee, you're
game!" denouement of a fight between the two. The film
features no major conflict, no villain, no slam-bang climax.
It is a simple, unhurried, nostalgic story about a group of
boys and how they come to care for each other and learn
something about themselves.

Perhaps this very simplicity was The Happy Years'
undoing, for Metro seemed lost as to what to do with the film
once it was completed. It was barely released even in major
cities and premiered on double bills in the few places it did
appear in. Most of the major newspapers did not even bother
reviewing it. Even Wellman must have thought it unimportant
for he apparently never mentioned the film in any interview,
even in passing. Odd, because of Wellman's nearly-80 films,
The Happy Years is one of the three or four best.

Unfortunately, the same can't be said for The Next
Voice You Hear, although that film can stand as a textbook
example on Wellman's strengths as a director even when given
preposterous material.

Dore Schary had found the story The Next Voice You
Hear by George Sumner Albee in a copy of Cosmopolitan Magazine in 1948 and was attracted to the parable about God's
voice being broadcast over the radio every night for a week.

The entire crew of The Next Voice You Hear gathers for a
publicity shot. Wellman sits, pointing, before the camera.
Standing to his right is producer Dore Schary. The actors
are James Whitmore, Nancy Davis, and Gary Gray.

The magazine story, however, presented seemingly insur-
mountable problems regarding its filming, notably scenes
showing atheists suddenly growing angels' wings and one de-
picting the continent of Australia sinking into the sea. He
felt that there was a good film in there somewhere, but for
the time being, he put the story on the shelf.

In 1949, Schary suddenly came upon an idea that might
make The Next Voice You Hear viable as a screen property.
He would cut back on the scope of the story and place the
emphasis on one family which he modeled after his own 1941
film, Joe Smith, American. He would excise the "miracles"
in favor of smaller, more realistic epiphanies in the lives of
his average family. He would, as he wrote, "bring this cos-
mic thing down to simple terms, a real story about real people to whom God will seem real.

With this outline completed, Schary turned the project over to screenwriter Charles Schnee. For a director, Schary had but one choice. "I wanted Bill Wellman," he wrote. "We had worked together very happily on Battleground" and the fact that Wellman brought in that major project under budget and ahead of schedule didn't hurt, either. Wellman was, Schary felt, "a rabid family man who feels things deeply, and is completely honest. Billy has great ability and experience in the business and is a man of enormous enthusiasm: if he would catch fire on the idea and agree to gamble his reputation on a short schedule, we'd be well along."

Wellman agreed to direct the film, but more as a challenge to his skill than in any sympathy with the picture's message. "I think it is a mistake to do anything as a message picture," he said, "especially if you hate messages the way I do." He said that he wanted to make The Next Voice You Hear because "I knew I could do it in three weeks and they had never made a picture at M-G-M in three weeks. There was an ego thing about it."

In fact, the film was made in an even shorter time than that. Schary wrote that Wellman "agreed to direct, promising he'd make it below the proposed schedule of twenty-two days and a budget of $650,000. He delivered it in fourteen days for the startling price of $430,000."

That The Next Voice You Hear is not ridiculous is due to Wellman's unvarnished, unsentimental style; the direct chain of events; and the simple, natural playing of the cast, particularly James Whitmore, Nancy Davis, and Gary Gray. Though the film is, at heart, a fantasy, Wellman directs it as though it were the simplest of family dramas; and there lies its strength. As ludicrous as the premise is and as unpromising, The Next Voice You Hear is a most respectable entry in Wellman's filmography, if only as a perfect example of "the deepest, worst angles" that Wellman did his "best shooting" from.

The Next Voice You Hear opened at Radio City Music Hall and did very good business; its low production cost and high receipts vindicated Schary once again, for another gamble was won. There were some ironies involved, too, as Schary wrote:

> When The Next Voice You Hear was reviewed favorably, I was pleasantly surprised to read Hedda Hop-

per's comments: "I've always been against message
in pictures but The Next Voice You Hear has one I
love--spirituality and love. Dore Schary and Bill
Wellman made this one for every member of the
family. In fact, for America. It can't miss."
      However, sic transit gloria mundi. After I was
propelled out of Metro, in November, 1956, Mrs.
Hopper decided to "make out my own list of best
and worst [pictures] and let the chips fall where
they may. Here we go:"

1st Best Picture of All Time:

Birth of a Nation

1st Worst Picture of All Time:

Next Voice You Hear

      With the successful release of The Next Voice You
Hear, Wellman was in the mood for a vacation. He got
Across the Wide Missouri, instead. However, since he was
still Schary's fair-haired boy, Wellman was able to parlay
the film assignment into a vacation of sorts. He wrote,

> I cannot remember (or did I ever know?) the story
> of the trouble on the picture. Everything apparently
> was ready to go, and they came up minus a direc-
> tor. I had finished my contractual number of pic-
> tures for the year, and they asked me to take over.
> I agreed, provided that they included all my family
> from the moment they left the house until they re-
> turned. This sounds simple, but it involved a wife
> and six kids. When I say "included," that means
> they pay everything. They agreed. This was an
> expensive agreement, for most of the picture was
> to be made on location at Durango, Colorado.

      With the exception of a handful of interiors done in the
studio, all of Across the Wide Missouri was shot on location
in the Rockies. The result was one of the most strikingly
beautiful Technicolor films that Wellman directed. Director
of photography William Mellor, who had worked with Wellman
on Reaching for the Sun, The Great Man's Lady, and The Next
Voice You Hear (and was to work with him again on Westward
the Women and My Man and I), wrote of the difficulties of
shooting on such an arduous location.

      For one sequence, we went in the way the trappers

did, hacking a path with axes. Cables, lights and
the Technicolor camera were packed in on muleback.
I figured lights would be necessary because of the
dense green foliage. Extreme contrast caused by
sunlight could be avoided by use of arcs. As it
turned out, the sun never even hit once where we
worked.

The main locations were at altitudes ranging from 9,000
to 14,000 feet and the company soon learned to live with the
constantly changing weather. Nearly every day brought equal
amounts of rain, snow, and sleet. Mellor wrote,

> When the storm clouds gathered, Bill Wellman would
> check with me on light, and even if we were in the
> middle of a long scene, he would switch to another
> sequence, picking up the interrupted shot later when
> light conditions matched. We worked all the time
> on this basis, with two stand-by set-ups. While we
> worked at "A," grips would be setting up "B" and
> "C" sites, giving us flexibility of choice. We had
> two portable generators on trucks. At some sites
> we had to "mush" in the generator on large wooden
> sleds.

Mellor's work was made much easier by a flexible
camera car called the Blue Goose, which was a four-wheel-
drive war surplus weapons carrier. On the front was mounted
a hydrolic lift capable of hoisting any weight up to three tons
to a height of twenty feet. The Blue Goose did everything
according to Mellor, "but play canasta."

Despite the hardships of the location, this sort of
movie-making was food and drink to Wellman and the fact
that he was able to bring his family along only added to its
appeal. The film that resulted was probably much better
originally than in its present form, for in addition to the
gorgeous photography, there are fine performances by a cast
of Wellman favorites--Clark Gable, Adolphe Menjou, George
Chandler, James Whitmore, Frankie Darro, J. Carroll Naish
--all of whom appeared in at least three of the director's
films.

[Opposite:] Left to right: George Chandler, Clark Gable,
Adolphe Menjou, John Hodiak, Alan Napier, and Henri Letondal in Across the Wide Missouri.

But of more importance than good performances is the
atmosphere that the film generates. The film has been de-
rided as "plotless" and it is that. But, like Buffalo Bill, beneath Across the Wide Missouri's glossy surface lies a touching portrayal of a man who starts the film as an Indian-fighter
but who comes to respect, then love, then prefer the company
and heritage of the Indian people.

However, the film is effective only in bits and pieces
and for that, one can turn to Dore Schary. Across the Wide
Missouri was, he wrote,

> rich in detail poured into it by William Wellman,
> but despite the wonderful characterizations of Clark
> Gable, Adolphe Menjou, the Indian actor Maria Elena
> Marques, Alan Napier, Jack Holt and Ricardo Mon-
> talban, individual incidents that were exciting and
> funny, beautiful locations, it did not hang together.
> There was a lack of tension. The film sagged and
> stumbled. We previewed in front of an audience
> that greeted the cast and other title cards with a
> welcoming roar, but halfway through the picture the
> customers lost interest.

After mulling over the problem, Schary called in producer Sam Zimbalist who came up with the solution. What
the picture lacked, said Zimbalist, was "a focal idea expressed in personal terms." Schary said,

> [Zimbalist's] solution was to frame the story of our
> chief mountain man, Gable [through the eyes of] his
> son, who, now grown, tells the story of his father
> and mother. Talbot Jennings, who had written the
> screenplay, wrote the narration. We rearranged
> the adventures and episodes in a straight narrative
> line, and presto--the good movie popped out and be-
> came a successful one, thanks to Zimbalist.

Ignored is the fact that the narration (spoken by Howard
Keel) hammers in points that were previously subtly alluded
to or it simply describes what is happening in plain sight
("My father turned and smiled," while on the screen, Gable
turns and smiles). While still ravishingly lovely to look at,
Across the Wide Missouri is now obvious and lumbering and,
at last, ends up being worth little.

"That's what the bastards did," said Wellman. "They

cut out all the action and put in a narration to fill the holes. That was a good, long picture the way I made it. I've never seen it and I never will. "

One element of Across the Wide Missouri that survived the worst that Schary and Zimbalist could do to it is the character of Gable's Indian wife, Kamiah, played by Maria Elena Marques. Though the emphasis is obstensibly on the rough, tough Mountain Men, Kamiah is shown throughout to be the men's equal or better in matters of tenacity, bravery, and intellect. When the trappers are engaged in the arduous trek across the Rockies, Kamiah is always at the head of the line and when they come upon a dangerous looking snowdrift, she unhesitatingly crosses it first to show that it's safe.

Wellman always complained about working with women. He said he preferred working with men "because they don't have to worry about being made up and put that God-damn hair in curls" but only someone who hasn't seen many of his films could fall for such a statement. Doubtless, he didn't like the time wasted on the set by hairdressers, but his admiration and respect for women was steadfast. Those who decry the lamentable bit of misogyny in The Public Enemy often don't take the time to see that Wellman spent the rest of his career making up for that grapefruit, whether consciously or not. In so many of his films (all of the Stanwyck pictures, especially The Great Man's Lady, Nothing Sacred, Woman Trap, Wild Boys of the Road, The Call of the Wild, A Star Is Born, Men with Wings, Lady of Burlesque, Magic Town, Gallant Journey, and Yellow Sky) women are shown to be the stronger, more intelligent and principled sex. In these films and others, women provide the moral and emotional center of the events and relationships.

Of course, there are Wellman women who have grown too strong, women whose strength has grown into iron will, and then into inflexibility, leaving them devoid of humanity. Ma Grier in The Ox-Bow Incident and Ma Bridges in Track of the Cat are perfect examples of women turned rigid and cold. (Of course, it's interesting to note that both of these characters were created by Walter Van Tilburg Clark and both are called "Ma, " which may tell us more about Clark than it does about Wellman--but that is the stuff of another study.)

Making Kamiah the major character of Across the Wide Missouri serves to set up Wellman's next project, Westward the Women. This film, based on an original story by Well-

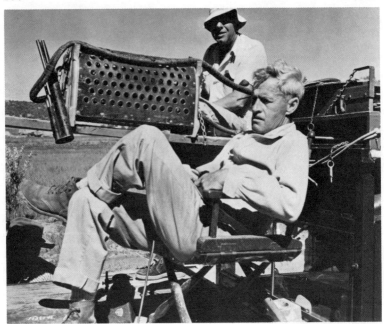

William Mellor and Wellman sit on "The Blue Goose," an extremely versatile camera car, during the filming of Westward the Women.

man's friend Frank Capra, concerned a wagontrain of women heading west to become the brides for a colony of male settlers there.   Capra has said that he got the idea from a magazine story about South American women who crossed the Isthmus for similar reasons and that he simply transferred the setting to the American West.

He was intrigued by the story and, since he had never made a western, tried to persuade Columbia to produce the film.   But, he said, "Columbia was no place for Westerns. They didn't have the background and the people for it.   They weren't equipped to make Westerns.   No horses."

Wellman, when Capra told him the story, became enthusiastic about it.   "That's a hell of a story," he told Capra. "I'd like to do that.   Maybe I could do it at M-G-M."   Wellman approached Schary with the idea and was given the go-ahead. Schary, in fact, caught Wellman's enthusiasm and decided to personally produce the picture.

A cast of two hundred women was gathered with the leads going to Robert Taylor (as the man who heads the train), Denice Darcel, Lenore Lonergan, Marilyn Erskine, Hope Emerson, Julie Bishop, and Beverly Dennis. In a moment right out of the screenplay, Wellman commenced production by calling all of the women together to advise them on what sort of undertaking they were embarking on. He told them that there would be no place for prima donnas, for the eleven-week schedule in the Utah Mountains and California desert would prove to be long, dirty and tiring. He offered everyone a last chance to back out of the picture. The women then began a three-week period of basic training, which involved calisthenics, rope skipping, softball, bullwhip cracking, horseback riding, mule team handling, firing frontier firearms, blacksmithing and assembling (and disassembling) covered wagons.

As on Across the Wide Missouri, nearly all of Westward the Women was shot on location, this time in a place called Surprise Valley in the Mojave Desert. This location was chosen for the beauty and unpredictability of the terrain. Mellor said,

> The Valley had every pictorial element we could ask for, from stark desert wastes to deep walled canyons, plus a stream that grew from a rivulet far up the canyon to a good-size river with many pictorial possibilities. Here in this valley we could shoot the greater part of the exteriors written into the script; do most of the picture here and save the studio considerable in production costs.

Wellman instructed Mellor to use filters as little as possible in order to accentuate the stark glaring look he was after. It works beautifully, for one almost feels the white heat of the desert sun in this shadowless land. Once again, Mellor used the Blue Goose to great effect in Surprise Valley and on this picture, he found another use for that versatile car: that of light parallel for his booster lights. By placing a brace of lights on the hydraulic lift, he could get his lights much higher than is averagely possible on location shooting. "Perhaps few directors have the respect and appreciation for 'continuity in lighting' that [Wellman] does," said Mellor. "Indeed, he considers this an important factor in pictorial perfection--something which marks every production he makes."

Capra described his story as "The Taming of the Shrew.
It was about one strong-willed woman who had to have her
way and the man had to finally knock her down.   Then she
finally learned her lesson." That might have been the story
that started the ball rolling, but it is definitely not the film
that finally made it to the screen.   Westward the Women is
that rare film that depicts extraordinary bravery and stamina
in women; it is a monument to women past and present, a
tribute to the pioneer spirit and to the indominability of the
human will.   Though the film has characters who make such
statements as "A woman'll go through a lot when there's a
wedding ring in sight," it's important that we do not confuse
the sentiments of a character with that of the director, for
Wellman's admiration for these women is evident in every
frame of this fine film.   Invariably, he shoots them from
below, with the camera (and the audience) literally looking up
to them.   It is a heroic composition, not unique to this film,
but generally reserved for presidents or other "great men."
The script can say what it wants, but Wellman's images tell
us how he feels.

There are many moments of great beauty in Westward
the Women, but perhaps the most striking comes after an Indian attack (typically, for Wellman, the attack is not seen,
only heard--just the aftermath is shown to us).   Taylor asks
for a roll-call of those who have been killed in the attack.
As each name is called and echoed about the canyon, the
prostrate figure of each dead woman is shown.   It is a
ghostly moment of elegy, a eulogy for all the women who
died blazing new trails.

One of Wellman's great pleasures in working on Westward the Women was directing his good friend Robert Taylor.

> I was crazy about Bob Taylor.   I think Bob Taylor's
> probably one of the finest men I've ever known in
> my whole life.   And he was an actor.   And he was
> probably handsomest one of them all.   He did every-
> thing I asked him to; he was wonderful.
> One day he asked me, "Well, who will I be?"
> I said, "Be me."   Maybe it helped him.

After completing Westward the Women, Wellman's career at M-G-M suddenly came to a screeching halt.   He directed one of eight episodes in Schary's patriotic opus, It's
a Big Country.   This omnibus film was in production for
nearly two years and Schary had various contract writers

Wellman and Shelley Winters on the set of My Man and I.

(William Ludwig, Allen Rivkin, George Wells) and directors
(Clarence Brown, Don Weis, Charles Vidor, John Sturges,
Anthony Mann, etc.) working on different episodes whenever
they found themselves between pictures.

Schary himself wrote the episode that Wellman directed,
titled The Minister in Washington. The story concerned a
young minister whose congregation includes the President of
the United States. The minister (Van Johnson) can't keep
himself from directing his messages at the president at the
expense of the rest of his church, until a kindly sexton
(Lewis Stone) talks some sense into him. The episode was
really no better nor worse than the rest of the film, which,
as a whole, was a rather dull affair.

Wellman's last film for M-G-M was virtually a "B"
picture, but, as usual, Wellman rose to the challenge of
turning the soapy script into a neat, well-acted melodrama.
The film started life as A Letter from the President, the
story of a Mexican migrant worker who takes pride in becoming a citizen of the United States and whose dearest possession is a letter he has received from the president. By
the time it was released, the title had been changed to My
Man and I (taken from a line in the song "Stormy Weather,"
which serves as the film's theme) presumably, a more commercial name.

Wellman took the slender story-line provided by writers John Fante and Jack Leonard and fashioned from it a surprisingly moving film about racial prejudice, patriotism and
the concerns of "little people"--not Capra-esque little guys
who fight against Big Evils and lick 'em, but ordinary, average people whose biggest triumph is learning to live together with trust and affection.

The scope of the film is so narrow, in fact, that one
wonders why it even occurred to anyone in the first place.
More than anything, it resembles the live drama which was
currently popular on television. My Man and I is not an important film, but it is a good one, filled with excellent performances and made to live through the courtesy of dozens of
Wellman's directorial touches. Ricardo Montalban, in his
third appearance with Wellman, was genuinely moving in the
role of Chu Chu Ramirez, and leads one to think that his
talents were never quite fully utilized in subsequent parts.
Shelley Winters, Claire Trevor, Wendell Corey, and Wellman's regular George Chandler were all at the top of their
forms.

My Man and I looks rather like a "B" film now and it struck Wellman so at the time. Though he made more than a creditable film of it, he resented the assignment. The year 1952 was when M-G-M released Singin' in the Rain, Ivanhoe, The Bad and the Beautiful, Pat and Mike, Lili, and other memorable films (not to mention a musical remake of Small Town Girl) and Wellman rightfully felt that other directors were getting the plum assignments while he, who had brought the studio buckets of money with Battleground and The Next Voice You Hear, was getting little pictures that any rookie director could handle. His three-year contract with the studio ran out that year and though Schary offered him a highly tempting contract to sign on again, Wellman refused. He already had in hand a great story about flying, Island in the Sky, and he had been approached to come over to Warner Bros. to work for a new production company, Wayne-Fellows Productions.

CHAPTER THIRTEEN

Wayne-Fellows Productions was formed in 1952 by actor John Wayne and producer Robert M. Fellows. Fellows had been a producer at Warner Bros., RKO, and Paramount since the late-1930's and had worked on such films as Virginia City (1940), They Died with Their Boots On (1941), Knute Rockne-- All American (1940), A Connecticut Yankee in King Arthur's Court (1949), and many others. Wayne had appeared in a Fellows' production, Back to Bataan, and the two found that they worked together well.

Wayne-Fellows Productions signed on with Warner Bros. and in May 1952 began shooting in Honolulu their first feature, Big Jim McClain. The film was a rather turgid piece of anti-Communist propaganda that was not greeted with favor by critics or the public. Wayne was somewhat stung by the failure and, while he acted in a non-Wayne-Fellows production, Trouble Along the Way (1953, Michael Curtiz), he began to cast about for a more sure-fire project.

That project came to him through Wellman. While golfing with literary agent Lester Linsk, Wellman was given a copy of Ernest K. Gann's novel Island in the Sky. The novel, about a plane downed in the Canadian wilderness and the frantic rescue operation that ensues, had already twice been sold to movie companies. First Stanley Kramer and Robert Stillman had bought the property, held the option for a year, then dropped it. Twentieth Century-Fox then paid Gann $5,000 for the rights but after a year, they, too, let the option expire.

Wellman, however, went crazy about the story. Not

242

only did it concern flying, his favorite subject, but the basic premise--a small group of people trapped in a cramped environment--was one that he repeatedly and fondly returned to: Beau Geste, Battleground, Safe in Hell, The Ox-Bow Incident, Track of the Cat, The High and the Mighty, Blood Alley, etc.

"Why, you son of a bitch," he cried to Linsk, "why have you been hiding this story from me? It will make a great movie!" His enthusiasm was caught up by Wayne and Fellows and Gann received yet another check for $5,000 from Warner Bros. Linsk said, "I hope nobody ever gets around to making this picture. If they do, we'll lose an annuity."

Wellman was impressed enough by the book to ask Gann to work on the screenplay. Gann remembered,

> There was elegance and dash about Wellman and it seemed to me he might have fitted in very well as one of Napoleon's dragons or as a Dumas musketeer. Wellman was an emotional child, mercurial in temper and unreasonable to the point of arrogance. But he was also exciting and inspiring and capable of true humility. Soon, his voice alternately booming and plaintive, he so captured my enthusiasm that I agreed "we" were about to father a film masterpiece.

Gann insisted on working at his home in Pebble Beach, but

> I seemed to hear Wellman even in my sleep. There were times when I thought Wellman was the most talented man I had ever met and other times when I became convinced he was crazy and was dragging me into his private asylum.

Because the film takes place in a snow-covered environment, Wellman chose Donner Lake, near Truckee, California for the location work. All of the aerial material was shot first, with a team of "rather beat-up DC-3's we had found in a Kansas surplus dump." William Clothier did all of the aerial photography (Wellman favorite Archie Stout was the cinematographer for the dramatic scenes) and Ernest Gann was signed on as technical director. Gann wrote,

> Wellman, flaunting tradition with his customary gusto, decided that his technical director should be responsible for all scenes which would demand authenticity. Therefore, I found myself directing Andy

<u>Island in the Sky</u>: the first of two successful ventures with
author Ernest K. Gann.

Devine, Lloyd Nolan, Jim Arness and even Duke
Wayne in several scenes where they were supposed
to be actually flying.

<u>Island in the Sky</u>, released on September 5, 1953,
turned out to be one of Wellman's strongest films with an aviation theme, though it always seems to pull back before the
frigid, isolated mood becomes too uncomfortable and, therefore, most effective. The bleak, unpretentious photography
of Archie Stout and the usual fine performances from the veteran cast are <u>Island in the Sky</u>'s strongest points, but the
constant interference of annoying flashbacks consistently jolt
the viewer out of involvement with the stranded crew's plight.

Wellman, in fact, thought that flashbacks were a necessity. "Of course, the introspective stuff presents certain
problems when it comes to getting it on film, but with narration and flashback, it isn't too difficult to present Gann's
heroes so they'll be understandable to the viewer." Wellman, himself, narrated the film.

Unfortunately, the same tendency marred Wellman and Gann's next film together, The High and the Mighty. While this Airport-forerunner stayed inside the plane, building on the tension felt by the occupants when they believe they are about to crash, The High and the Mighty is taut, firm, and effective. However, every passenger on the commercial aircraft has a story, and those stories are told in excruciating detail.

Once again, Gann wrote the script, but this time Wellman tried to involve himself. The director commented,

> If I bought a book or a story and I loved it, I wanted to do the book, but Ernie kept wanting to change it because he said, "I can improve on it." I said, "Look, Ernie, let's just stick to the book. That's all I want." And we almost had a fist fight about it on one occasion. "Look," I said, "I am going to get hold of Gann who wrote this novel and tell him what this silly son of a bitch who is writing the script is trying to do." It worked.

Very possibly, Gann would have "improved" some of the flashbacks out of the film, for what works effectively in a novel is not necessarily what will best work on screen. As it is, the film The High and the Mighty is remarkably faithful to the novel, the great majority of the dialog is repeated verbatim and the parts are even cast with actors who strongly resemble descriptions in the book. The only major change is the addition of a character, a little boy who sleeps through the entire crisis. Wellman chose his five-year-old son Michael for the role (Mike and his brother Tim had made their screen debuts the year before, playing Andy Devine's sons in Island in the Sky). "I've often said that if some of the actors had a little more of Mike in them," Wellman said, "they'd be much better. He slept when I wanted him to. We woke him up when we wanted to. He did the thing and there was no trouble at all. Gorgeous performance."

When the screenplay was completed, Gann was rather confused to notice that Wellman seemed to be drawing away from him. "Suddenly I was not made privy to his production plans; I was shunted away from casting meetings and any suggestions I might have had for even the smaller parts were unheard."

Wellman did not hire Gann as technical director on The

High and the Mighty and, indeed, did not seek to involve the
writer in any way. Suddenly, everything became clear. Gann
wrote,

> Just before production began, I saw the covers of
> the newly typed script. I had labored hard and long
> on both the book and the scenario--not a word of
> either version was written by anyone else. The
> story, based on a true event, was part of my fly-
> ing life. Now, in bold letters I read:
>
> WILLIAM WELLMAN'S
>
> THE HIGH AND THE MIGHTY
>
> I knew then the chilling ways of Hollywood and left
> town immediately.

If it's true that Wellman had decided to shunt Gann
aside (as it seems he did with Carson a dozen years before),
he never stinted in his praise for the writer. He told reporter Howard McClay, "Mac, there are some terrific characters in this one. If you read the book, you'll know what I

John Wayne and George Chandler in The High and the Mighty.

mean! Gann's carefully-drawn characterizations provide the
kind of material that any director would cluck over." Still,
the main title of the work reads: William Wellman's The
High and the Mighty.

The film was released to enormous success. By the
end of its first run, The High and the Mighty had grossed
over $8,000,000, a considerable sum in 1954. Appropriately,
Wellman was nominated for an Academy Award for his direction of the film, though The High and the Mighty was not nominated as Best Picture. Other nominations included Ralph
Dawson, for editing and Dimitri Tiomkin for both Best Score
and Best Song (with Ned Washington). Tiomkin's score won
The High and the Mighty's only Oscar.

The picture was such a huge hit that Wellman was given
carte blanche on his next project. Wayne let him know that
if he chose to film the telephone book, Batjac would produce
it and Warner Bros. would release it. Wellman didn't want
to shoot the telephone book, but the movie he eventually made
turned out to be the commercial equivalent. "For seven
years, if I remember correctly," Wellman said, "I'd looked
for a story that I could do--and this sounds silly--in black-
and-white in color. And I found it in Track of the Cat."

Track of the Cat was based on a story by Walter Van
Tilburg Clark, who had written The Ox-Bow Incident. It was
a psychological drama about a family in a snow-bound farmhouse, whose cattle are being attacked and killed by a dangerous black panther. The claustrophobic setting and the finite
boundaries of emotion and tension struck Wellman as the perfect vehicle for his color experiment. He wanted the film to
be an externalization of the characters' feelings, the frugal
color scheme to mirror their own spiritual and emotional isolation. Wellman wrote,

> Bill Clothier, than whom there is no better, was
> my cameraman. He shared my enthusiasm and the
> result, photographically, was fantastic. Never have
> I seen such beauty, a naked kind of beauty. Bill
> and I saw the first print back from the lab. We
> sat there, drooling. We had it at last.

The film was photographed so that everything appeared
either black or white. Trees were back-lit so that they photographed black, all the clothes were black or white, the
farmhouse, the interiors, the exteriors--there was no color

in the film except a red mackinaw and a yellow scarf. Clothier recalled,

> We'd check every piece of wardrobe that was worn
> in the picture. There were two things that we
> missed--he didn't see it and neither did I until we
> were in the projection room. We had a scene in
> the kitchen and Mitchum picked up a pair of snow-
> shoes that were reasonably new and varnished.
> They were a yellow color and we didn't realize
> there was color to it until we saw it on the screen.

To Clothier, the color scheme was a way to make the
colors that did make it onto the screen really stand out.

> You can go see a picture made in color and you
> may like it, [but I'd ask] you, "What's the color
> of the girl's eyes?" and you'd probably say, "I
> don't know." But when you have the subdued color,
> the only color's in the face and eyes, you immedi-
> ately see this and they stand out.

Besides the color scheme, Track of the Cat is the
most mannered film that Wellman ever made. The pace is
slow and precise, the acting stylized and the atmosphere grim
and depressing. In addition, Track of the Cat, like The High
and the Mighty was shot in CinemaScope and the expanse of
the frame allowed Wellman to virtually dispense with the stac-
cato editing that he preferred; Track of the Cat is shot in
long takes and much attention is given to space and position.
For this reason, Track of the Cat is rendered (like all wide-
screen films) nearly incomprehensible when viewed on television; sadly, that's about the only way that the film can be
seen now.

Wellman's use of CinemaScope in these films (and in
Ring of Fear and Blood Alley to follow) is a good example of
his original approach to new techniques. As he had taken
sound and Technicolor in stride in the 1930's, so he now conducted business as usual with the new aspect ratio, instinctively adapting himself to the new compositional possibilities.
For a process that must have seemed ideal for photographing
great vistas and wide-open spaces, CinemaScope, in Wellman's
films, found itself being used to explore finite spaces, en-
closed areas, the territories of the mind and emotion.

Track of the Cat boasted several fine performances,

This still conveys the stark, rather depressing mood of Wellman's Track of the Cat.   Pictured are Beulah Bondi (left),
Diana Lynn, Tab Hunter, and Carl "Alfalfa" Switzer (front).

notably Robert Mitchum as the arrogant and selfish Curt and
Beulah Bondi as the cold, self-righteous matriarch of the
troubled family.   Mitchum had, of course, been catapulted
to stardom in Wellman's The Story of G.I. Joe nine years
earlier and he and his director saw Track of the Cat as a
decided change of pace.

Bondi had never worked with Wellman and found herself locking horns with him on the first day's shooting.   Wellman was never known to mince words and his comments to
Bondi were expressed in ways that she found objectionable.
She immediately let him know that she would not stand for
such language and Wellman (who, like so many of his protagonists, had something of a mother complex) apologized.

Bondi found the part of the mother more challenging
than most roles she had undertaken.   She explained,

It was a very difficult role. The woman was complex. I tried to go back and think what her beginning was in the early days. The woman was within
herself. She held onto the Bible--it was the only
straw that she had left for any faith or any belief
in anything. Her children were disappointing, her
husband was a drunken sot. She had to avoid turning into something that was brutal. She still had
love for her children and a certain concern for them
and their danger. But she was warped, very warped.

Track of the Cat garnered favorable, but rather puzzled, reviews. Bosley Crowther in The New York Times
called it,

a sort of Eugene O'Neill-ized Western drama ... at
several points in [the] presentation the black enor-
mity of the selfishness of man comes into the center
of the picture like a gust of the winter outside....
Then, a feeling of tragic frustration seeps out of
the CinemaScope screen, and the shadow of an
O'Neill character flickers on the fringe.

By virtue of its cast--Mitchum, Bondi, Theresa Wright,
Tab Hunter, Diana Lynn, Philip Tonge, William Hopper and
Carl (Alfalfa) Switzer (as a 100-year-old Indian!)--Track of
the Cat did respectably at the box-office, but it was no High
and the Mighty.

In 1954, Wellman had two occasions to be involved with
television. The first came in September of the year when
David Selznick called Wellman to ask if he would be inter-
ested in being one of several directors to work on Light's
Diamond Jubilee, a celebration of the 75th anniversary of
Edison's invention of the light bulb. Wellman wrote,

The last twenty minutes were to be devoted to President Eisenhower; and of all the directors in the
motion picture business, [Selznick] had chosen me.
It was to be a job of love, not money, and as he
said, something for my memoirs. I jumped at the
chance.

Wellman went to Denver, Colorado to shoot the scene
and his part of the total production only came to about two
minutes of air time. Light's Diamond Jubilee was broadcast
on the evening of October 24, 1954, on all four networks

(NBC, ABC, CBS, and Dumont) and featured such stars as
Judith Anderson, Lauren Bacall, Walter Brennan, Joseph
Cotton, David Niven, and Robert Benchley, along with dozens
more.

In addition to Wellman, other directors who worked on
the broadcast were King Vidor, Norman Taurog, Roy Rowland,
and Christian Nyby, and "live" segments were directed by
Bud Yorkin and Alan Handley. Selznick wrote that he

> did this show for the express purpose of learning
> what the medium was all about, and in preference
> to a Selznick Theater of the Air and various other
> proposals that had been made to me through the
> years for a continuing series.
> This show was budgeted at $350,000; actually,
> the cost ran substantially over this. The cost was
> swollen greatly by the fact that I deliberately ex-
> perimented for purposes of my own education, in
> blending film and live, and, of course, the film
> was much more expensive. But nevertheless it was
> a lesson in the cost of a first-rate show.

Of directing the President, Wellman wrote, "Everything
went so smooth, it was unbelievable, and the president acted
like an old timer who was making his fiftieth picture, completely relaxed, oblivious to the camera, and with a natural
gift of timing."

About two months later, on the evening of December
7, 1954, Wellman went over to Warner Bros. to work on the
trailer for Track of the Cat. He was to meet John Wayne
and stars Tab Hunter and Theresa Wright there to go over
some special material that was to be incorporated into the
trailer. As they sat around a table in a conference room,
Wellman was shocked to hear a voice come from a hidden
speaker say, "William A. Wellman, This Is Your Life!"

Within moments, he found himself trotting toward the
stage of Ralph Edwards' embarrassing television show to have
his past trotted out before him. Among the guests who came
on to talk about their relationships with "Wild Bill" were John
Wayne, James Cagney, Hedda Hopper, his buddy from the
Lafayette Flying Corps Reggie "Duke" Sinclair, Claire Trevor
(who reported that her eyebrows had still not grown back in
from the time Wellman had her shave them for a scene in
The High and the Mighty), and, most importantly, his mother,

Hedda Hopper is among the surprise guests to greet Wellman on "This Is Your Life," hosted by Ralph Edwards (left).

Celia, and his older brother, Arthur. Wellman bore the ordeal in good humor and was genuinely delighted to see his mother and brother, and especially Sinclair--this meeting was to rekindle their friendship and they would continue to see each other frequently until Wellman's death.

When, for the big finish, Dottie brought all seven Wellman children onto the stage, all ended well, but for Edwards, there was at least one rocky moment. When Sinclair came on stage, Wellman was asked if he was surprised. Wellman replied, "You're damn right I am!" Edwards, flustered (this was on live television), said to the audience, "Well, we told you he was unpredictable!"

*   *   *

While Wellman was casting around for his next project, Wayne and Fellows approached him about a circus picture currently being directed by Wayne's verbose writer James Edward Grant, Ring of Fear. Grant had heretofore directed one film, Angel and the Badman, which had turned out quite well. However, it was apparent to everyone that Ring of Fear was almost irredeemably bogged down. Wellman was asked to step in and fix it up. "I had made enough for that year," Wellman wrote, "so I consented, provided that I didn't get paid and I didn't get credit. That was agreeable to all, so I got a couple of writers and went to work."

The film, which starred Clyde Beatty and Mickey Spillane (as themselves), was enormously successful. At a party celebrating the happy ending, Wayne, "in an unconscious moment, sat down and wrote me a little gift," Wellman said, "a small percentage of the profits, if any. There was, and still is, and I have often wondered what his true feelings are when he has to sign those checks to the half-wit that wanted to do it for nothing."

In January 1955, Wellman was headed for San Francisco to begin filming an adventure set in China called Blood Alley. John Wayne had bought out Robert Fellows and Wayne-Fellows became Batjac Productions. Blood Alley was Batjac's first film. The picture was to star Robert Mitchum and Lauren Bacall, but during the first week of shooting, Mitchum was suddenly fired. The official reason given was that the actor had pushed the company's transportation manager, George Coleman, into the San Francisco Bay. Wellman told the press that such pranks were "detrimental to the making of

our film." The mind reels at "Wild Bill's" making such a
statement; Hollywood's leading prankster clucking over a
practical joke! At any rate, Mitchum was removed from
the project and John Wayne was forced to step in as the
lead, after Gregory Peck and Humphrey Bogart had proved
"too expensive."

Sid Fleischman wrote the screenplay from his own
novel and he described the story to a reporter during shooting:

> We have this whole Chinese village, disgusted with
> Communism. They decide to escape to freedom in
> the ferry boat, along with Lauren Bacall, who plays
> the daughter of a missionary.
> Well, the villagers can't escape without John
> Wayne, the only one around who knows how to op-
> erate the ferry. He plays the part of a ship's cap-

John Wayne and Mike Mazurki subdue two Chinese Communists
in Blood Alley.

tain who is stuck in China. They dress him up in
a Russian officer's uniform, sneak him aboard and
they start down Blood Alley--that's the Formosa
Straits.

Virtually the entire film was shot on location in China
Camp, (near San Francisco), in Stockton, and in Point San
Pablo. The majority of extras were real Chinese, but, in
true Hollywood style (reminiscent of The Hatchet Man), most
of the leading roles were played by Caucasian actors such as
Paul Fix, Mike Mazurki, and Anita Ekberg.

Blood Alley, like Track of the Cat, is quite beautiful
photographically and eerily effective atmospherically. Unlike
Track of the Cat, however, Blood Alley is entirely conventional and predictable. Though entertaining enough and certainly well-made, Blood Alley remains a minor chapter in the
careers of Wellman, Wayne, and Bacall.

Wellman's final film for Batjac was one of his favorite
movies, Goodbye, My Lady. This gentle film starred Brandon
de Wilde, Walter Brennan, Phil Harris, Louise Beavers, and
Sidney Poitier. Based on a novel by James Street (the script
was by Sid Fleischman), Goodbye, My Lady was "a financial
fiasco. I don't know why," Wellman wrote. "The story was
beautiful, the performances superb. How could you miss?
But I did."

The film was shot on location near Albany, Georgia,
which was made to stand in for the Mississippi swamps that
are the setting of the film. Here, Wellman got a firsthand
look at some of the South's biases. He recalled,

> We moved in, took over a hotel. The first night,
> I looked around at dinner and I said, "Where's
> Poitier?" And they said, "They won't let him eat
> in the dining room. He's out in the kitchen." So
> I went in the kitchen and I ate with Poitier. To
> me this was a little strange, so I finally went up
> to the stupid son of a bitch who was running the
> hotel and I said, "Look, what I resent is that after
> I take over your hotel, you are going to tell me
> how to run my business. I'm bringing a couple of
> hundred thousand dollars into your lovely little town
> and I'm going to get out unless you let me do what
> I want with my own company." So they did.

The film is about a fourteen-year-old boy who finds a

stray dog, a Basenji, which he keeps.   He names her Lady.
After he has become strongly attached to the dog, he finds
that she belongs to someone else, who is offering a large re-
ward for her return.   The remainder of the plot hinges on
his choice between keeping the dog he has grown to love or
returning her to her rightful owner.   The result was one of
Wellman's best movies and one that is, like The Happy Years,
frustratingly hard to find.   Wellman wrote,

> We went down in the swamps in Albany, Georgia,
> all through the peanut fields, with the snakes and
> the heat, and worked like Trojans.   For what?
> For a plaque that reads:

> > "To William A. Wellman for his outstanding con-
> > tribution to the technique of Motion Picture Di-
> > rection and for Goodbye, My Lady the National
> > Society, Daughters of the American Revolution
> > awards its CERTIFICATE OF HONOR for pro-
> > ducing the Best Children's Picture of the year
> > 1956.
> >   [signed]
> >   Josephine T. Nash--National
> >   Chairman--Motion Picture
> >   Committee
> >   Allene W. Graves--President
> >   General"

Wellman himself produced Goodbye, My Lady and decided to produce/direct his next feature as well.   His contract with Batjac was at an end, but Wellman elected to stay
at Warner Bros.

[Opposite:]   Brandon de Wilde and Lady, a Basenji hound, in
Goodbye, My Lady.

CHAPTER FOURTEEN

By 1956, Wellman was thinking seriously of retiring from filmmaking. His arthritis was getting worse and the changing nature of the movie business was becoming less palatable to him all the time. At heart, Wellman was a studio director--he was at his best in a studio atmosphere, working within the limited structures that the system offered. As the studios began changing or (in some cases) closing, Wellman was no longer comfortable. He told an interviewer at about this time, "I can tell you right now, it's no longer much fun making pictures."

Since he had left M-G-M in 1953, there was some part of him that approached each film with the feeling that it might be his last. He knew that if there was a "dream project" that he wanted to get off the ground, now was the time to do it; there weren't going to be too many more opportunities.

In fact, he had been carrying such a dream project around in his mind ever since he first started in the motion picture business. The story was "of this pal of mine" in the Lafayette Flying Corps.

> He married a little "femme de la nuit" and she gave up her profession. They had a complete understanding. He and I went to Avord together for our basic training. The Frenchmen made the horrible mistake of trying to make us drill. There was this stinking little sous-lieutenant who had a very active quirt in his hand. My pal forgot to salute him once and got the quirt in his face and

the lieutenant got knocked on his butt. [My pal]
could have been sent to Devil's Island or shot or
whatever, and they put him in jail. That night we
went down and broke in [to the jail]. We let him,
and everybody else in the jail, out. He got over
the fence and got to Paris.
His little gal, who had given up her career,
was now a little black-uniformed conductress in the
subway and they were living across the river and
had to hide out. At the end, he got into the American Air Corps. He got through his training. He
went to the front, and on the way he got lost and
a couple of Fokkers dove on him and killed him.
And when his little wife found out about it, she
jumped into the Seine and committed suicide. On
her wrist was his identification tag.
Now, to me, this is a hell of a story.

Since the early thirties Wellman had been trying to interest producers in this "hell of a story," but there were no
takers. Wellman had to be content with inserting little moments of autobiography in his other flying films, notably The
Conquerors, Legion of the Condemned, and Men with Wings.

After he completed his obligations with John Wayne and
Batjac, Wellman elected to stay on at Warner Bros. and tried
to interest Jack Warner in filming this story, which he called
C'est La Guerre. Warner, like his predecessors, was not
impressed. This was the 1950's. Nobody was interested in
World War I and nobody was going to come see a picture with
a name like C'est La Guerre. Wellman was adamant: he
begged, pleaded, cajoled, shouted, threatened. Finally,
Warner agreed. There were, of course, conditions. The
first condition was that, upon completion of the filming of
C'est La Guerre, Wellman was to make another film, sight
unseen. Secondly, he was to direct C'est La Guerre at no
salary, but would receive fifty percent of the profits, if any.
Wellman signed on the dotted line and began casting C'est La
Guerre.

That was the one picture I wanted to make, [Well-
man remembered,] as the greatest thing I've ever
made in my life. To finish off a whole career,
realizing that I was a sick guy, it was the one I
most wanted to make. And it was the worst picture I ever made.

Filming began in November 1956 in Santa Maria, California at a small, abandoned airport there. The presence of
star Tab Hunter caused quite a stir in the community and the
company was constantly plagued by hordes of breathless teen-
aged girls, out to catch a glimpse of their hero.

The script of C'est La Guerre is perhaps the most un-
compromisingly autobiographical that ever emerged from the
Hollywood studio system. Wellman wrote of the men he knew
in the Lafayette Flying Corps and Tom Hitchcock, Duke Sinclair, David Judd, Dave Putnam, and young Billy Wellman
made up the cast of characters. "It's all true," Wellman
told a visitor to the set, "even those old crates that we flew.
Why I recall some of the pilots I flew with as if it had all
happened only yesterday. I've tried to cast those roles with
actors who have personalities like the pilots they play." All,
that is, except the young man chosen to play young Bill Well-
man--Bill Wellman, Jr., then 19. "I make him a nice character," Wellman said. "Not like me. I wasn't a nice guy."

Oddly, Wellman himself had not chosen his son to play
the role; the idea came from a Warner Bros.' casting director. Wellman thought the idea a good one, though. He told
Bill, Jr., "Listen, if you're gonna do this part, you're gonna
know your lines, be on time and do the thing right. I won't
have anybody think I'm playing favorites. I'll be rougher on
you than on anybody else!"

Once Bill Wellman, Jr. was cast, the studio got a
great publicity idea: they would hire some other sons of
famous fathers for roles in C'est La Guerre. So, cast as
Tommy Hitchcock was Joel McCrea's son Jody and as Red
Scanlon, Andy Devine's son Dennis. The rest of the cast
did not seem particularly special at the time, but is full of
names that have since become quite well-known: David Janssen, Clint Eastwood, and Tom Laughlin.

As in the making of Men with Wings in 1938, Wellman's staff spent a great deal of time locating appropriate
aircraft for the film. Some of the "penguins" were built by
studio craftsmen. Other planes, including the rare Bleriots,
were found in museums.

The Bleriot aircraft presented a problem to photographer Bill Clothier. The plane's top speed was around 40
miles per hour and Clothier could not find a camera plane
that could go that slowly. Finally, by mounting the camera

in a small pusher-type craft with a special propeller and flying at stalling speeds for short periods, Clothier was able to
obtain the scenes. In addition, the Bleriots were extremely
light, fragile aircraft that were strongly affected by wind
changes. Subsequently, the bulk of the flying scenes were
shot at dawn, when wind velocity was at its lowest.

     C'est La Guerre had another, stronger link with Men
with Wings. All of the dog-fights in the film used footage
from the earlier movie. Bill Wellman, Jr. said, "They just
took out the inserts of Ray Milland and Fred MacMurray in
the cockpits and put in new ones of us."

     In December 1956, C'est La Guerre was first shown
to a sneak preview audience. Though the actors felt that the
audience had reacted well to the tragic story, the Warner
Bros. executives present felt the ending was too downbeat.
Wellman himself got a more direct reaction. He told a reporter,

> When we previewed it, we sensed that the audience
> was restless and unhappy. When it was over, a
> bevy of beautiful girls, just like my daughters, fol-
> lowed me out into the parking lot. "Are you the
> director of this picture?" they said. I said I was.
> "Then you ought to be ashamed of yourself," they
> said. "You killed Tab Hunter." Well, you are in
> pictures to make money. So we did three more
> days of takes and made a happy ending. I'm not
> complaining. It was a sensible thing to do. After
> all, I own a piece of the picture.

     Fifteen years later, in speaking to another interviewer,
his movie career behind him, Wellman's version of the night's
events had changed a bit.

> I had made it as a tragedy, which it was. It was
> previewed as a tragedy; it was the only preview I
> ever had where people stood up as the picture ended
> and said nothing. Then there was a beat and a
> beat and a beat and they suddenly started cheering.
>   And that dirty rotten bastard (Jack Warner) de-
> cided that killing Tab Hunter--don't laugh--was im-
> possible. So they changed it to a happy ending and
> called it Lafayette Escadrille: it didn't have a damn
> thing to do with the Lafayette Escadrille. All the
> guys (from the original Lafayette Escadrille) that

were still alive thought I was nuts. I told Warner
if I ever caught him alone, which in his case is
damn near impossible, that I'd put him in the hospital. I have never hated a man as much as I hate
him.

This sequence of events became a favorite in Wellman's
standard repertoire of anecdotes. He claimed less and less
responsibility in the "raping" of Lafayette Escadrille as the
years went by and shifted more and more of the blame on
Warner Bros. in general and Jack Warner in particular.

However, the sequence of events seems to have gone
like this: at about the time of Lafayette Escadrille's first
preview, Tab Hunter had released a hit record that had sold
extraordinarily well. He followed it up with another single
of slightly less popularity, but of sufficient potency to make
Warner Bros. feel that they had a redhot property in young
Hunter. They decided to hold back on the release of Lafayette Escadrille (which also went through a phase of being
called With You in My Arms) until Hunter's popularity reached
a fever pitch. Unfortunately, his first single had been the
fever-pitch part of the career and by summer 1957, it became apparent that Hunter alone would not draw in the crowds
that the film would have if released six months earlier. So,
in August 1957, Wellman went back into the studio with Hunter
and Etchika Choreau to shoot one additional scene which, with
some reshuffling, reediting, and deleting other scenes, would
transform the tragic ending to a happy ending.

Wellman spent much time in his later life complaining
about the title of the film and the fact that, as he is quoted
above, "it didn't have a damn thing to do with the Lafayette
Escadrille." This turns out to be wisdom in hindsight, for
in all contemporary interviews Wellman refers to the film as
being about the Lafayette Escadrille and strongly infers that
he, himself, was in the Escadrille. It was only after his retirement from the business that one starts to find Wellman
correcting interviewers by pointing out that he was in the Lafayette Flying Corps.

Though the characters in the film refer to their squadron familiarly as, simply, "Lafayette," the narration, written
and spoken by Wellman, specifically names the setting of the
film as the Lafayette Escadrille.

This brings to mind another instance in a Wellman film

where he purposely blurred the line between Escadrille and
Flying Corps: in Men with Wings, Fred MacMurray goes off to
join the Lafayette Escadrille at the outbreak of World War I (it's
even written up in the papers), yet the plane he is shown flying is
a replica of Wellman's "Celia V, " complete with the Squadron N.
87 "Black Cat" insignia. In other words, Wellman shows his
own plane in the film and places it in the Lafayette Escadrille.

When the final scene was shot, Wellman was already filming Darby's Rangers, a film about the special assault troops which
Colonel William Orlando Darby (played by James Garner) led
in the North African landings, the invasion of Sicily, and the
Italian campaign.

Darby's Rangers, based on the book of the same name
by Major James Altieri, was Wellman's contractual obligation
for the privilege of having directed Lafayette Escadrille. His
lack of enthusiasm for the project shows in every frame of
this tired film and Darby's Rangers marks a sad, anticlimac-
tic ending to his career. Not that he didn't try to make an
authentic picture. A Newsweek article describes the "Training Schedule for All Ranger Actors" which included,

> 0800 to 0900: Wardrobe fittings. 0900 to 0930:
> Welcoming of troops and orientation to their mis-
> sion. 0930 to 1000: Ranger film footage taken at
> Fort Benning for orientation and inspiration. 1000
> to 1100: Assignment of actors to squads, issuing
> of weapons, alignment of platoons. 1100 to 1200:
> Close-order drill. 1200 to 1300: Lunch. 1300 to
> 1400: Weapons training--how to hold and carry M-1
> rifle, BAR, tommy guns, mortars, etc.

In addition to this training, the actors in Darby's
Rangers also took instruction in "grenade throwing, barbed-
wire falling, etc. Procedures in firing of bazooka mortars,
street-fighting tactics, falling off truck and rolling on ground,
demonstration of knife fighting. "

Though Wellman went to extraordinary pains to make
his actors look like genuine fighting men, he once more placed
his action in the stylized atmosphere of the sound stage. As
usual, Wellman was eloquent in his use of the artificial sur-
roundings and nearly the only interesting scenes in Darby's
Rangers take place in the unusually still fog of a quiet battle-
field. Wellman said,

I have this low-hanging fog, waist-high. The Rang-

James Garner and Jack Warden in Darby's Rangers.

ers sneak into it, like slithering snakes, in complete silence. I'm not even going to have music in
it. Then there's the damnedest barrage you ever
heard--they are ambushed. We bloody near blew
the studio away. When it's over, you see the fog
hanging and [feel] the lonesomeness of it.

Darby's Rangers was a moderate success at the box-
office, due mainly to the star, James Garner, then popular
on television as Maverick, but all in all, the desire to retire
from motion pictures was only strengthened in Wellman's
heart and mind. The film was released in April 1958 and
two months later was followed into the theatres by the ill-
fated Lafayette Escadrille. Despite the new, happier ending,
the film flopped abysmally.

Wellman's son Bill (who had also had a part in Darby's
Rangers) wrote, "Dad had made unsuccessful pictures before,
but this one nearly broke his heart." Wellman recalled,

I made a deal. I shot the happy ending [to Lafayette Escadrille] and came home to Dottie and said,

"Dottie, I'm tired. I've worked too hard and I made a deal with a man I hate, knowing he's wrong. I'm never going to make another picture as long as I live."

She said, "I don't want you to make another."

And I never have.

CHAPTER FIFTEEN

In fact, Wellman's exit from the movie business was not quite so abrupt. Though he was bitterly discouraged by the failure of Lafayette Escadrille, he had been directing too long to simply give it up all at once. After a short vacation, Wellman began work on a comic western called The Rounders at M-G-M. After several versions of the script had been submitted, the studio decided against the picture and struck it from the 1960 roster.

The Rounders was eventually filmed in 1965 by director Burt Kennedy and starred Henry Fonda and Glenn Ford. When Wellman saw the result, his anger at having the property pulled out from under him five years earlier was tempered with his relief at not having been involved with the bland, forgettable film.

In October 1961, Wellman signed on at Universal ("I finally reached that!" he said later) to direct a picture called The S. O. B. 's about "incorrigibles in the Navy Air Force." After eighteen months of developing the picture, it, too, was abruptly cancelled. On March 1, 1962, he announced to the press that, in addition to the cancelling of The S. O. B. 's, he was retiring from show business. As an explanation of the termination of the film, Wellman told reporters that "Ed Muhl (Universal-International's vice-president in charge of production) didn't like the story." He later told an interviewer,

> I went out [to Universal] on a story that I was nuts
> about, and the man who was in charge of the thing
> was an ex-lawyer. Now that is great training for

266

a producer--a lawyer. He didn't like the story, so I spent three of four months out there doing nothing. You never can prove whether you are right or whether you are wrong if you don't make the picture.

So, three years after the release of his final film, Wellman retired from directing. He said to his friend Hedda Hopper, "I'm not the most popular man in town, but I did have sense enough to save my money. I don't like the stories they're making now--I much prefer the company of my grandchildren."

He settled in at his spacious Brentwood home and began living the easy life of a retired gentleman. His son Bill wrote,

He is very happy enjoying his seven children and eleven grandchildren, doing some writing, playing golf, hunting garden ants, trapping gophers, clobbering moles, directing the gardeners, swimming twenty to forty laps per day, watching sports on television and once in a while ... drinking a little beer.

Even in retirement, though, Wellman's restless energy would not let him sit back and do nothing, so he started writing his autobiography. In 1960, he had been hospitalized when his back, always troublesome, went out on him. He underwent surgery to correct his spine, broken in that plane crash over fifty years earlier. The broken back had been partially responsible for the arthritis that had troubled him since the early thirties and the symptoms had worsened into a condition known as radiculitis, a name which delighted Wellman: "Fits me perfectly." He later said,

I spent four weeks in the hospital, and three months upstairs [at home] in bed. I kept a nurse's report, because that's what they have to keep in the hospital --you know, your bowel movements, what you ate-- and [on the report] there's a column for remarks.
Well, the only thing that kept me sane was writing my remarks there.

In 1963, after a year of retirement, a representative of Hawthorn Books, Inc. in New York, approached Wellman to write an autobiography. According to the director,

>I started to write it, but I didn't take the money.
>The man told me to give him the first forty-five
>pages. I said "Good, I'll try it." So, I wrote
>forty-five pages. Finally, he called me up and
>said he was coming out to see me and I told him
>it was a little too late. He came out anyway and
>said, "Where are the forty-five pages?" and I said,
>"They're in the fireplace." I had burned them up
>the night before.
>   I had sat down and read it--and really, when
>you write an autobiography, it's a little presumptu-
>ous and you suddenly say to yourself, "Goddam!
>This man I'm writing about I'm in love with!" So
>I threw it all away--burned it up.

He walked around "in a goofy state" for awhile, wondering if he would, in fact, be able to put together an autobiography. Suddenly, he remembered the nurse's reports
from his hospital stay, "these crazy things I'd written.
'Cause I was crazy! [I was] half nuts, half full of dope.
[Under those circumstances] you think of things that you
wouldn't, or couldn't think of under ordinary circumstances."

So, using the nurse's reports as a guide, Wellman began on his memoirs again. For nine months he worked on
the volume "thinking of things I hadn't remembered in years!"
and upon its completion, showed it to his publisher.

"He didn't like it," Wellman recalled. "He wanted me
to go back and do the thing in chronological order" but Wellman refused. In late 1964, the book was announced on Hawthorn's schedule, but in fact it was another ten years before
A Short Time for Insanity, as he called it, ever saw the light
of day.

Wellman continued to get offers to return to directing,
but he turned all of them down without considering any of them
very seriously. In 1965, he was offered a flying film called
The Flight of the Phoenix, about a plane that crashes in the desert and the attempts of the stranded crew to get the craft flying again. This was a strong temptation and after mulling it
over for some weeks, Wellman told Twentieth Century-Fox
that he would direct the film. As he was about to begin the
pre-production work, his doctors stepped in and forbade his
working again. The film was made by Robert Aldrich, who
had been Wellman's assistant director on The Story of G.I.
Joe.

The stunt pilot on Flight of the Phoenix was Paul
Mantz, the man who had flown for Wellman many times in
films like The Conquerors, Central Airport, Men with Wings,
Thunder Birds and Gallant Journey. Flight of the Phoenix
would have been a welcome reunion between Wellman and
Mantz, for they had remained close friends. After July 8,
1965, though, Flight of the Phoenix became more to Wellman
than simply another picture that he might have made, for on
that day, while filming in Arizona's Buttercup Valley (the location for Beau Geste, among other pictures), Mantz crashed
the Phoenix and was killed.

After the mid-sixties, Wellman continued to get offers,
but now he simply turned them down without even considering
them. He was out of the business for good.

Ironically, Wellman had retired from motion pictures
at just about the same time that American cinema was starting to be re-evaluated, first by French critics, then by American writers. To Wellman's surprise, there started in the
mid-1960's an unending stream of film scholars wishing to
interview him about his past. A natural, enthusiastic (if
often inaccurate) story-teller, Wellman quite enjoyed this unexpected popularity. "It's all right, " he said. "It's a switch
from before, that's for sure. I never had a publicity man in
my whole life--everybody else did, but I never did. I figured
the money should be spent publicizing the people I was photographing: the Stars."

In the late sixties and early seventies there were more
interviews with and articles about Wellman than in his entire
career to that point. And the honors started to come. Always rather disappointed at never having won an Academy
Award for direction, Wellman was gratified to receive the
Directors Guild of America's D. W. Griffith Award at their
25th awards dinner in 1972. Frank Capra, Wellman's friend
and neighbor of years standing, made the presentation. Capra
said in his introduction,

> A producer-director reveals himself in his work.
> The sum total of a filmmaker's films is a pictorial
> life-story--each film a chapter in his autobiography.
> Any man who makes films cannot long remain in-
> cognito.
>   As a director, he fought many a battle, some
> with his fists, for the right to make his films the
> way he thought he should make them. And make

them he did. As he wanted to make them. And
in doing so, he accomplished almost the impossible.
Because Bill did not have his own independent production company. He made his films in many studios under the heavy-handed overlordship of many
superegos.

That same year, Wellman received the biggest boost
in making his name known to the public at large when he appeared in an episode of Richard Schickel's PBS series, The
Men Who Made the Movies. Wellman's humor, charm, and
magnetic personality gave his segment an edge that the others
lacked.

In 1973, Hawthorn finally brought out A Short Time for
Insanity, with an introduction by Richard Schickel. The book
received good, if rather confused, notices--Variety called it
"a crazy-quilt of recollections, both fascinating and annoying"
complaining that one would prefer "more precise dates and
details." Wellman's fought-for "dopey" structure had been
retained, though it delayed the book's publication for ten
years. At the time of its publication, Bill Wellman, Jr.
organized the largest retrospective of Wellman's work to
date--39 of Wellman's 79 films--at the West Los Angeles
Royal Theater. The series was underwritten by Tom Laughlin and Delores Taylor and all the box-office proceeds went
to the recently-formed William Wellman scholarship fund in
the Cinema Department at the University of California, Los
Angeles.

The series was not particularly successful. Bill recalled,

> We wanted to put the series into a theater--as op-
> posed to a museum or something--because we wanted
> them to be seen in the atmosphere in which they
> were intended to be seen. The crowds were not
> that good, maybe because some of the films are so
> easy to see on television--especially in Los Angeles.

Later in 1972, the British Film Institute mounted an
even more extensive retrospective and the Wellmans flew to
London for the very successful series. Wellman was treated
with a respect as a filmmaker in England that, despite his new
popularity, he had not been shown in this country. His brief
stay in London was filled with television guest spots, radio
appearances, and dozens of interviews.

William and Dorothy Coonan Wellman in 1972.

       Back in the states, Wellman found himself in fairly
constant demand as a talk-show guest, appearing on The Merv
Griffin Show several times as well as ABC specials on Clark
Gable and Henry Fonda. The latter special was Wellman's
last appearance before a camera. In it, he told of directing
Fonda in The Ox-Bow Incident, as he had told it so many
times before and once again noted that Fonda was "perhaps
the best actor I ever directed and probably the most dedicated." The special was broadcast on April 12, 1976, but
by that time, William A. Wellman had been dead for four
months.

       In the last months of his life, Wellman had been work-
ing on a second volume of memoirs called Growing Old Disgracefully and had made a last trip to Massachusetts to visit

his brother Arthur. In late summer 1975, he was diagnosed
as having leukemia and his degeneration was swift. By November, he was hospitalized but, realizing that he was dying,
he asked to be brought home. There, on Tuesday, December
9, 1975, he died.

     The last paragraph of A Short Time for Insanity read:
"I want to be cremated and emptied high above the smog--
high enough to join a beautiful cloud--not one that brings a
storm, one that brings peace and contentment and beauty."
The instructions were carried out.

     Growing Old Disgracefully was never published. Copies
were privately printed and distributed to his wife and each of
their children. The major re-evaluation of his work which
seemed imminent at the time of his death never came about
either, and most film scholars have been content to place
Wellman back in his previous position of able, but ultimately
inconsequential, craftsman.

     He was more than that, of course, for Wellman's work
is marked by the personality of its creator, which is the real
difference between a simple "job of work" and a work of art.
As Capra said, Wellman did not "remain incognito"; he put
himself on the screen as surely as if he had made nothing but
self-portraits. His work has continuity, consistency, recurring themes, a recognizable style. The films are generally
unpretentious (not always), but they are anything but anonymous, assembly-line pieces of product and their director was
anything but a servile, compliant company man. Whatever
the film, whatever the depth of his commitment to it, Wellman made it his own. He made works of art that were entertaining, enjoyable, exciting, moving; he made entertain-
ments that were accurately observed, flawlessly constructed,
intelligent and meaningful: in a word, artistic.

     The circumstances that bred Wellman and his contem-
poraries are, of course, gone for good. The average film
director today does well to release a film per year; often
there is a much longer space between pictures. Wellman,
Hawks, Ford, Dwan, Walsh often released four or more
films each year, a process that might have given them the
impression that they were simply workers on an assembly
line, but which allowed them to try something different, ex-
pand their abilities, try on a new attitude. The Hollywood
of the Studio Era was a place where Wellman could release
The Ox-Bow Incident and Lady of Burlesque back to back and

come up with two films that seem totally opposite and yet, under examination, reveal themselves to be inextricable threads of the fabric of his career. Wellman prized versatility and he respected the opinions of the public--no matter how good the reviews, if a picture failed at the box-office, chances are Wellman would remain convinced throughout his life that it was a "stinker." But this attitude, ultimately, is the secret behind the inordinately high quality of his output. He was skilled enough to make them real. More importantly, he had the unique gift of being able to get his own enthusiasm on the screen, his own attitudes, prejudices, sense of humor; Wellman is among the most personal filmmakers to have come from the studio system.

The re-evaluation of Wellman's career is still to come and he continues to be underrated, but rediscovery is inevitable. A career that includes Wings, You Never Know Women, Beggars of Life, The Man I Love, The Public Enemy, Wild Boys of the Road, The Robin Hood of El Dorado, A Star Is Born, Nothing Sacred, Beau Geste, The Light That Failed, Roxie Hart, The Ox-Bow Incident, Lady of Burlesque, The Story of G.I. Joe, Battleground, The Happy Years, Westward the Women, The High and the Mighty, and Goodbye, My Lady is one that demands respect. These titles alone represent a far greater accomplishment than most directors have to their credit. The fact that Wellman directed over sixty more films of similar quality irreversibly names him as one of Hollywood's greatest directors.

BOOKS

Agee, James. Agee on Film Vol. I, McDowell Obolensky, 1958.
Bergman, Andrew. We're in the Money, New York University Press, 1971.
Brownlow, Kevin. The Parade's Gone By, Alfred A. Knopf, 1969.
Brownlow, Kevin. The War, the West and the Wilderness, Alfred A. Knopf, 1978.
Cagney, James. Cagney on Cagney, Doubleday, 1976.
Cohen, Henry, ed. The Public Enemy, University of Wisconsin Press, 1981.
Colman, Juliet Benita. Ronald Colman, A Very Private Person, William Morrow, 1975.
Dickens, Homer. The Films of Gary Cooper, Citadel, 1970.
Dwiggens, Don. Hollywood Pilot: The Biography of Paul Mantz, Doubleday, 1967.
Eyles, Allen. John Wayne and the Movies, A. S. Barnes, 1976.
Farber, Manny. Negative Space, Praeger, 1971.
Fenin, George N., and William K. Everson. The Western: From Silents to the Seventies, Grossman, 1973.
Ferguson, Otis. The Film Criticism of Otis Ferguson, Temple University Press, 1971.
Gann, Ernest K. A Hostage to Fortune, Alfred A. Knopf, 1978.
Grace, Dick. I Am Still Alive, Rand McNally, 1931.
Greene, Graham. Graham Greene on Film, Simon and Schuster, 1972.
Gussow, Mel. Don't Say Yes Until I Finish Talking, Doubleday, 1971.
Haver, Ronald. David O. Selznick's Hollywood, Alfred A. Knopf, 1980.
Hecht, Ben. A Child of the Century, Simon and Schuster, 1954.
Hirschorn, Clive. The Warner Bros. Story, Crown, 1979.
Katz, Ephraim. The Film Encyclopedia, Crowell, 1979.
Lambert, Gavin. On Cukor, G. P. Putnam's Sons, 1972.
Marill, Alvin H. Robert Mitchum on Screen, A. S. Barnes, 1978.
Munden, Kenneth W., ed. American Film Institute Catalog: Feature Films 1921-1930, R. R. Bowker, 1971.

Nemcek, Paul. The Films of Nancy Carroll, Lyle Stuart, 1969.
Quirk, Lawrence J. The Films of Ronald Colman, Citadel, 1977.
Rotha, Paul. The Film Till Now, Funk and Wagnalls, 1949.
Schary, Dore. Heyday, Little, Brown, 1979.
Schary, Dore, and Charles Palmer. Case History of a Movie, Ran-
    dom House, 1950.
Schickel, Richard. The Men Who Made the Movies, Atheneum, 1975.
Sennett, Ted. Warner Brothers Presents, Castle, 1971.
Shale, Richard. Academy Awards, Ungar, 1978.
Silke, James R. Here's Looking at You, Kid, Little, Brown, 1976.
Skogsberg, Bertil. Wings on the Screen, A. S. Barnes, 1981.
Smith, Ella. Starring Miss Barbara Stanwyck, Crown, 1974.
Stack, Robert, and Mark Evans. Straight Shooting, Macmillan, 1980.
Steen, Mike. Hollywood Speaks, G. P. Putnam's Sons, 1974.
Suid, Lawrence H. Guts and Glory, Addison-Wesley, 1978.
Thomas, Bob. Selznick, Doubleday, 1970.
Thomas, Tony. The Great Adventure Films, Citadel, 1976.
Thomas, Tony, and Rudy Behlmen. Hollywood's Hollywood, Citadel,
    1975.
Thomson, David. A Biographical Dictionary of Film, William Mor-
    row, 1976.
Thrasher, Frederic. Okay for Sound, Duell, Sloan and Pierce, 1946.
Tuska, John, ed. Close-Up: The Hollywood Director (Wellman
    chapter by David Wilson), Scarecrow Press, 1978.
Wellman, William A. Go Get 'Em!, Page Co., 1918.
Wellman, William A. A Short Time for Insanity, Hawthorn, 1974.
White, David Manning, and Richard Averson. The Celluloid Weapon,
    Beacon Press, 1972.
Zmijewsky, Steve; Boris Zmijewsky; and Mark Ricci. The Films of
    John Wayne, Citadel, 1970.

                            ARTICLES

Brooks, Louise. "On Location with Billy Wellman," Film Culture
    (Spring 1972).

Champlin, Charles. "Another Kind of Hollywood Hero," The Los
    Angeles Times (December 12, 1975).

Eyman, Scott. "'Wild Bill' William A. Wellman," Focus on Film
    (March 1978).

Fox, Julian. "It's a Man's World," Films and Filming (March and
    April 1973).

Gallagher, John. "Wild Bill Wellman," Grand Illusions (February
    1977).

_____. "William Wellman," Films in Review (May and June 1982).

Gilliat, Penelope. "Wings," The New Yorker (September 25, 1972).

Hopper, Hedda. "Wellman's Spirit Still Flames," The Los Angeles Times (October 3, 1954).

_____. "Bill Wellman Quits Picture Business," The Los Angeles Times (March 5, 1962).

Krebs, Alvin. "William A. Wellman Dies; Directed Movie Classics," The New York Times (December 12, 1975).

Mellor, William. "No Time for Weather," American Cinematographer (January 1952).

Miller, Ed Mack. "Yank in the Black Cat Squadron," Flying (August 1961).

Parton, Lemuel F. "A Pugnacious Movie Director," The New York Times (June 22, 1939).

Peak, Mayme Ober. "Billy Wellman Was All Started for Career As Wool Salesman in Boston When War Mixed Things Up," Boston Globe (October 16, 1927).

Peary, Gerald. "More Than Meets the Eye," American Film (March 1976).

Pringle, Henry F. "Screwball Bill," Collier's (February 26, 1938).

Pryor, Thomas M. "Bill Wellman's Hodgepodge Recall," Variety (May 18, 1974).

Rau, Neil. "He Helped Live a Story," Los Angeles Herald Examiner (February 17, 1957).

Rowan, Arthur. "Westward the Women," American Cinematographer (January 1952).

Smith, Darr. "Column," New York Daily News (October 19, 1949).

Smith, John M. "The Essential Wellman," Brighton Film Review (January 1970).

Sterritt, David. "A Director of Yesterday's Hits Looks at Today's Films," The Christian Science Monitor (May 16, 1975).

Tallmer, Jerry. "When Movies Were Better Than Ever," The New York Post (August 3, 1974).

Thompson, Frank T. "Wellman's Westerns," American Classic Screen (Winter 1980).

_____. "William Wellman: The Paramount Years," American Classic Screen (Summer 1980).

Townsend, Dorothy. "William Wellman, Colorful Director of 82 Films, Dies," The Los Angeles Times (December 10, 1975).

Wellman, William A. "The Birth of a Celebrated Mug Shot," The Los Angeles Times Calendar (November 26, 1978).

Wellman, William A. (with Lonnie Raidor). "Wellman de les Chats Noir," Cross and Cockade Journal (Autumn 1976).

Wellman, William A., Jr. "William A. Wellman, Director Rebel," Action (March-April 1970).

Wicking, Christopher. "William A. Wellman," John Player Lecture Brochure (July 23, 1972).

Williams, Whitney. "Deemed Hollywood 'Immortal,' Wm. A. Wellman Dies at 79," Variety (December 17, 1975).

Young, Jordan. "Chatauqua to Eastwood ... And Still Going," The Los Angeles Times Calendar (January 14, 1979).

FILMOGRAPHY*

Compiled by Frank Thompson and John Gallagher

Wellman appeared as an actor in the following film:

THE KNICKERBOCKER BUCKAROO (1919) Artcraft. A Douglas Fairbanks Pictures Production. Written and Produced by Douglas Fairbanks. Directed by Albert Parker. Photography: Victor Fleming.
Production Manager: Theodore Reed. Publicity Director: Bennie
F. Ziedman. 6 Reels. Opened at the Rivoli Theatre, New York,
on May 26, 1919.
    The Cast: Douglas Fairbanks (Teddy Drake), Marjorie Daw
(Mercedes), William Wellman (Henry), Frank Campeau, James Mason
(the villains).

Wellman worked as an actor in the following film, though it
is doubtful that his part survived into the finished film:

EVANGELINE (1919) Fox. Presented by William Fox. Produced
and Directed by Raoul Walsh. Scenario: Raoul Walsh, based on the
poem by Henry Wadsworth Longfellow. Photography: J. D. Jennings. 5 Reels. Opened at the 44th St. Theatre, New York, on
August 19, 1919.
    The Cast: Miriam Cooper (Evangeline), Albert Roscoe (Ga-
briel), Spottiswoode Aitken (Benedict Bellefontaine), James Marcus
(Basil), Paul Weigel (Father Felician), William Wellman (British
Officer).

In 1920, Wellman worked as assistant propman on the follow-
ing films: JUBILO, JES' CALL ME JIM, CUPID THE COW-
PUNCHER, THE HONEST PUNCH. All directed by Clarence
Badger and starring Will Rogers.

---

*All dates given are for New York release.

When Head Propman James Flood was promoted to assistant director, Wellman was promoted to Head Propman on the following film:

GUILE OF WOMEN (1920) Goldwyn Pictures. Directed by Clarence Badger. Continuity Writer: Edfrid A. Bingham. Author: Peter Clark MacFarlane. Photography: Marcel Picard. Assistant Director: James Flood.
The Cast: Will Rogers (Yal), Mary Warren (Hulda), Bert Sprotte (Skole), Lionel Belmore (Armstrong), Charles A. Smiley (Captain Larsen), Nick Cogley (Captain Stahl), Doris Pawn (Annie), John Lince (butler), Jane Starr (maid). Released December 26, 1920.

In early 1921, Wellman was promoted to Assistant Director. The exact number of films on which he worked in this capacity is not known. The list offered here is certainly incomplete and, in some cases, probably inaccurate; screen credits for assistant directors were rare in the 1920's and a lot of archival records are incomplete in these items. Consequently, this list was compiled from various sources: studio records, recollections of artists who also worked on the films, and clues left by Wellman in interviews and his own writings. I would appreciate having any corrections or additions forwarded to me via the publisher.

HOLD YOUR HORSES (1921) Goldwyn Pictures. Directed by E. Mason Hopper. Scenario: Gerald C. Duffy. Photography: John Mescall.
The Cast: Tom Moore (Daniel Canavan), Sylvia Ashton (Honora Canavan), Naomi Childers (Beatrice Newness), Bertram Grassby (Rodman Cadbury), Mortimer E. Stinson (Jim James), Sydney Ainsworth (Horace Slayton). Released January 28, 1921.

JUST OUT OF COLLEGE (1921) Goldwyn Pictures. Directed by Alfred Green. Scenario: Arthur F. Statter. Camera: George Webber.
The Cast: Jack Pickford (Ed Swinger), Molly Malone (Caroline Pickering), George Hernandez (Septimus Pickering), Edythe Chapman (Mrs. Pickering), Otto Hoffman (Professor Bliss), Irene Rich (Miss Jones), Maxfield Stanley (Herbert Poole), Maurice B. Flynn (Paul Greer), Loretta Blake (Genevieve). Released February 11, 1921.

BOYS WILL BE BOYS (1921) Goldwyn Pictures. Directed by Clarence G. Badger. Scenario: Edfrid A. Bingham. Photography: Marcel Le Picard.
The Cast: Will Rogers (Peep O'Day), Irene Rich (Lucy), C. E. Mason (Tom Minor), Sydney Ainsworth (Sublette), Edward Kimball

(Judge Priest), H. Milton Ross (Bagby), C. E. Thurston (Sheriff Breck), May Hopkins (Kitty), Cordelia Callahan (Mrs. Hunter), Nick Cogley (Aunt Mandy), Burton Halbert (Farmer Bell). Released May 14, 1921.

FOOTFALLS (1921) Fox Film Corporation. Presented by William Fox. Scenarist-Director: Charles J. Brabin. Photography: George W. Lane.

The Cast: [Frederick] Tyrone Power (Hiram Scudder), Tom Douglas (Tommy), Estelle Taylor (Peggy Hawthorne), Gladden James (Alec Campbell). Released November 1921.

THE DEVIL WITHIN (1921) Fox Film Corp. Presented by William Fox. Directed by Bernard J. Durning. Scenario: Arthur J. Zellner. Photography: Don Short.

The Cast: Dustin Farnum (Captain Briggs), Virginia Valli (Laura), Nigel De Brulier (Dr. Philiol), Bernard Durning (Hal), Jim Farley (Scurlock), Tom O'Brien (Wansley), Bob Perry (Crevay), Charles Gorman (Bevins), Otto Hoffman (Ezra), Kirk Incas (cabin boy), Evelyn Selbie (witch), Hazel Deane (young witch). Released November 20, 1921.

THE BROADWAY PEACOCK (1922) Fox Film Corp. Presented by William Fox. Directed by Charles J. Brabin. Story-Scenario: Julia Tolsva. Photography: George W. Lane. 5 Reels.

The Cast: Pearl White (Myrtle May), Joseph Striker (Harold Van Tassel), Doris Eaton (Rose Ingraham), Henry Southard (Jerry Gibson), Elizabeth Garrison (Mrs. Van Tassel). Released February 19, 1922.

IRON TO GOLD (1922) A Fox Film. Presented by William Fox. Directed by Bernard J. Durning. Scenario: Jack Strumwasser. Based on a story by Owen Baxter. Photography: Dan Short. Stunts: Harvey Parry. 5 Reels.

The Cast: Dustin Farnum (Tom Curtis), Marguerite Marsh (Anne Kirby), William Conklin (George Kirby), William Elmer (Bat Piper), Lionel Belmore (Sheriff), Glen Cavender (Sloan), Robert Perry (Creel), Dan Mason (Lem Baldwin). Released March 21, 1922.

MONTE CRISTO (1922) Fox Film Corp. Presented by William Fox. Directed by Emmett J. Flynn. Scenario: Bernard McConville. Story: Alexander Salvini. Additional Story: Charles Fechter. Photography: Lucien Andriot. 10 Reels.

The Cast: John Gilbert (Edmond Dantes, Count of Monte Cristo), Estelle Taylor (Mercedes, Countess de Morcerf), Robert McKim (De Villefort), William V. Mong (Caderousse), Virginia Brown Faire (Haidee), George Siegmann (Luigi Vampa), Spottiswoode Aitkin (Abbe Faria), Ralph Cloninger (Fernand), Albert Prisco (Baron Danglars), Gaston Glass (Albert de Morcerf), Al Filson (Morrel), Harry Lonsdale (Dantes), Francis MacDonald Benedetto), Jack Cosgrove (Governor of Chateau d'If), Maude George (Baroness Danglars), Renée Adorée (Eugenie Danglars), George Campbell (Napoleon), Willard Koch (tailor at Chateau d'If), Howard Kendall (surgeon). Released April 1922.

VERY TRULY YOURS (1922) Fox Film Corp. Presented by William Fox. Directed by Harry Beaumont. Scenario: Paul Schofield. Story: Hannah Hinsdale. Photography: John Arnold. 5 Reels.
    The Cast: Shirley Mason (Marie Tyree), Allan Forrest (Bert Woodmansee), Charles Clary (A. L. Woodmansee), Otto Hoffman (Jim Watson), Harold Miller (Archie Small), Helen Raymond (Mrs. Evelyn Grenfall), Hardee Kirkland (Dr. Maddox). Released April 30, 1922.

STRANGE IDOLS (1922) Fox Film Corp. Presented by William Fox. Directed by Bernard J. Durning. Scenario: Jules Furthman. Story: Emil Forst. Photography: Dan Short. 5 Reels.
    The Cast: Dustin Farnum (Angus MacDonald), Doris Pawn (Ruth Mayo), Philo McCullough (Ted Raymond), Richard Tucker (Malcolm Sinclair). Released May 28, 1922.

LIGHTS OF THE DESERT (1922) Fox Film Corp. Presented by William Fox. Directed by Harry Beaumont. Scenario: Paul Schofield. Story: Gladys E. Johnson. Photography: Frank Good. 5 Reels.
    The Cast: Shirley Mason (Yvonne Laraby), Allan Forrest (Clay Truxall), Edward Burns (Andrew Reed), James Mason (Slim Saunders), Andree Tourneur (Marie Curtis), Josephine Crowell (Ma Curtis), Lillian Langdon (Susan Gallant). Released June 11, 1922.

A FOOL THERE WAS (1922) Fox Film Corp. Presented by William Fox. Directed by Emmett J. Flynn. Scenario: Bernard McConville. Photography: Lucien Andriot. 7 Reels.
    The Cast: Estelle Taylor (Gilda Fontaine), Lewis Stone (John Schuler), Irene Rich (Mrs. Schuyler), Muriel Dana (Muriel Schuyler), Marjorie Daw (Avery Parmelee), William V. Mong (Boggs), Harry Lonsdale (Parks). Released June 18, 1922.

OATH BOUND (1922) Fox Film Corp. Presented by William Fox. Directed by Bernard J. Durning. Scenario: Jack Strumwasser and Edward J. LeSaint. Story: Edward J. LeSaint. Photography: Dan Short. 5 Reels.
    The Cast: Dustin Farnum (Lawrence Bradbury), Ethel Grey Terry (Connie Hastings), Fred Thomson (Jim Bradbury), Maurice B. Flynn (Ned Hastings), Norman Selby (Hicks), Aileen Pringle (Alice), Bob Perry (The Gang Leader), Herschell Mayall (Captain Steele). Released August 13, 1922.

THE FAST MAIL (1922) Fox Film Corp. Presented by William Fox.
Directed by Bernard J. Durning. Scenario: Agnes Parsons and
Jacques Jacard. Based on the play by Lincoln Carter. Photography:
George Schneidermann and Dan Short. 6 Reels.
    The Cast: Charles "Buck" Jones (Stanley Carson), Eileen
Percy (Virginia Martin), James Mason (Lee Martin), William Steele
(Pierre LaFitte), Adolphe Menjou (Cal Baldwin), Harry Dunkinson
(Harry Joyce). Released August 20, 1922.

YOSEMITE TRAIL (1922) Fox Film Corp. Presented by William Fox.
Directed by Bernard J. Durning. Scenario: Jack Strumwasser.
Based on the novel One Way Trail by Ridgwell Cullon. Photography:
Dan Short. 5 Reels.
    The Cast: Dustin Farnum (Jim Thorpe), Irene Rich (Eve
Marsham), Walter McGrail (Ned Henderson), Frank Campeau (Jerry
Smallbones), W. J. Ferguson (Peter Blunt), Charles French (The
Sheriff). Released September 24, 1922.

WITHOUT COMPROMISE (1922) Fox Film Corp. Presented by Wil-
liam Fox. Directed by Emmett J. Flynn. Scenario: Bernard Mc-
Conville. Photography: Dev Jennings. Based on the novel by Lil-
lian Bennett-Thompson and George Hubbard. 6 Reels.
    The Cast: William Farnum (Dick Leighton), Lois Wilson (Jean
Ainsworth), Robert McKim (David Ainsworth), Tully Marshall (Samuel
McAllister), Hardee Kirkland (Judge Gordon Randolph), Otis Harlan
(Dr. Evans), Willi Walling (Bill Murray), Alma Bennett (Nora Fos-
ter), Eugene Pallette (Tommy Ainsworth), Fred Kohler (Cass Blake),
Jack Dillon (Jackson). Released October 29, 1922.

LIGHTS OF NEW YORK (1922) Fox Film Corp. Presented by Wil-
liam Fox. Directed by Charles J. Brabin. Story and Scenario by
Charles J. Brabin. Photography: George W. Lane. 6 Reels. This
film is comprised of two separate stories of New York life.
    The Cast (First story): Clarence Nordstrom (Robert Reid),
Margaret Seddon (Mrs. Reid), Frank Currier (Daniel Reid), Florence
Short (Mary Miggs), Charles Gerard (Jim Slade). (Second story):
Marc MacDermott (Charles Redding), Estelle Taylor (Mrs. George
Burton). Released November 12, 1922.

WHILE JUSTICE WAITS (1922) Fox Film Corp. Presented by William
Fox. Directed by Bernard J. Durning. Scenario: Edwin B. Tilton
and Jack Strumwasser. Story: Charles A. Short and Dan Short.
Photography: Dan Short. 5 Reels. Working title: A MAN THINK-
ETH.
    The Cast: Dustin Farnum (Dan Hunt), Irene Rich (Nell Hunt),
Earl Metcalf (George Carter), Junior Delamater (Hunt, Jr.), Frankie
Lee (Joe), Hector Sarno (A man), Peaches Jackson (his daughter),
Gretchen Hartman (Mollie Adams). Released November 19, 1922.

THREE WHO PAID (1923) Fox Film Corp. Presented by William
Fox. Directed by Colin Campbell. Scenario: Joseph Franklin Po-
land. Based on the story in Western Story Magazine by George Owen
Baxter. Photography: Dan Short. 5 Reels.
    The Cast: Dustin Farnum (Riley Sinclair), Fred Kohler (Jim
Quade), Bessie Love (John Caspar/Virginia Cartwright), Frank Campeau (Edward Sanderson), Robert Daly (Sam Lowrie), William Conklin (Jude Cartright), Robert Agnew (Hal Sinclair). Released January
7, 1923.

THE BUSTER (1923) Fox Film Corp. Presented by William Fox.
Directed by Colin Campbell. Scenario: Jack Strumwasser. Based
on the novel by William Patterson White. Photography: David Abel.
5 Reels.
    The Cast: Dustin Farnum (Bill Coryell), Doris Pawn (Char-
lotte Rowland), Francis MacDonald (Swing), Gilbert Holmes (Light
Laurie), Lucille Hutton (Yvonne). Released February 18, 1923.

BUCKING THE BARRIER (1923) Fox Film Corp. Presented by William Fox. Directed by Colin Campbell. Scenario: Jack Strumwasser. Story: George Goodchild. Photography: Lucien Andriot. 5
Reels.
    The Cast: Dustin Farnum (Kit Carew), Arline Pretty (Blanche
Cavendish), Leon Bary (Luke Cavendish), Colin Chase (Frank Farfax),
Hayford Hobbs (Cyril Cavendish), Sidney D'Albrook (Tyson). Released April 1, 1923.

THE ELEVENTH HOUR (1923) Fox Film Corp. Presented by William
Fox. Directed by Bernard J. Durning (and, uncredited, Wellman).
Scenario: Louis Sherwin. Photography: Dan Short. 7 Reels.
    The Cast: Shirley Mason (Barbara Hackett), Charles "Buck"
Jones (Brick McDonald), Richard Tucker (Herbert Glenville), Alan
Hale (Prince Stefan deBernie), Walter McGrail (Dick Manley), June
Elvidge (Mordecai Newman), Fred Kohler (Barbara's uncle). Re-
leased July 20, 1923.

        Wellman directed the following films:

THE MAN WHO WON (1923) Fox Film Corp. Presented by William
Fox. Directed by William A. Wellman. Screenplay: Ewart Adam-
son. Based on the novel The Twins of Suffering Creek by Ridgwell
Cullom. Photography: Joseph August. Assistant Director: Edward
Bernoudy. Originally released with color tints. 5 Reels.
    The Cast: Dustin Farnum (Wild Bill), Jacqueline Gadsden
(Jessie), Lloyd Whitlock ("Lord" James), Ralph Cloninger (Scipio),
Mary Warren (Birdie), Pee Wee Holmes (Toby Jenks), Harvery Clark
(Sunny Oaks), Lon Poff (Sandy Joyce), Andy Waldron (Minkie), Ken

Maynard (Conroy), Muriel McCormack, Mickey McBan (The twins),
Bob Marks (the drunkard), Pedre Leon (stuntman for Farnum). Released August 26, 1923.

SECOND HAND LOVE (1923) Fox Film Corp. Presented by William
Fox. Directed by William A. Wellman. Screenplay: Charles Kenyon. Story: Shannon Fife. Photography: Dan Short. Originally
released with color tints. 5 Reels.
    The Cast: Charles "Buck" Jones (Andy Hanks), Ruth Dwyer
(Angela Trent), Charles Coleman (Dugg), Harvey Clark (Scratch, the
detective), Frank Weed (Deacon Seth Poggins), James Quinn (Dugg's
partner), Gus Leonard (the constable). Released August 26, 1923.

BIG DAN (1923) Fox Film Corp. Presented by William Fox. Directed by William A. Wellman. Story and Screenplay: Frederick
and Fanny Hatton. Photography: Joseph August. Originally released with color tints. 6 Reels.
    The Cast: Charles "Buck" Jones (Dan O'Hara), Marian Nixon
(Dora Allen), Ben Hendricks (Cyclone Morgan), Charles Coleman
(Doc Snyder), Lydia Yeamans Titus (Aunt Kate Walsh), Monte Collins (Tom Walsh), Charles Smiley (Father Quinn), Harry Lonsdale
(Stephen Allen), Mattie Peters (Ophelia), J. P. Lockney (Pat Mayo),
Jack Herrick (Muggs Murphy). Released October 14, 1923.

CUPID'S FIREMAN (1923) Fox Film Corp. Presented by William
Fox. Directed by William A. Wellman. Screenplay: Eugene B.
Lewis. Based on the story, "Andy M'Gee's Chorus Girl" in Van
Bibber and Others by Richard Harding Davis. Photography: Joseph
August. Originally released with color tints. 5 Reels.
    The Cast: Charles "Buck" Jones (Andy McGee), Marian Nixon
(Agnes Evans), Brooks Benedict (Bell Evans), Eileen O'Malley (Eliza-
beth Stevens), Lucy Beaumont (Mother), Al Fremont (Fire Chief),
Charles McHugh (Old Man Turner), Mary Warren (Molly Turner),
L. H. King (veteran). Released December 16, 1923.

NOT A DRUM WAS HEARD (1924) Fox Film Corp. Presented by
William Fox. Directed by William A. Wellman. Screenplay: Doty
Hobart. Based on a story by Ben Ames Williams. Photography:
Joseph August. 5 Reels.
    The Cast: Charles "Buck" Jones (Jack Mills), Betty Bouton
(Jean Ross), Frank Campeau (Banker Rand), Rhody Hathaway (James
Ross), Al Fremont (the sheriff), William Scott (Bud Loupel), Mickey
McBan (Jack Loupel, Jr.). Released January 27, 1924.

THE VAGABOND TRAIL (1924) Fox Film Corp. Presented by William Fox. Directed by William A. Wellman. Screenplay: Doty Hobart. Based on the novel Donnegan by George Owen Baxter. Photography: Joseph August. 5 Reels.

The Cast: Charles "Buck" Jones (Donnegan), Marian Nixon (Lou Macon), Charles Coleman (Aces), L. C. Shumnay (Lord Nick), Virginia Warwick (Nellie LeBrun), Harry Lonsdale (Col. Macon), Frank Nelson (Slippy), George Reed (George), George Romain. Released March 9, 1924.

THE CIRCUS COWBOY (1924) Fox Film Corp. Presented by William Fox. Directed by William A. Wellman. Screenplay: Doty Hobart. Story: Louis Sherwin. Photography: Joseph Brotherton. Originally released with color tints. 5 Reels.

The Cast: Charles "Buck" Jones (Buck Saxon), Marian Nixon (Bird Taylor), Jack McDonald (Ezra Bagley), Ray Hallor (Paul Bagley), Marguerite Clayton (Norma Wallace), George Romain (Slovini). Released May 11, 1924.

WHEN HUSBANDS FLIRT (1925) A Columbia Picture. Presented by Harry Cohn. Directed by William A. Wellman. Story and Continuity: Paul Gangelin and Dorothy Arzner. Photography: Sam Landers. 6 Reels.

The Cast: Doroty Revier (Violet Gilbert), Forrest Stanley (Henry Belcher), Maude Wayne (Charlotte Germaine), Frank Weed (Percy Snodgrass), Erwin Connelly (Joe McCormick). Released November 23, 1925.

THE BOOB (1926) A Metro-Goldwyn-Mayer Picture. Directed by William A. Wellman. Story: George Scarborough and Annette Westbay. Adaptation: Kenneth B. Clarke. Titles: Katherine Hilliker and H. H. Caldwell. Photography: William Daniels. Art Direction: Cedric Gibbons and Ben Carre. Editor: Ben Lewis. Assistant Director: Nick Grinde. 64 minutes. Working title: I'LL TELL THE WORLD. British title: THE YOKEL.

The Cast: Gertrude Olmstead (Amy), George K. Arthur (Peter Good), Joan Crawford (Jane), Charles Murray (Cactus Jim), Antonio D'Algy (Harry Benson), Hank Mann (Village soda jerk), Babe London (Fat girl). Released May 19, 1926.

THE CAT'S PAJAMAS (1926) Famous Players-Lasky Company. Released by Paramount Pictures. Presented by Adolph Zukor and Jesse L. Lasky. Directed by William A. Wellman. Screenplay: Hope Loring and Louis D. Lighton. Story: Ernest Vajda. Photography: Victor Milner. Props: Charles Barton. 6 Reels.

The Cast: Betty Bronson (Sally Winton), Ricardo Cortez (Don Cesare Gracco), Arlette Marchal (Riza Dorina), Theodore Roberts (Sally's father), Gordon Griffith (Jack), Tom Ricketts (Mr. Briggs). Released August 29, 1926.

YOU NEVER KNOW WOMEN (1926) Famous Players-Lasky Company. Released by Paramount Pictures. Presented by Adolph Zukor and

Jesse L. Lasky. Directed by William A. Wellman. Screenplay:
Benjamin Glazer. Story: Ernest Vajda. Photography: Victor Mil-
ner. Associate Producers-West Coast: B. P. Schulberg and Hector
Turnbull. Props: Charles Barton. 6 Reels.
    The Cast: Florence Vidor (Vera), Lowell Sherman (Eugene
Foster), Clive Brook (Norodin), El Brendel (Toberchik), Roy Stewart
(Dimitri), Joe Bonomo (The Strong Man), Irma Kornelia (Olga), Sid-
ney Bracy (Manager), Eugene Pallette (dinner guest). Released Sep-
tember 22, 1926.

WINGS (1927) Paramount Famous Lasky Corporation. Presented by
Adolph Zukor and Jesse L. Lasky. Produced by Lucien Hubbard.
Associate Producer: B. P. Schulberg. Directed by William A.
Wellman. Screenplay: Hope Loring and Louis D. Lighton. Story
and novelization: John Monk Saunders. Titles: Julian Johnson.
Engineering Effects: Roy Pomeroy. Photography: Harry Perry.
Additional Photography: E. Burton Steene, William Clothier, Cliff
Blackston, Russell Harlan, Bert Baldridge, Frank Cotner, Faxon M.
Dean, Ray Olse, Herman Schoop, L. Guy Wilky, Al Williams.
Aerial Photography: Schoop, Dean, Harlon, Blackston, Baldridge,
Wilky, Cotner, Gene O'Donnell, Paul Perry, Art Lane, Harry Ma-
son, Ray Olsen, Al Meyers, Guy Bennett, Ernest Laszlo, William
Clothier. Edited by Lucien Hubbard. Editor-In-Chief: E. Lloyd
Sheldon. Art Director: Laurence Hitt. Production Manager:
Frank Blount. Costumes: Edith Head. Musical Score: John S.
Zamecnik. Song "Wings" by Zamecnik and Ballard MacDonald.
Props: Charles Barton. Assistant Directors: Richard Johnston,
Norman Z. McLeod and Charles Barton. Stunt Pilot: Dick Grace.
Supervision of Flying Sequences: S. C. Campbell, Ted Parson,
Carl Von Hartmann, James A. Healy. Stills Photographer: Otto
Dyar. Originally released in color tints. Portions of the film
utilized Magnascope. 13 Reels.
    The Cast: Clara Bow (Mary Preston), Charles "Buddy" Rog-
ers (Jack Powell), Richard Arlen (David Armstrong), Jobyna Ralston
(Sylvia Lewis), Gary Cooper (Cadet White), Arlette Marchal (Celeste),
El Brendel (Herman Schwimpf), Gunboat Smith (The Sergeant), Rich-
ard Tucker (Air Commander), Roscoe Karns (Lt. Cameron), Julia
Swayne Gordon (Mrs. Armstrong), Henry B. Walthall (Mr. Armstrong), George Irving (Mr. Powell), Hedda Hopper (Mrs. Powell),
Nigel De Brulier (Peasant), James Pierce (MP), Carl Von Hartmann
(German Officer), Dick Grace, Rod Rogers, Tommy Carr (Aviators),
William Wellman (dying soldier), Charles Barton (doughboy hit by
ambulance), Margery Chapin Wellman (peasant woman), Gloria Wellman (peasant child). Silent version released August 12, 1927. Sound
effects and musical score (Movietone) version released January 5,
1929. Academy Awards: Best Picture, Best Engineering Effects
(Roy Pomeroy).

LEGION OF THE CONDEMNED (1928) Paramount Famous Lasky Corporation. Presented by Adolph Zukor and Jesse L. Lasky. Produced and Directed by William A. Wellman. Associate Producer:

E. Lloyd Sheldon. Screenplay: John Monk Saunders and Jean De-Limur. Based on an original story by Wellman and Saunders. Novelized by Eustace Hale Ball. Titles: George Marion. Photography: Henry Gerrard. Art Director: Laurence Hitt. Editor: Alyson Schaeffer. Editor-In-Chief: E. Lloyd Sheldon. Assistant Director: Richard Johnston. Second Assistant Director: Charles Barton. Props: Joseph Youngerman. 8 Reels.

The Cast: Fay Wray (Christine Charteris), Gary Cooper (Gale Price), Barry Norton (Byron Dashwood), Lane Chandler (Lane Holabird), Francis MacDonald (Gonzolo Vasquez), Albert Conti (Von Hohendorff), Charlotte Bird (Celeste, Tart in cafe), Voya George (Robert Montagnal), Freeman Wood (Richard DeWitt), E. H. Calvert (Commandant), Toto Guette (Mechanic). This film utilized stock footage from WINGS. Released March 18, 1928.

LADIES OF THE MOB (1928) Paramount Famous Lasky Corporation. Presented by Adolph Zukor and Jesse L. Lasky. Directed by William A. Wellman. Screenplay: John Farrow. Based on story by Ernest Booth in The American Mercury. Adaptation: Oliver H. P. Garrett. Titles: George Marion. Photography: Henry Gerrard. Editor: Alyson Schaeffer. Assistant Director: Charles Barton. 7 Reels.

The Cast: Clara Bow (Yvonne), Richard Arlen (Red), Helen Lunch (Marie), Mary Alden (Soft Annie), Carl Gerrard (Joe), Bodil Rosing (The Mother), Lorraine Rivero (Little Yvonne), James Pierce (The Officer). Released May 17, 1928.

BEGGARS OF LIFE (1928) Paramount Famous Lasky Corporation. Presented by Adolph Zukor and Jesse L. Lasky. Produced and Directed by William A. Wellman. Screenplay: Benjamin Glazer and Jim Tully. Based on a novel by Jim Tully. Photography: Henry Gerrard. Edited by Alyson Schaeffer. Assistant Director: Charles Barton. Stunt Double for Louise Brooks: Harvey Parry. 9 Reels.

The Cast: Wallace Beery (Oklahoma Red), Louise Brooks (Nancy), Richard Arlen (Jim), Edgar "Blue" Washington (Mose), H. A. Morgan (Skinny), Andy Clark (Skelly), Mike Donlin (Bill), Roscoe Karns (Hopper), Robert Perry (The Arkansas Snake), Johnnie Morris (Rubin), George Kotsonaros (Baldy), Jacques "Jack" Chapin (Ukie), Robert Brower (Blind Sims), Frank Brownlee (Farmer), Guinn "Big Boy" Williams (bakery cart driver), Harvey Parry (Hobo). Released September 18, 1928. Originally released with musical score, sound effects and some dialog sequences (Movietone).

CHINATOWN NIGHTS (1929) Paramount Famous Lasky Corporation. Presented by Adolph Zukor and Jesse L. Lasky. Associate Producer: David O. Selznick. Directed by William A. Wellman. Screenplay: Ben Grauman Kohn. Based on the story "Tong War" by Samuel Ornitz. Dialogue: William B. Jutte. Titles: Julian Johnson. Adaptation: Oliver H. P. Garrett. Photography: Henry Gerrard. Edited by Alyson Schaeffer. Technical Director: Tom Gubbins. As-

sistant Director: Charles Barton. Props: Joseph Youngerman. 8
Reels.
The Cast: Wallace Beery (Chuck Riley), Florence Vidor (Joan
Fry), Warner Oland (Boston Charley), Jack McHugh (The Shadow),
Jack Oakie (Reporter), Tetsu Komai (Woo Chung), Frank Chew (Gam-
bler), Mrs. Wong Wing (Maid), Pete Morrison (Reporter), Freeman
Wood (Gerald). Released March 30, 1929. Often called Wellman's
first talkie, CHINATOWN NIGHTS is, in fact, advertised as "65%
Dialogue." It was also released in a silent version.

THE MAN I LOVE (1929) Paramount Famous Lasky Corporation.
Presented by Adolph Zukor and Jesse L. Lasky. Associate Pro-
ducer: David O. Selznick. Directed by William A. Wellman.
Screenplay: Percy Heath and Herman J. Mankiewicz. Story and
Dialog: Herman J. Mankiewicz. Photography: Henry Gerrard.
Edited by Alyson Shaeffer. Song "Celia" by Leo Robin and Richard
Whiting. Assistant Director: Charles Barton. Props: Joseph
Youngerman. 7 Reels.
The Cast: Richard Arlen (Dum Dum Brooks), Mary Brian
(Celia Fields), Olga Baclanova (Sonia Barondorff), Harry Green (Curly
Bloom), Jack Oakie (Lew Layton), Pat O'Malley (D. J. McCarthy),
Leslie Fenton (Carlo Vesper), Charles Sullivan (Champ Mahoney),
Sailor Vincent (K. O. O'Hearn), Robert Perry (Gateman), William
Wellman (voice of "Bill"). Released May 27, 1929. Wellman's first
full-talkie. Also released in a silent version with titles by Joseph
L. Mankiewicz.

WOMAN TRAP (1929) Paramount Famous Lasky Corporation. Presented by Adolph Zukor and Jesse L. Lasky. Directed by William
A. Wellman. Screenplay and Dialogue: Bartlett Cormack. Scenario:
Louise Long. Based on the play Brothers by Edwin Burke. Photography: Henry Gerrard. Edited by Alyson Schaeffer. Recording Engineer: Earl Hayman. Assistant Director: Charles Barton. Props:
Joseph Youngerman. Sound by Movietone. 7 Reels.
The Cast: Hal Skelly (Dan Malone), Chester Morris (Ray Malone), Evelyn Brent (Kitty Evans), William B. Davidson (Watts), Effie Ellsler (Mrs. Malone), Guy Oliver (Mr. Evans), Leslie Fenton
(Eddie Evans), Charles Giblyn (Smith), Joseph L. Mankiewicz (Reporter), Wilson Hummell (Detective Captain), William "Sailor Billy"
Vincent (Himself, a Boxer), Virginia Bruce (Nurse). Released August 30, 1929. Also released in a silent version.

DANGEROUS PARADISE (1930) Paramount Famous Lasky Corporation.
Presented by Adolph Zukor and Jesse L. Lasky. Directed by William
A. Wellman. Screenplay and Dialogue: William Slavens McNutt and
Grover Jones. Photography: Archie J. Stout. Based on "Incidents
from" Victory by Joseph Conrad. Assistant Director: Charles Bar-
ton. Props: Joseph Youngerman. Song "Smiling Skies" by Leo
Robin and Richard Whiting. Sound by Movietone. 6 Reels. Working
title: FLESH OF EVE.

The Cast: Nancy Carroll (Alma), Richard Arlen (Heyst), Warner Oland (Scomberg), Gustav Von Seyffertitz (Mr. Jones), Francis McDonald (Ricardo), George Kotsonaros (Pedro), Dorothea Wolbert (Mrs. Schomberg), Clarence H. Wilson (Zangiacomo), Evelyn Selbie (his wife), Willie Fung (Wang), Wong Wing (his wife), Lillian Worth (Myrtle). Other versions of VICTORY were released in 1919 (dir. Maurice Tourneur) and 1940 (dir. John Cromwell). DANGEROUS PARADISE was also released in a silent version.

YOUNG EAGLES (1930) Paramount Famous Lasky Corporation. Presented by Adolph Zukor and Jesse L. Lasky. Directed by William A. Wellman. Screenplay and Dialogue: William Slavens McNutt and Grover Jones. Photography: Archie J. Stout. Editor: Allyson Scheffer. Based on two stories in Red Book by Elliot White Springs: "The One Who Was Clever" and "Sky High." Song "The Sunrise and You" by Arthur A. Penn. Recording Engineer: Eugene Merritt. Assistant Director: Charles Barton. Props: Joseph Youngerman. Stunt Pilot: Dick Grace. Sound by Movietone. 8 Reels.

The Cast: Charles "Buddy" Rogers (Lt. Robert Banks), Jean Arthur (Mary Gordon), Paul Lucas (Von Baden), Stuart Erwin (Pudge Higgins), Virginia Bruce (Florence Welford), Gordon De Main (Major Lewis), James Finlayson (Scotty), Frank Ross (Lt. Graham), Jack Luden (Lt. Barker), Freeman Wood (Lt. Mason), George Irving (Col. Wilder), Stanley Blystone (Capt. Deming), Newell Chase, Lloyd Whitlock. Released March 21, 1930. Also released in a silent version. Some stock footage from WINGS was utilized.

MAYBE IT'S LOVE (1930) Warner Bros. Pictures. Directed by William A. Wellman. Screenplay and Dialogue: Joseph Jackson. Story: Mark Canfield (Darryl Zanuck). Photography: Robert Kurrle. Editor: Edward McDermott. Songs "Maybe It's Love" and "All American" by Sidney Mitchell, Archie Gottler, George W. Meyer. Television title: ELEVEN MEN AND A GIRL. 8 Reels.

The Cast: Joan Bennett (Nan Sheffield), Joe E. Brown (Speed Hanson), James Hall (Tommy Nelson), Laura Lee (Betty), Anders Randolph (Mr. Nelson), Sumner Getchell (Whiskers), George Irving (President Sheffield), George Bickel (Professor), Howard Jones (Coach Bob Brown), Bill Banker (Bill), Russell Saunders ("Racehorse" Russell), Tim Moynihan (Tim), W. K. Schoonover (Schoony), E. N. Sleight (Elmer), George Gibson (George), Ray Montgomery (Ray), Otto Pommerening (Otto), Kenneth Haycraft (Ken), Howard Harpster (Howard), Paul Scull (Paul), Stuart Erwin (Brown of Harvard). The cast includes members of the 1928 and 1929 All-American football teams. Released October 4, 1930.

OTHER MEN'S WOMEN (1931) Warner Bros. Pictures. Directed by William A. Wellman. Scenario and Dialogue: William K. Wells. Story and Adaptation: Maude Fulton. Photography: Chick McGill. Editor: Edward McDermott. Vitaphone Orchestra Conducted by Louis Silvers. Musical Director: Erno Rapee. Wardrobe: Earl Luich.

Sound by Vitaphone.   70 minutes.   Originally titled STEEL HIGH-
WAY.
   The Cast: Grant Withers (Bill), Regis Toomey (Jack), Mary
Astor (Lily), James Cagney (Ed), Joan Blondell (Marie), Fred Kohler
(Haley), J. Farrell MacDonald (Pegleg), Walter Long (Bixby), Lillian
Worth (Waitress), Bob Perry, Lee Morgan, Kewpie Morgan, Pat
Hartigan (Railroad workers).   Released April 19, 1931.

THE PUBLIC ENEMY (1931) Warner Bros. Picture.   Production
Supervisor: Hal B. Wallis.   Produced by Darryl F. Zanuck.   Di-
rected by William A. Wellman.   Based on the story "Beer and
Blood" by Kubec Glasmon and John Bright.   Adaptation and Dialogue:
Harvey Thew.   Photography: Dev Jennings.   Editor: Edward Mc-
Dermott.   Art Director: Max Parker.   Vitaphone Orchestra con-
ducted by David Mendoza.   Costumes: Earl Luick and Edward Ste-
venson.   Makeup: Perc Westmore.   Sound by Vitaphone.   83 min-
utes.   British Title: ENEMY OF THE PUBLIC.
   The Cast: James Cagney (Tom Powers), Jean Harlow (Gwen
Allen), Eddie Woods (Matt Doyle), Joan Blondell (Mame), Donald
Cook (Mike Powers), Leslie Fenton (Nails Nathan), Beryl Mercer
(Ma Powers), Robert Emmett O'Conner (Paddy Ryan), Murray Kin-
nell (Putty Nose), Mae Clarke (Kitty), Rita Flynn (Molly Doyle),
Snitz Edwards (Hack), Ben Hendricks, Jr. (Bugs Moran), Frank
Coghlan, Jr. (Tommy as a boy), Frankie Darro (Matt as a boy),
Robert E. Homans (Officer Pat Burke), Dorothy Gee (Nails' girl),
Purnell Pratt (Officer Powers), Lee Phelps (Steve, a bartender),
Mia Marvin (Jane), Clark Burroughs (Dutch), Adele Watson (Mrs.
Doyle), Helen Parrish, Dorothy Gray, Nancie Price (Little Girls),
Ben Hendricks, III (Bugs as a child), George Daly (machine-gunner),
Eddie Kane (Joe, the headwaiter), Charles Sullivan (Mug), Douglas
Strauss (Pawnbroker).   Released April 23, 1931.

NIGHT NURSE (1931) Warner Bros. Pictures.   Directed by William
A. Wellman.   Adaptation and Screenplay: Oliver H. P. Garrett.
From the novel by Dora Macy (pseudonym for Grace Perkins Ours-
ler).   Additional Dialogue: Charles Kenyon.   Photography: Barney
"Chick" McGill.   Art Director: Max Parker.   Editor: Edward Mc-
Dermott.   Costumes: Earl Luick.   Technical Director: Dr. Harry
Martin.   Sound by Vitaphone.   72 minutes.
   The Cast: Barbara Stanwyck (Lora Hart), Ben Lyon (Mortie),
Joan Blondell (Maloney), Charles Winninger (Dr. Bell), Charlotte
Merriam (Mrs. Richey), Edward Nugent (Eagan), Allan Lane (Intern),
Blanche Frederici (Mrs. Maxwell), Vera Lewis (Miss Dillon), Ralf
Harolde (Dr. Ranger), Clark Gable (Nick), Walter McGrail (Drunk),
Betty May (nurse), Marcia Mae Jones (Nanny), Betty Jane Graham
(Desney).   Released July 16, 1931.

STAR WITNESS (1931) Warner Bros. Pictures.   Directed by William
A. Wellman.   Story, Adaptation and Dialogue: Lucien Hubbard.
Photography: James Van Trees.   Edited by Hal McLernon.   Sound

by Vitaphone. Working titles: THE MAN WHO DARED, THIS IS
THE ANSWER and PRECIOUS LITTLE THING. 7 Reels.
The Cast: Walter Huston (Whitlock), Charles "Chic" Sale
(Grandpa Summerville), Dickie Moore (Donny Leeds), Grant Mitchell
(Pa Leeds), Frances Starr (Ma Leeds), Ralph Ince (Maxey Campo),
Sally Blane (Sue Leeds), Edward J. Nugent (Jack Leeds), Tom Dugan
(Brown), Robert Elliot (Williams), Noel Madison (Hogan), George
Ernest (Ned Leeds), Nat Pendleton (Big Jack), Russell Hopton (Dep-
uty Thorpe), Mike Donlin (Mickey), Fletcher Norton (Dopey), Guy
O'Ennery (Jack Short), Ed Dearing (Sackett), Allen Lane (Clerk),
William Wellman (voice of lineman). Released August 3, 1931. Re-
ceived Academy Award nomination for Best Writing--Original Story
(Lucien Hubbard).

SAFE IN HELL (1931) First National. Directed by William A. Well-
man. Story: Houston Branch. Adaptation and Dialogue: Joseph
Jackson and Maude Fulton. Photography: Barney "Chick" McGill.
Editor: Owen Marks. Sound by Vitaphone. British title: THE
LOST LADY. 8 Reels.
The Cast: Dorothy Mackaill (Gilda Karlson), Donald Cook
(Carl), Ralf Harolde (Piet), John Wray (Egan), Ivan Simpson (Crunch),
Victor Varconi (Gomez), Morgan Wallace (Bruno), Nina Mae McKin-
ney (Leonie), Gustav Von Seyffertitz (Larson), Cecil Cunningham
(Angie), Charles Middleton (Jones), Noble Johnson (Bobo), George
Marion, Sr. (Jack), Clarence Muse (Newcastle). Released Decem-
ber 18, 1931.

THE HATCHET MAN (1932) First National. Directed by William A.
Wellman. Screenplay: J. Grubb Alexander. Based on the play "The
Honourable Mr. Wong" by David Belasco and Achmed Abdullah. Pho-
tography: Sid Hickox. Editor: Owen Marks. Gowns: Earl Luick.
Vitaphone Orchestra Conducted by Leo F. Forbstein. 74 minutes.
The Cast: Edward G. Robinson (Wong Low Get), Loretta Young
(Toya San), Dudley Digges (Nag Hong Fah), Leslie Fenton (Harry En
Lai), Edmund Breese (Yu Chang), Tully Marshall (Long Sen Yat),
Noel Madison (Charley Kee), Blanche Frederici (Madame Si-Si), J.
Carroll Naish (Sun Yat-Sen), Toshia Mori (Miss Ling), Charles Mid-
dleton (Lip Hot Fat), Ralph Ince (Malone), Otto Yamioka (Chung Ho),
Evelyn Selbie (Wah Li), E. Allyn Warren (Soo Notary), Anna Chang
(Sing Girl), Gladys Lloyd Robinson (Fan Yi), James Leong (Tong
Member). Released February 3, 1932.

SO BIG (1932) Warner Bros. Pictures. Produced by Darryl F. Zan-
uck. Directed by William A. Wellman. Based on the novel by Edna
Ferber. Adaptation and Dialogue: J. Grubb Alexander and Robert
Lord. Production Supervisor: Lucien Hubbard. Photography: Sid
Hickox. Music: W. Franke Harling. Editor: William Holmes.
Art Director: Jack Okey. Costumes: Orry-Kelly. Make-up: Perc
Westmore. Sound by Vitaphone. 82 minutes.
The Cast: Barbara Stanwyck (Selina Peakie), George Brent

(Roelf), Dickie Moore (Dirk as a boy), Guy Kibbee (August Hemple), Bette Davis (Dallas O'Mara), Mae Madison (Julie Hemple), Hardie Albright (Dirk as a man), Robert Warwick (Simeon Peake), Arthur Stone (Jan Steen), Earle Foxe (Pervus DeJong), Alan Hale (Klaus Pool), Dorothy Peterson (Maartje), Dawn O'Day--later Anne Shirley --(Selina as a girl), Dick Winslow (Roelf as a boy), Harry Beresford (Adam Ooms), Eulalie Jensen (Mrs. Hemple), Elizabeth Patterson (Mrs. Tebbitts), Rita LeRoy (Paula), Blanche Frederici (Widow Parrlenburg), Willard Robertson (Doctor), Harry Holman (Country Doctor), Lionel Belmore (Rev. Dekker). Released April 29, 1932. Other versions of SO BIG were released in 1924 (dir. Charles Brabin) and 1953 (dir. Robert Wise).

LOVE IS A RACKET (1932) First National. Produced by Hal B. Wallis. Directed by William A. Wellman. Based on a novel by Rian James. Adaptation: Courtenay Terrett. Photography: Sid Hickox. Editor: William Holmes. Art Director: Jack Okey. Makeup: Perc Westmore. Sound: Vitaphone. 70 minutes.

The Cast: Douglas Fairbanks, Jr. (Jimmy Russell), Ann Dvorak (Sally), Lee Tracy (Stanley Fiske), Frances Dee (Mary), Lyle Talbot (Shaw), Warren Hymer (Burney), William Burress (Ollie), George Raft (Sneaky), Andre Luquet (Max Boncour), Terence Ray (Seeley), Marjorie Peterson (Hat Check Girl), Edward Kane (Captain), Cecil Cunningham (Hattie), John Marston (Curley). Released June 10, 1932.

THE PURCHASE PRICE (1932) Warner Bros. Pictures. Produced by Hal B. Wallis. Directed by William A. Wellman. Screenplay: Robert Lord. Based on the story "The Mud Lark" by Arthur Stringer. Photography: Sid Hickox. Editor: William Holmes. Art Director: Jack Okey. Makeup: Perc Westmore. Sound by Vitaphone. Working title: THE NIGHT FLOWER. 68 minutes.

The Cast: Barbara Stanwyck (Joan Gordon), George Brent (Jim Gilson), Lyle Talbot (Ed Fields), David Landau (Bull McDowell), Leila Bennett (Emily), Murray Kinnell (Spike Forgan), Crauford Kent (Peters), Hardie Albright (Don Leslie), Matt McHugh (Waco), Clarence Wilson (Justice of the Peace), Lucille Ward (his wife), Dawn O'Day--later Anne Shirley--(farmer's daughter), Victor Potel (Clyde), Adele Watson (Mrs. Tipton), Snub Pollard (Joe), Mae Busch. Released July 15, 1932.

THE CONQUERORS (1932) RKO-Radio Pictures. Executive Producer: David O. Selznick. Directed by William A. Wellman. Screenplay: Robert Lord. Based on a story by Howard Estabrook. Photography: Edward Cronjager. Montage: Slavko Vorkapich. Aerial Photography: William Clothier. Musical Director: Max Steiner. Editor: William Hamilton. Art Director: Carroll Clark. Assistant Directors: Dolph M. Zimmer and James Anderson. Sound: John Tribby. Makeup: Ern Westmore. Working title: FRONTIER. Television title: PIONEER BUILDERS. 88 minutes.

The Cast: Richard Dix (Roger Standish/Roger Lennox), Ann Harding (Caroline Ogden Standish), Edna May Oliver (Matilda Blake), Guy Kibbee (Dr. Daniel Blake), Julie Hayden (Frances Standish), Donald Cook (Warren Lennox), Harry Holman (Stubby), Richard "Skeets" Gallagher (Benson), Walter Walker (Mr. Ogden), Wally Albright, Jr. and Marilyn Knowlden (twins), Jason Robards (Lane), Jed Prouty (auctioneer), E. H. Calvert (Doctor), J. Carroll Naish (agitator), Robert Greig (Mr. Downey), Elizabeth Patterson (Landlady). Released November 20, 1932.

FRISCO JENNY (1933) First National. Production Supervisor: Raymond Griffith. Directed by William A. Wellman. Screenplay: Wilson Mizner and Robert Lord. Based on a story by Gerald Beaumont, Lillie Hayward and John Francis Larkin. Photography: Sid Hickox. Editor: James Morley. Sound: Vitaphone. Makeup: Perc Westmore. Gowns: Orry-Kelly. Working title: COMMON GROUND. 8 Reels.

The Cast: Ruth Chatterton (Jenny), Donald Cook (Dan Reynolds), James Murray (Dan McAllister), Louis Calhern (Steve Dutton), Hallam Cooley (Willie Gleason), Pat O'Malley (O'Houlihan), Robert Warwick (Kelly), Harold Huber (Weaver), Helen Jerome Eddy (Amah), Frank McGlynn, Sr. (Good Book Charlie), J. Carroll Naish (Harris), Noel Francis (Rose), Robert Emmett O'Connor (Jim Sandoval), Sam Godfrey (Kilmer), Franklin Parker (Martel), William Wellman (reporter). Released January 6, 1933.

CENTRAL AIRPORT (1933) First National. Produced by Hal B. Wallis. Directed by William A. Wellman. Screenplay and Adaptation: Rian James and James Seymour. Based on the story "Hawk's Mate" by Jack Moffitt. Photography: Sid Hickox. Technical Effects: Fred Jackman. Stunt Pilot: Paul Mantz. Sound: Vitaphone. Makeup: Perc Westmore. Editor: James Morley. Art Director: Jack Okey. Working title: GRAND CENTRAL AIRPORT. 70 minutes.

The Cast: Richard Barthelmess (Jim Blaine), Sally Eilers (Jill Collins), Tom Brown (Neil Blaine), Glenda Farrell (girl in wreck), Harold Huber (Swarthy Man), Grant Mitchell (Mr. Blaine), James Murray (Eddie Hughes), Claire McDowell (Mrs. Blaine), Willard Robertson (Havana manager), Arthur Vinton (Amarillo manager), Charles Sellon (man in wreck), John Wayne (man in wreck), J. Carroll Naish (nervous passenger), William Wellman (voice of airport flight announcer). Released May 3, 1933.

LILLY TURNER (1933) First National. Produced by Hal B. Wallis. Directed by William A. Wellman. Screenplay: Gene Markey and Kathryn Scola. From the play by Philip Dunning and George Abbott, based on a story by Frances Fox Dunning. Photography: James Van Trees. Sound: Vitaphone. Makeup: Perc Westmore. Art Direction: Jack Okey. Gowns: Orry-Kelly. Editor: James Gibbon. Vitaphone Orchestra Conducted by Leo F. Forbstein. 7 Reels.

The Cast: Ruth Chatterton (Lilly Turner), George Brent (Bob

Chandler), Frank McHugh (Dave Dixon), Ruth Donnelly (Edna), Guy Kibbee (Doc McGill), Gordon Westcott (Rex Durkee), Marjorie Gateson (Mrs. McGill), Arthur Vinton (Sam), Robert Barrat (Fritz), Grant Mitchell (Dr. Hawley), Margaret Seddon (Mrs. Turner), Hobart Cavanaugh (Earle), Mayo Methot (Mrs. Durkee), Catherine Claire Ward (Mrs. Flint), Lucille Ward (Mother), Mae Busch (Hazel). Released June 14, 1933.

MIDNIGHT MARY (1933) Metro-Goldwyn-Mayer. Associate Producer: Lucien Hubbard. Directed by William A. Wellman. Screenplay: Gene Markey and Kathryn Scola. Original Story: Anita Loos. Photography: James Van Trees. Editor: William S. Gray. Musical Score: Dr. William Axt. Art Director: Cedric Gibbons. Recording Director: Douglas Shearer. 71 minutes. Also released as LADY OF THE NIGHT.

The Cast: Loretta Young (Mary Martin), Ricardo Cortez (Leo Darcy), Franchot Tone (Tom Mannering), Andy Devine (Sam Travers), Una Merkel (Bunny), Frank Conroy (District Attorney), Warren Hymer (Angelo Ricci), Ivan Simpson (Tindle), Harold Huber (Puggy), Sandy Roth (Blimp), Martha Sleeper (Barbara), Charles Grapewin (Clerk), Halliwell Hobbes (Churchill), Robert Emmett O'Connor (Cop). Released July 14, 1933.

HEROES FOR SALE (1933) First National. Produced by Hal B. Wallis. Directed by William A. Wellman. Story and Screenplay: Robert Lord and Wilson Mizner. Photography: James Van Trees. Editor: Howard Brotherton. Makeup: Perc Westmore. Gowns: Orry-Kelly. Vitaphone Orchestra Conducted by Leo F. Forbstein. 76 minutes. Originally titled BREADLINE.

The Cast: Richard Barthelmess (Tom Holmes), Loretta Young (Ruth Holmes), Aline MacMahon (Mary Dennis), Gordon Westcott (Roger Winston), Robert Barrat (Max), Charley Grapewin (Pa Dennis), Berton Churchill (Mr. Winston), Grant Mitchell (George Gibson), Robert McWade (Dr. Briggs), James Murray (Blind Man), Ward Bond (Red), Douglass Dumbrille (Chief Engineer), Edwin Maxwell (President of Laundry), Margaret Seddon (Mrs. Holmes), Arthur Vinton (Captain Joyce), John Marston (The Judge), Lee Phelps (Ed Brady), Dewey Robinson (Arguer), Milton Kibbee (Teller), Guy Usher (Constable), Robert Elliot, Willard Robertson, George Pat Collins. Released July 21, 1933.

WILD BOYS OF THE ROAD (1933) First National. Produced by Darryl F. Zanuck. Directed by William A. Wellman. Production Supervisor: Robert Presnell. Screenplay: Earl Baldwin. Based on the story "Desperate Youth" by Danny Ahearn. Photography: Arthur Todd. Editor: Thomas Pratt. Art Director: Esdras Hartley. Makeup: Perc Westmore. Sound: Vitaphone. 73 minutes. British title: DANGEROUS DAYS.

The Cast: Frankie Darro (Eddie Smith), Dorothy Coonan (Sally), Edwin Philips (Tommy), Rochelle Hudson (Grace), Ann Hovey

(Lola), Arthur Hohl (Dr. Heckel), Grant Mitchell (Mr. Smith), Claire McDowell (Mrs. Smith), Sterling Holloway (Ollie), Robert Barrat (Judge White), Shirley Dunstead (Harriet), Minna Gombel (Aunt Carrie), Ward Bond (Red), Willard Robertson (Captain of Detectives), Charley Grapewin (Mr. Cadmust), Adrian Morris (Buggie Haylin). Released September 21, 1933.

COLLEGE COACH (1933) Warner Bros. Production Supervisor: Robert Lord. Directed by William A. Wellman. Story and Screenplay: Niven Busch and Manuel Seff. Photography: Arthur Todd. Editor: Thomas Pratt. Art Director: Jack Okey. Makeup: Perc Westmore. Sound: Vitaphone. Gowns: Orry-Kelly. Vitaphone Orchestra Conducted by Leo F. Forbstein. 75 minutes. British title: FOOTBALL COACH.
    The Cast: Dick Powell (Dick Sargent), Ann Dvorak (Claire Gore), Pat O'Brien (Coach Gore), Arthur Byron (Dr. Philip Sargent), Lyle Talbot (Buck Weaver), Hugh Herbert (J. Marvin Barnett), Arthur Hohl (Seymour Young), Guinn "Big Boy" Williams (Matthews), Nat Pendleton (Petrowski), Donald Meek (Spencer Trask), Berton Churchill (Otis), Harry Beresford (Professor), Joseph Sawyer (Holcomb), Herman Bing (Glantz), Phillip Reed (Westerman), Ward Bond (Assistant Coach), John Wayne, Philip Faversham, Charles C. Wilson. Released November 10, 1933.

LOOKING FOR TROUBLE (1934) A Twentieth Century Picture released through United Artists. A Darryl F. Zanuck Production. Presented by Joseph M. Schenck. Associate Producers: William Goetz and Raymond Griffith. Directed by William A. Wellman. Screenplay: Leonard Praskins and Elmer Harris. Based on an original story by J. R. Bren. Photography: James Van Trees. Editor: Peter Fritch. Art Directors: Richard Day and Joseph Wright. Musical Director: Alfred Newman. 80 minutes. Working title: TROUBLE SHOOTERS.
    The Cast: Spencer Tracy (Joe Graham), Jack Oakie (Casey), Constance Cummings (Ethel Greenwood), Arline Judge (Maizie), Judith Wood (Pearl LaTour), Morgan Conway (Dan Sutter), Paul Harvey (James Regan), Joseph Sawyer (Max Stanley), Franklin Ardell (Martin), Paul Porcasi (Cabaret Manager), Robert Homans (Cop). Released April 11, 1934.

STINGAREE (1934) An RKO-Radio Picture. Presented by Merian C. Cooper. Produced by Pandro S. Berman. Directed by William A. Wellman. Associate Producer: David Lewis. Screenplay: Becky Gardiner. Adaptation: Lynn Riggs and Leonard Spigelgass. Based on a series of stories by E. W. Hornung. Photography: James Van Trees. Editor: James B. Morley. Musical Director: Max Steiner. Music and Lyrics by Steiner and Edward Eliscu and Gus Kahn and W. Franke Harling. Sound Effects: Murray Spivack. Extracts from the operas "Faust" and "Martha." Photographic Effects: Vernon E. Walker. Costumes: Walter Plunkett. Recorded by John E. Trilby. 76 minutes.

The Cast: Irene Dunne (Hilda Bouverie), Richard Dix (Stingaree), Mary Boland (Mrs. Clarkson), Conway Tearle (Sir Julian Kent),
Andy Devine (Howie), Henry Stephenson (Mr. Clarkson), Una O'Connor (Annie), George Barraud (Inspector Bradford), Reginald Owen
(Governor General), Snub Pollard (Victor). Released May 17, 1934.

THE PRESIDENT VANISHES (1934) A Walter Wanger Production. Released by Paramount Pictures. Produced by Walter Wanger. Directed by William A. Wellman. Screenplay: Carey Wilson and Ce-
dric Worth. Dialogue: Lynn Starling. Based on the novel by Rex
Stout, published anonymously. Photography: Barney "Chick" McGill.
Directors of Special Photographic Effects: Slavko Vorkapich and John
Hoffman. Editor: Hanson Fritch. Art Director: Sidney M. Ull-
man. Musical Settings, Hugo Reisenfeld. Assistant Director: Dolph
Zimmer. Sound: Hugo Grenzbach. Filmed at General Service Stu-
dios, Hollywood. 86 minutes.
The Cast: Arthur Byron (President Craig Stanley), Paul Kelly
(Chick Moffat), Peggy Conklin (Alma Cronin), Edward Arnold (Lewis
Wardell), Andy Devine (Val Orcott), Janet Beecher (Mrs. Stanley),
Osgood Perkins (Harris), Sidney Blackmer (D. L. Voorman), Edward
Ellis (Lincoln Lee), Irene Franklin (Mrs. Orcott), Charley Grapewin
(Richard Norton), Rosalind Russell (Sally Voorman), Robert McWade
(Molleson), De Witt Jennings (Edward Cullen), Walter Kingsford (Mar-
tin Drew), Douglas Wood (Roger Grant), Charles Richman (Judge Cor-
coran), Paul Harvey (Skinner), Jason Robards (Kilbourne), Harry
Woods (Kramer), Tommy Dugan (Nolan), Martha Mayo (Mrs. Dell-
ing), J. Carroll Naish (communist agitator), Robert Homans (Pat the
Cop), Clara Blandick. Released December 7, 1934.

THE CALL OF THE WILD (1935) A Twentieth Century Picture. Re-
leased through United Artists. A Darryl F. Zanuck Production.
Presented by Joseph M. Schenck. Directed by William A. Wellman.
Adaptation and Screenplay: Gene Fowler and Leonard Praskins.
Based on the novel by Jack London. Photography: Charles Rosher.
Musical Director: Alfred Newman. Art Director: Richard Day.
Editor: Hanson Fritch. Buck's Trainer: Carl Spitz. 95 minutes.
The Cast: Clark Gable (Jack Thornton), Loretta Young (Claire
Blake), Jack Oakie (Shorty Hoolihan), Frank Conroy (John Blake),
Reginald Owen (Smith), Sidney Toler (Joe Groggins), Katherine De-
Mille (Marie), Lalo Encinas (Kali), Charles Stevens (Francois),
James Burke (Ole), Duke Green (Frank), John T. Murray ("Heavy"
on stage), Bob Perry (Stage Manager), Marie Wells (Hilda), Sid
Grauman (Poker Player), Herman Bing (Sam), Wade Boteler, Arthur
Aylesworth, John Ince (miners), Joan Woodbury (girl crossing street),
Sid Saylor (Picolo player), Buck the Dog (himself), Tommy Jackson,
Russ Powell, George McQuarrie. Released August 14, 1935. Other
filmed versions of the London novel: 1923 (dir. Fred Jackman) and
1972 (dir. Ken Annakin). Scenes from the Wellman version were incorporated into MYRA BRECKINRIDGE (1970, dir. Michael Sarne).

THE ROBIN HOOD OF EL DORADO (1936) A Metro-Goldwyn Mayer Picture. Produced by John Consodine, Jr. Directed by William A. Wellman. Screenplay: William A. Wellman, Joseph Calleia and Melvin Levy. Based on the biography of Joaquin Murrietta by Walter Noble Burns. Photography: Chester Lyons. Musical Score: Herbert Stothart. Art Director: David Townsend, Gabriel Scognamillo. Recording Director: Douglas Shearer. Editor: Robert J. Kern. Working title: I AM JOAQUIN!. 86 minutes.
The Cast: Warner Baxter (Murrietta), Ann Loring (Juanita de la Cuesta), Bruce Cabot (Bill Warren), Margo (Rosita), J. Carroll Naish (Three-Fingered Jack), Soledad Jiminez (Madre Murrietta), Carlos de Valdez (Jose Murrietta), Eric Linden (Johnnie Warren), Edgar Kennedy (Sheriff Judd), Charles Trowbridge (Ramon de la Cuesta), Harvey Stephens (Captain Osborne), Ralph Remley (Judge Perkins), George Regas (Tomas), Harry Woods (Pete), Francis Mc-Donald (Pedro the Spy), Kay Hughes (Louise), Paul Hurst (Wilson), Boothe Howard (Tabbard). Released March 13, 1936.

SMALL TOWN GIRL (1936) A Metro-Goldwyn-Mayer Picture. Produced by Hunt Stromberg. Directed by William A. Wellman. Screenplay: John Lee Mahin, Frances Goodrich, Albert Hackett, Edith Fitzgerald. Based on the novel by Ben Ames Williams. Photography: Charles Rosher. Musical Score: Herbert Stothart and Edward Ward. Lyrics: Gus Kahn. Art Director: Cedric Gibbons. Editor: Blanche Sewell. Recording Director: Douglas Shearer. 90 minutes. Re-titled for television: ONE HORSE TOWN.
The Cast: Janet Gaynor (Kay Brannan), Robert Taylor (Bob Dakin), Binnie Barnes (Priscilla), Lewis Stone (Dr. Dakin), Andy Devine (George), Elizabeth Patterson (Ma Brannan), Frank Craven (Pa Brannan), James Stewart (Elmer), Douglas Fowley (Chick), Isabel Jewell (Emily), Charley Grapewin (Dr. Fabre), Nella Walker (Mrs. Dakin), Robert Greig (Childers), Edgar Kennedy (Captain Mack), Willie Fung (So-So), Agnes Ayres (Catherine), Mary Forbes (Mrs. Hyde), Frank Sully (Bill), Ethel Wales (Mrs. Johnson), Ivan Simpson (Hyde Butler), Edna Bennett (Nurse), Eddie Kane (Proprietor), Charles Wilson (Chief Engineer). Released April 10, 1936. Remade as a musical in 1953 (dir. Leslie Kardos).

A STAR IS BORN (1937) A Selznick International Picture. Released by United Artists. Produced by David O. Selznick. Directed by William A. Wellman. Screenplay: Dorothy Parker, Alan Campbell, Robert Carson (and, uncredited, Selznick, Wellman, Ring Lardner, Jr., Budd Schulberg, John Lee Mahin). Color: Technicolor. Photography: W. Howard Greene. Color Consultant: Natalie Kalmus. Color Design: Lansing Holden. Musical Score: Max Steiner. Musical Director: Louis Forbes. Art Director: Lyle Wheeler. Associate Art Director: Edward G. Boyle. Supervising Film Editor: Hal C. Kern. Film Editor: James E. Newcom. Associate Film Editor: Anson Stevenson. Costumes: Omar Kiam. Assistant Director: Eric Stacey. Second-Unit Director: Richard Rosson.

Special Effects: Jack Cosgrove. Sound: Oscar Lagerstrom. Production Manager: Raymond Klune. Production Secretary and Production Assistant: Barbara Keon. Location Manager: Mason Litson. Construction Superintendent: Harold Fenton. Property Man: Robert Lander. Head Grip: Fred Williams. Makeup: Paul Stanhope and Eddie Voight. Publicity Director: Russell Birdwell. Head Electrician: James Potevin. 111 minutes.

The Cast: Janet Gaynor (Esther Blodgett/Vickie Lester), Fredric March (Norman Maine), Adolphe Menjou (Oliver Niles), Andy Devine (Danny McGuire), May Robson (Lettie), Lionel Stander (Libby), Owen Moore (Casey Burke), Elizabeth Jenns (Anita Regis), J. C. Nugent (Theodore Smythe), Clara Blandick (Aunt Mattie), A. W. Sweatt (Alex, Esther's brother), Peggy Wood (Miss Philips, Central Casting Clerk), Clarence Wilson (Justice of the Peace), Adrian Rosley (Harris, makeup man), Arthur Hoyt (Ward, makeup man), Guinn "Big Boy" Williams (Posture Coach), Vince Barnett (Otto Fried, photographer), Paul Stanton (Academy Awards Speaker), Franklin Pangborn (Billy Moon), Jonathon Hale (Night Court Judge), Edgar Kennedy (Pop Randall), Pat Flaherty (Cuddles), Dr. Leonard Walker (Orchestra Leader in Hollywood Bowl), Edwin Maxwell (Voice Coach), Marshall Neilan (Bert), Jed Prouty (Artie Carver), Trixie Friganza, Jane Barnes (waitresses in commissary), Charles Williams (assistant cameraman), Robert Emmett O'Connor (bartender at Santa Anita), Olin Howard (Jud Baker), Carleton Griffin (Cameraman), Claude King, Eddie Kane, Dennis O'Keefe (Burke party guests), George Chandler (delivery boy), Francis Ford (first night court drunk), Kenneth Howell (second night court drunk), Chris-Pin Martin (Rodriquez, third night court drunk), Lana Turner, Carole Landis (extras in Santa Anita bar), Snowflake (witness), Irving Bacon (Station Agent), Billy Dooley (Painter), Helene Chadwick. Released April 22, 1937. Academy Awards to Wellman and Carson for Best Writing--Original Story and Special Award to Greene for the color photography. Nominated for Best Picture, Best Actor, Best Actress, Best Direction, Assistant Direction, Screenplay. Other versions: 1954 (dir. George Cukor) and 1976 (dir. Frank Pierson).

NOTHING SACRED (1937) A Selznick International Picture. Released by United Artists. Produced by David O. Selznick. Directed by William A. Wellman. Screenplay: Ben Hecht (and, uncredited, Selznick, Wellman, Ring Larder, Jr., George Oppenheimer, Sidney Howard, Moss Hart, George Kaufman). Suggested by the story "Letter to the Editor" by James H. Street. Color: Technicolor. Photography: W. Howard Greene. Aerial Photography: Wilfrid Cline. Color Consultant: Natalie Kalmus. Editor: James E. Newcom. Art Director: Lyle Wheeler. Set Decorator: Edward G. Boyle. Musical Score: Oscar Levant. Novelty Swing Music: Raymond Scott. Musical Director: Louis Forbes. Special Effects: Jack Cosgrove. Assistant Director: Frederick Spencer. Sound Recording: Fred J. Lau. Main Titles: Sam Berman. Miss Lombard's Costumes: Travis Banton. Other Costumes: Walter Plunkett. Production Manager: Raymond A. Klune. Production Secretary and Scenario Assistant: Barbara Keon. Publicity Director: Russell Birdwell. Working title: LET ME LIVE. 75 minutes.

The Cast: Carole Lombard (Hazel Flagg), Fredric March (Wall Cook), Charles Winninger (Dr. Enoch Downer), Walter Connolly (Oliver Stone), Sig Rumann (Dr. Emile Egglehoffer), Frank Fay (master of ceremonies), "Slapsie" Maxie Rosenbloom (Max Levinsky), Margerey Hamilton (drug store lady), Troy Brown (Ernest Walker), Hattie McDaniel (Mrs. Walker), Olin Howland (baggage man), George Chandler (photographer), Claire DuBrey (Miss Rafferty, nurse), John Qualen (Swedish fireman), Charles Richman (Mayor), Art Lasky (mug), Alex Schoenberg (Dr. Kerchinwasser), Monty Wooley (Dr. Vunch), Alex Novinsky (Dr. Marachuffsky), Katherine Shelton (Dr. Downer's Nurse), Ben Morgan, Hans Steinke (wrestlers), Aileen Pringle (Mrs. Bullock), Hedda Hopper (shipboard dowager), Dick Rich (Moe), A. W. Sweatt (office boy), Clarence Wilson (Mr. Watson), Betty Douglas ("Helen of Troy"), Eleanor Troy ("Catherine of Russia"), Monica Bannister ("Pocahontas"), Jinx Falkenberg ("Katinka"), Margeret Lyman ("Salome"), Shirley Chambers ("Lady Godiva"), Ernest Whitman, Everett Brown (policemen), Vera Lewis (Miss Sedgewick), Ann Doran (telephone girl), Bill Dunn, Lee Phelps (Electricians), Cyril Ring (pilot), Mickey McMasters (referee), Bobby Tracey (announcer), Billy Barty (little boy), Nora Cecil (schoolteacher), Raymond Scott and his Quintet. Re-made as LIVING IT UP (1954, dir. Norman Taurog).

MEN WITH WINGS (1938) A Paramount Picture. A William A. Wellman Production. Produced and Directed by William A. Wellman. Screenplay: Robert Carson. Color Consultant: Natalie Kalmus. Color: Technicolor. Assistant Director: Joseph Youngerman. Photography: W. Howard Greene. Aerial Photography: Wilfrid Cline. Music: W. Franke Harling and Gerard Carbonara. Stunt Pilots: Frank Clarke and Paul Mantz. Musical Direction: Boris Morros. Art Direction: Hans Dreier and Robert Odell. Film Editor: Thomas Scott. Sound Recording: Gene Merritt and John Cope. Costumes: Edith Head. Interior Decorations: A. E. Freudeman. Special Photographic Effects: Gordon Jennings, A. S. C. Process Photography: Farciot Edouart, A. S. C.

The Cast: Fred MacMurray (Patrick Falconer), Ray Milland (Scott Barnes), Louise Campbell (Peggy Ranson), Andy Devine (Joe Gibbs), Lynne Overman (Hank Rinebow), Porter Hall (Hiram F. Jenkins), Walter Abel (Nick Ranson), Kitty Kelly (Martha Ranson), Virginia Weidler (Peggy Ranson as a child), Donald O'Connor (Pat Falconer as a child), Billy Cook (Scott Barnes as a child), James Burke (J. A. Nolan), Williard Robertson (Major General Hadley), Dennis Morgan (Galton), Charles Trowbridge (Alcott), Jonathon Hale (Long), Juanita Quigley (Patricia Falconer at age six), Joan Brodel (Patricia Falconer at age eleven), Mary Brodel (Patricia at age seventeen), Archie Twitchell (Nelson), Dorothy Tennant (Mrs. Nelson). 105 minutes. Released August 2, 1938.

BEAU GESTE (1939) A Paramount Picture. A William A. Wellman Production. Produced and Directed by William A. Wellman. Screenplay: Robert Carson. Based on the novel by Percival Christopher Wren. Photography: Theodor Sparkhul and Archie J. Stout. Editor:

Thomas Scott. Art Direction: Hans Dreier and Robert Odell. Musical Score: Alfred Newman. Orchestrations: Edward B. Powell. Assistant Director: Joseph Youngerman. Second Unit Director: Richard Talmadge. Technical Advisor: Louis Van Der Ecker. Sound Recording: Hugi Grenzbach and Walter Oberst. Costumes: Edith Head. Makeup: Wally Westmore. 120 minutes (cut to 114 minutes upon 1950 re-release, which version is now the only one available).

   The Cast: Gary Cooper (Michael "Beau" Geste), Ray Milland (John Geste), Robert Preston (Digby Geste), Brian Donlevy (Markoff), Susan Hayward (Isobel Rivers), J. Carroll Naish (Rasinoff), Albert Dekker (Schwartz), Broderick Crawford (Hank Miller), Charles T. Barton (Buddy McGonigle), James Stephenson (Major Henri DeBeaujolais), Heather Thatcher (Lady Patricia Brandon), G. P. Huntley, Jr. (Augustus Brandon), James Burke (Lt. Dufour), Henry Brandon (Renouf), Arthur Aylesworth (Renault), Harry Woods (Renoir), Harold Huber (Vousin), Stanley Andrews (Maris), Donald O'Connor (Beau as a child), Billy Cook (John as a child), Martin Spellman (Digby as a child), Ann Gillis (Isobel as a child), David Holt (Augustus as a child), Harvey Stephens (Lt. Martin), Barry McCollom (Krenke), Ronnie Rondell (bugler), Frank Dawson (Burdon, the butler), George Chandler (Cordier), Duke Green (Glock), Thomas Jackson (Colonel in the recruiting office), Jerome Storm (Sergeant-Major), Joseph Whitehead (Sergeant), Harry Worth, Nestor Paiva (Corporals), George Regas, Francis McDonald (Arab Scouts), Carl Voss, Joe Bernard, Robert Perry, Larry Lawson, Henry Sylvestor, Joseph William Cody (Legionnaires), Joe Colling (Trumpeter), Gladys Jean (girl in Port Said cafe), Otto Mezetti (stuntman for J. Carroll Naish). Bob Kortman, Gino Corrado. Released August 2, 1939. Academy Award nominations went to Donlevy (Best Supporting Actor) and Dreier and Odell (Interior Design). Other versions: 1926 (dir. Herbert Brenon), 1966 (dir. Douglas Heyes), THE LAST RE-MAKE OF BEAU GESTE (1977, dir. Marty Feldman). The Feldman film incorporated footage from Wellman's version.

THE LIGHT THAT FAILED (1939) A Paramount Picture. A William A. Wellman Production. Produced and Directed by William A. Wellman. Screenplay: Robert Carson. Based on the novel by Rudyard Kipling. Second Unit Director: Joseph Youngerman. Photography: Theodor Sparkhul. Art Direction: Hans Dreier and Robert Odell. Editor: Thomas Scott. Music: Victor Young. Stunt Coordinator: Yakima Canutt. 97 minutes.

   The Cast: Ronald Colman (Richard Heldar), Walter Huston (Torpenhow), Muriel Angelus (Maisie), Ida Lupino (Bessie Broke), Dudley Digges (The Nilghai), Ernest Cossart (Beeton), Ferike Boros (Madame Binat), Pedro De Cordoba (M. Binat), Colin Tapley (Gardner), Ronald Sinclair (Dick as a boy), Sarita Wooten (Maisie as a girl), Halliwell Hobbes (Doctor), Francis McDonald (George), George Regas (Gassavetti), Wilfred Roberts (Barton), George Chandler (correspondent), Charles Irwin, Clyde Cook, James Aubrey, Charles Bennett, David Phursby (soldiers), Colin Kenny (Doctor). Released December 22, 1939.

REACHING FOR THE SUN (1941) A Paramount Picture. A William
A. Wellman Production.   Produced and Directed by William A. Well-
man.   Screenplay: W. L. River.   Based on the story "F. O. B. De-
troit" by Wessel Smitter.   Photography: William C. Mellor, A. S. C.
Process Photography: Farciot Edouart, A. S. C.   Art Direction:
Hans Dreier and Earl Hedrick.   Music: Victor Young.   Editor:
Thomas Scott.   Sound Recording: Harry Mills and Walter Oberst.
Second Unit Director: Joseph C. Youngerman.   Second Unit Cam-
eraman: Dewey Wrigley, A. S. C.   Assistant Director: John Coonan.
90 minutes.

The Cast: Joel McCrea (Russ Eliot), Ellen Drew (Rita), Ed-
die Bracken (Benny Hogan), Albert Dekker (Herman), Billy Gilbert
(Amos), Bodil Ann Rosing (Rita's mother), James Burke (Norm),
Charles D. Brown (Johnson), Michael Duggan (Little Benny), Regis
Toomey (Interne), Hobart Cavanaugh (Front Office Man), Charles
Williams (Truck Driver), Nella Walker (Nurse), Warren Hymer
(Percy Shelley), Billy Fletcher (Butch Svoboda), George Chandler
(Jerry).

ROXIE HART (1942) Twentieth Century-Fox.   Produced by Nunnally
Johnson.   Directed by William A. Wellman.   Screenplay: Nunnally
Johnson.   Based on the play Chicago by Maurine Watkins.   Photogra-
phy: Leon Shamroy.   Art Direction: Richard Day and Wiard B.
Ihnen.   Editor: James B. Clark.   Music: Alfred Newman.   Dance
Director: Hermes Pan.   75 minutes.

The Cast: Ginger Rogers (Roxie Hart), George Montgomery
(Homer Howard), Adolphe Menjou (Billy Flynn), Lynne Overman
(Jake Callahan), Nigel Bruce (E. Clay Benham), Phil Silvers (Babe),
George Chandler (Amos Hart), Sara Allgood (Mrs. Morton), William
Frawley (O'Malley), Spring Byington (Mary Sunshine), Ted North
(Stuart Chapman), Helene Reynolds (Velma Wall), Charles D. Brown
(Charles E. Murdock), Morris Ankrum (Martin S. Harrison), George
Lessey (Judge), Iris Adrian (Two-Gun Gertie), Milton Parsons (An-
nouncer), Billy Wayne (Court Clerk), Charles Williams (Photographer),
Frank Darien (Finnegan), Jeff Corey (Orderly), Arthur Aylesworth
(Mr. Wadsworth), Margaret Seddon (Mrs. Wadsworth).   Previously
filmed as CHICAGO (1927, dir. Frank Urson).

THE GREAT MAN'S LADY (1942) A Paramount Picture.   Produced
and Directed by William A. Wellman.   Screenplay: W. L. River.
Original story: Adela Rogers St. John and Seena Owen.   Based on
a short story by Vina Delmar.   Photography: William C. Mellor,
A. S. C.   Music: Victor Young.   Art Direction: Hans Dreier and
Earl Hedrick.   Costumes: Edith Head.   Makeup: Wally Westmore.
Assistant Director: Joseph C. Youngerman.   90 minutes.

The Cast: Barbara Stanwyck (Hannah Semplar), Joel McCrea
(Ethan Hoyt), Brian Donlevy (Steely Edwards), Katherine Stevens
(biographer), Thurston Hall (Mr. Semplar), Lloyd Corrigan (Mr.
Cadwallader), Lillian Yarbo (Mandy), Damian O'Flynn (Burns),
Charles Lane (Pierce), George Chandler (Forbes), Anna Q. Nils-
son (Paula Wales), George P. Huntley (Quentin), Milton Parsons

(Froman), Etta McDaniels (Delilah), Mary Treen (Persis), Helen
Lynd (Bettina), Lucien Littlefield (city editor), Frank M. Tomas
(Frisbee), William B. Davidson (Senator Knobs), Fred Toones--
Snowflake--(Pogey), John Hamilton (Senator Grant). Released April
29, 1942.

THUNDER BIRDS (1942) A Twentieth Century-Fox Picture. Produced
by Lamar Trotti. Directed by William A. Wellman. Screenplay:
Lamar Trotti. Based on a story by Melville Crossman (i.e. Darryl
F. Zanuck). Photography: Ernest Palmer. Art Direction: Richard
Day, James Basevi. Editor: Allen McNeil. Music: David Buttolph.
Stunt Pilot: Paul Mantz. Color: Technicolor. Commentary: John
Gunther. 79 minutes.
     The Cast: Preston Foster (Steve Britt), Gene Tierney (Kay
Saunders), John Sutton (Peter Stackhouse), Jack Holt (Colonel Mc-
Donald), Dame Mae Whitty (Lady Stackhouse), George Barbier (Grand-
pa), Richard Haydn (George Lockwood), Reginald Denny (Barrett), Ted
North (Cadet Hackzell), Janis Carter (Blonde), Archie Got and Law-
rence Ung (Chinese Cadets), Montague Shaw (Doctor), Nana Bryant
(Mrs. Black), Viola Moore (Nurse), Connie Leon (Ellen), Walter Tet-
ley (Messenger), Billy McGuire, Richard Woodruff (British Cadets),
Joyce Compton (Saleswoman), Bess Flowers (Nurse), Peter Lawford
(British Cadet), Selmar Jackson (Man), Charles Tannen (Recording),
Harry Strang (Forest Ranger). Released October 28, 1942.

THE OX-BOW INCIDENT (1943) A Twentieth Century-Fox Picture.
Produced by Lamar Trotti. Directed by William A. Wellman.
Screenplay: Lamar Trotti. Based on the novel by Walter Van Til-
burg Clark. Photography: Arthur Miller. Music: Cyril J. Mock-
ridge. Editor: Allen McNeil. Art Direction: Richard Day and
James Basevi. Set Decoration: Thomas Little and Frank Hughes.
Costumes: Earl Luick. Makeup: Guy Pearce. Sound Recording:
Alfred Bruzlin and Roger Heman. British Title: STRANGE INCI-
DENT. 75 minutes.
     The Cast: Henry Fonda (Gil Carter), Dana Andrews (Donald
Martin), Mary Beth Hughes (Rose Mapen), Anthony Quinn (Juan Mar-
tines), William Eythe (Gerald Tetley), Henry Morgan (Art Croft),
Jane Darwell (Ma Grier), Matt Briggs (Judge Tyler), Harry Daven-
port (Arthur Davies), Frank Conroy (Major Tetley), Marc Lawrence
(Farnley), Paul Hurst (Monty Smith), Victor Kilian (Darby), Chris-
Pin Martin (Poncho), Dick Rich (Mapes), Ted North (Joyce), George
Meeker (Mr. Swanson), Almira Sessions (Mrs. Swanson), Margaret
Hamilton (Mrs. Larch), Francis Ford (Old Man), Stanley Andrews
(Bartlett), Billy Benedict (Greene), Rondo Hatton (Hart), Paul Burns
(Winder), Leigh Whipper (Sparks), George Lloyd (Moore), George
Chandler (Jimmy Cairnes), Hank Bell (Red), Forrest Dillon (Mark),
George Plues (Alec Small), Willard Robertson (Sheriff), Tom London
(Deputy). Released May 8, 1943. Re-made as a television special
in 1955 (dir. Gerd Oswald). Nominated for Academy Award as Best
Picture. National Board of Review Awards: Best Picture, Director,
Actor (Morgan).

LADY OF BURLESQUE (1943) A Hunt Stromberg Production. Released by United Artists. Presented and Produced by Hunt Stromberg. Directed by William A. Wellman. Screenplay: James Gunn. Based on the novel The G-String Murders by Gypsy Rose Lee. Photography: Robert DeGrasse. Musical Score: Arthur Lange. Editor: James E. Newcom. Songs by Sammy Cahn and Harry Akst. Art Direction: Bernard Herzbrun. Dance Direction: Danny Dare. Miss Stanwyck's Costumes: Edith Head. Other Costumes: Natalie Visart. Production Design: Joseph Platt. 91 minutes.

The Cast: Barbara Stanwyck (Dixie Daisy), Michael O'Shea (Biff Brannigan), J. Edward Bromberg (S. B. Foss), Iris Adrian (Gee Gee Graham), Gloria Dickson (Polly Baxter), Virginia Faust (Lolita LaVerne), Stephanie Bachelor (Princess Nirvena), Charles Dingle (Inspector Harrigan), Marion Martin (Alice Angel), Eddie Gordon (Officer Pat Kelly), Frank Fenton (Russell Rogers), Pinky Lee (Mandy), Frank Conroy (Stacchi), Lew Kelly (Hermit), Lee Trent (Lee), Beal Wong (Wong), Claire Carleton (Sandra), Janis Carter (Janine), Gerald Mohr (Louis Grindero), Bert Hanlon (Sammy), Sid Marion (Joey), Lou Lubin (Moey), Don Lynn (Don), Freddie Walburn (Messenger boy), Isabel Withers (Teletype operator), George Chandler. Released May 13, 1943. Academy Award Nomination: Music-- Scoring of a Dramatic or Comedy Picture (Lange).

BUFFALO BILL (1944) A Twentieth Century-Fox Picture. Produced by Harry Sherman. Directed by William A. Wellman. Screenplay: Aeneas MacKenzie, Clements Ripley and Cecile Kramer. Based on a story by Frank Winch. Photography: Leon Shamroy. Color: Technicolor. Music: David Buttolph. Art Direction: James Basevi and Lewis Creber. Editor: James B. Clark. Musical Director: Emil Newman. Second Unit Director: Otto Brower. 90 minutes.

The Cast: Joel McCrea (Buffalo Bill Cody), Maureen O'Hara (Louise Cody), Linda Darnell (Dawn Starlight), Thomas Mitchell (Ned Buntline), Edgar Buchanan (Sgt. Chips), Anthony Quinn (Yellow Hand), Moroni Olsen (Senator Frederici), Frank Fenton (Murdo Carvell), Matt Briggs (General Blazier), George Lessey (Mr. Vandevere), Frank Orth (Sherman), George Chandler (Trooper Clancy), Chief Many Treaties (Tall Bull), Nick Thompson (Medicine Man), Chief Thundercloud (Crazy Horse), Sidney Blackmer (Theodore Roosevelt), Evelyn Beresford (Queen Victoria), Cecil Weston (Maid), Vincent Graeff (crippled boy), Fred Graham (Editor), Harry Tyler, Arthur Loft, Syd Saylor (Barkers), Robert Homans (Muldoon), Cordell Hickman, Gerald Mackey, Eddie Nichols, Fred Chapman, George Nokes (boys), John Reese (tough guy), John Dilson (Rutherford B. Hayes), Edwin Stanley (Doctor), Tatzumbia Dupea (old Indian woman), Margaret Martin (Indian Servant), George Bronson (strong man). Released April 19, 1933. This feature utilized footage from John Ford's DRUMS ALONG THE MOHAWK (Fox, 1939). In turn, footage from the Battle of War Bonnet Gorge was used in the following features: PONY SOLDIER (1952, dir. Joseph M. Newman) and SIEGE AT RED RIVER (1954, dir. Rudolph Mate).

THIS MAN'S NAVY (1945) A Metro-Goldwyn-Mayer Picture. Produced by Samuel Marx. Directed by William A. Wellman. Story and Screenplay: Borden Chase. Based on an idea by Commander Herman Halland, USN Ret. Photography: Sidney Wagner. Musical Score: Nathaniel Shilkret. Editor: Irvine Warburton. Art Direction: Cedric Gibbons and Howard Campbell. Set Decoration: Edwin B. Willis. Associate: Glen Barner. Recording Director: Douglas Shearer. Special Effects: A. Arnold Gillespie and Donald Jahraus. Montage Effects: Peter Ballbusch. Technical Advisor: Hugh Allen, Goodyear Aircraft. Costume Supervision: Irene. Associate: Kay Dean. Working titles, AIRSHIP SQUADRON #4 and THEY ALSO WEAR WINGS. 106 minutes.
     The Cast: Wallace Beery (Ned Trumpet), Tom Drake (Jess Weaver), James Gleason (Jimmy Shannon), Jan Clayton (Cathy Cortland), Selena Royle (Maude Weaver), Noah Beery, Sr. (Joe Hodum), Henry O'Neill (Lt. Cdr. Roger Graystone), Steve Brodie (Tim Shannon), George Chandler (Bert Bland), Donald Curtis (Operations Officer), Arthur Walsh (Cadet Rayshek), Will Fowler (David), Richard Crockett (Sparks), Frank Fenton (Capt. Grant), Paul Cavanaugh (Sir Anthony Tivall). Released April 15, 1946.

THE STORY OF G.I. JOE (1945) A William A. Wellman Production. Presented and Produced by Lester Cowan. Directed by William A. Wellman. Released through United Artists. Associate Producer: David Hall. Screenplay: Leopold Atlas, Guy Endore and Philip Stevenson. Based on the books Here Is Your War and Brave Men by Ernie Pyle. Photography: Russell Metty. Art Direction: James Sullivan. Supervising Film Editor: Otho Lovering. Film Editor: Albracht Joseph. Assistant Director: Robert Aldrich. Musical Score: Ann Ronell and Louis Applebaum. Musical Director: Louis Forbes. Songs, "Linda" by Jack Lawrence and Ann Ronell, "I'm Coming Back" and "Infantry March" by Ann Ronell. Production Manager: Ray Heinz. Set Decorations: Edward G. Boyle. Sound Recording: Frank McWhorter. Makeup: Bud Westmore. Research: Paigne Cavanaugh. 109 minutes.
     The Cast: Burgess Meredith (Ernie Pyle), Robert Mitchum (Lt. Walker), Freddie Steele (Sgt. Warnicki), Wally Cassell (Private Dondaro), Bill Murphy (Private Mew), William Self (Cookie), Dick Rich (Sgt. at Showers), Billy Benedict (Whitey), Dorothy Coonan Wellman (nurse), George Chandler (Soldier), Jimmy Lloyd (Private Spencer), Tito Renaldo (Lopez), William Self (Gawky Henderson), Yolanda Lacca (Amelia) and, as themselves, combat veterans of the campaigns in Africa, Sicily and Italy. Released October 5, 1945.

GALLANT JOURNEY (1946) A Columbia Picture. Produced and Directed by William A. Wellman. Screenplay: Byron Morgan and William A. Wellman. Photography: Burnett Guffey, George Meehan, Jr. and Elmer Dyer. Editor: Al Clark. Art Direction: Stephen Goossen and Carl Anderson. Musical Director: Morris W. Stoloff. Musical Score: Marlin Skiles. Based on a story by Byron Morgan and William A. Wellman. Technical Advisor: Col. C. A. Shoop.

Stills Photographer: Joe Walters. Chief Pilot: Paul Mantz. 86 minutes.
The Cast: Glenn Ford (John Montgomery), Janet Blair (Regina Cleary), Charles Ruggles (Jim Montgomery), Henry Travers (Thomas Logan), Arthur Shields (Father Kenton), Willard Robertson (Zachary Montgomery), Selena Royle (Mrs. Montgomery), Robert DeHaven (Jim Montgomery as a boy), Loren Tindall (Jim Logan), Byron Morgan (John Logan), Eula Morgan (Mrs. Logan), Michael Towne (Raymond Walker), Paul Marion (Tony Dondaro), Henry Rowland (Cornelius Rheinlander), Robert Hoover (Dick Ball as a boy), Paul E. Burns (Peacock Fox), Chris-Pin Martin (Pedro Lopez), Fernando Alvarado (Juan Morales), Bobby Cooper (Tom), Rudy Wissler (Hep), Tommy Cook (Cutty), Buddy Swan (Sharkey), Conrad Binyon (Snort). Released October 9, 1946.

MAGIC TOWN (1947) A William A. Wellman Production. Presented by Robert Riskin. Released by RKO-Radio Pictures. Written and Produced by Robert Riskin. Directed by William A. Wellman (and, uncredited, Robert Riskin). Based on a story by Robert Riskin and Joseph Krumgold. Photography: Joseph Biroc. Editor: Sherman Todd and Richard G. Wray. Musical Score: Roy Webb. Musical Director: Constantin Bakaleinikoff. Montage: William Hornbeck. Production Associate: William S. Holmes. Assistant Director: Arthur Black. Sound Recording: John Tribby and Terry Kellum. Miss Wyman's Gowns: Milo Anderson. Songs: "Magic Town" by Mel Torme and Bob Wells; "My Book of Memory" lyrics by Edward Heyman. Working title: THE MAGIC CITY. 103 minutes.
The Cast: James Stewart (Rip Smith), Jane Wyman (Mary Peterman), Kent Smith (Hoopendecker), Ned Sparks (Ike Sloan), Wallace Ford (Lou Dicketts), Regis Toomey (Ed Weaver), Ann Doran (Mrs. Weaver), Donald Meek (Mr. Twiddle), E. J. Ballentine (Moody), Ann Shoemaker (Ma Peterman), Mickey Kuhn (Hank Nickleby), Howard Freeman (Nickleby), Harry Homan (Mayor), Mary Currier (Mrs. Frisby), Mickey Roth (Bob Peterman), Frank Fenton (Birch), George Irving (Senator Wilson), Selmar Jackson (Stringer), Robert Dudley (Dickey), Julia Dean (Mrs. Wilson), George Chandler (Bus Driver), Frank Darien (Quincy), Larry Wheat (Sam Fuller), Jimmy Crane (Shorty), Dick Elliott (Man being interviewed), Richard Belding (Junior Dicketts), Danny Mummert (Benny), Tom Kennedy, William Haade, Frank Marlowe, Richard Wessel (movers). Released October 7, 1947.

THE IRON CURTAIN (1948) A Twentieth Century-Fox Picture. Produced by Sol C. Siegel. Directed by William A. Wellman. Screenplay: Milton Krims. Based on the memoirs of Igor Gouzenko. Photography: Charles C. Clarke. Editor: Louis Loeffler. Music: Dmitri Shostakovich, Serge Prokofieff, Aram Khachaturian, Nicholas Miakovsky. Musical Director: Alfred Newman. Art Direction: Lyle Wheeler and Mark Lee Kirk. Set Decorations: Thomas B. Little. Assistant Director: William Eckhardt. Special Photographic Effects: Fred Sersen. Sound Recording: Bernard Freericks and

Harry M. Leonard.   Costumes: Bonnie Cashin.   Makeup: Ben Bye.
Television title: BEHIND THE IRON CURTAIN.   87 minutes.
    The Cast: Dana Andrews (Igor Gouzenko), Gene Tierney (Anna
Gouzenko), June Havoc (Karanova), Berry Kroeger (Grubb), Edna
Best (Mrs. Foster), Stefan Schnabel (Ranev), Nicholas Joy (Dr. Nor-
man), Eduard Franz (Major Kulin), Frederick Tozere (Col. Trigorin),
Noel Cravat (Bushkin), Christopher Robin Olsen (Andrei), Peter Whit-
ney (Winikov), Leslie Barrie (Editor), Mauritz Hugo (Leonard Loetz),
John Shay (Sergeyev), Victor Wood (Captain Class), Anne Curson
(Helen Tweedy), Helena Dare (Mrs. Kulin), Eula Morgan (Mrs. Trigorin), Reed Hadley (Commentator), John Ridgeley (Policeman Murphy), John Davidson (Secretary), Joe Whitehead (William Hollis),
Michael J. Dugan (Policeman), Harry Carter (Fairfield), Robert Adler (Wilson), Arthur E. Gould-Porter (Foster), Matthew Boulton (Inspector Burns).   Released May 12, 1948.

YELLOW SKY (1948) A Twentieth Century-Fox Picture.   Written and
Produced by Lamar Trotti.   Directed by William A. Wellman.   Based
on a story by W. R. Burnett.   Photography: Joe MacDonald.   Art
Direction: Lyle Wheeler and Albert Hogsett.   Set Decoration: Thom-
as Little.   Editor: Harmon Jones.   Musical Director: Alfred New-
man.   Special Photographic Effects: Fred Sersen.   98 minutes.
    The Cast: Gregory Peck (Stretch), Anne Baxter (Mike), Rich-
ard Widmark (Dude), Robert Arthur (Bull Run), John Russell (Lengthy),
Henry Morgan (Half Pint), James Barton (Grandpa), Charles Kemper
(Walrus), Robert Adler (Jed), Victor Kilian (Bartender), Paul Hurst
(Drunk), William Gould (Banker), Norman Leavitt (Bank Teller), Chief
Yowlachie (Colorado), Eula Guy (woman), Harry Carter (Lieutenant),
Hank Worden (Rancher), Jay Silverheels (Indian).   Released February
1, 1949.   Remade in 1967 as THE JACKALS (dir. Robert Webb).

BATTLEGROUND (1949) A Metro-Goldwyn-Mayer Picture.   Produced
by Dore Schary.   Directed by William A. Wellman.   Story and
Screenplay: Robert Pirosh.   Photography: Paul C. Vogel.   Associate Producer: Robert Pirosh.   Musical Score: Lennie Hayton.
Editor: John Dunning.   Art Direction: Cedric Gibbons and Hans
Peters.   Special Photographic Effects: Peter Ballbusch.   Set Decorations: Edwin B. Willis; Associate: Alfred E. Spencer.   Record-
ing Director: Douglas Shearer.   Technical Advisor: H. W. O. Kin-
nard, Lt. Col.   Makeup: Jack Dawn.   118 minutes.
    The Cast: Van Johnson (Holley), John Hodiak (Jarvess), Ri-
cardo Montalban (Rodriquez), George Murphy (Ernest "Pop" Stazak),
Marshall Thompson (Jim Layton), Jerome Courtland (Abner Spudler),
Don Taylor (Standiford), Bruce Cowling (Wolowicz), James Whitmore
(Kinnie), Douglas Fowley ("Kipp" Kippton), Leon Ames (Chaplain),
Guy Anderson (Hansan), Thomas E. Breen (Doc), Denise Darcel
(Denise), Richard Jaeckel (Bettis), Jim Arness (Garby), Scotty Beck-
ett (William J. Hooper), Brett King (Lt. Teiss), Roland Varno (Ger-
man Lieutenant), Edmon Ryan (Major), Michael Browne (Levinstein),
Jim Drum (Supply Sgt.), Dewey Martin, Tom Noonan, David Holt
(G. I. stragglers), George Offerman, Jr. and William Self (G. I. 's),

Steve Pendleton (Sgt.), Jerry Paris (German Sgt.), Tommy Bond
(Runner), Nan Boardman (Belgian woman volunteer), Ivan Triesault
(German Captain), Henry Rowland (German), John Mylong (German
major), Ian MacDonald (American Colonel), William Lester (Tank
Destroyer Man), George Chandler (Mess Sgt.), Dick Jones (Tanker),
Chris Drake (Medic), Tommy Kelly (Casualty), and the original
"Screaming Eagles" of the 101st Airborne Division. Released No-
vember 11, 1949. Academy Awards for Best Writing and Best Cine-
matography (black and white). Academy Award nominations for Best
Picture, Director, Supporting Actor (Whitmore), Film Editing. New
York Times Ten Best List. Photoplay Gold Medal Award.

THE HAPPY YEARS (1950) A Metro-Goldwyn-Mayer Picture. Produced by Carey Wilson. Directed by William A. Wellman. Screen-
play: Harry Ruskin. Based on the "Lawrenceville School Stories"
by Owen Johnson. Photography: Paul C. Vogel. Color: Techni-
color. Editor: Jack Dunning. Art Direction: Cedric Gibbons and
Daniel B. Cathcart. Set Decorations: Edwin B. Willis. Recording
Director: Douglas Shearer. Music: Leigh Harline. 110 minutes.
Working title: YOU'RE ONLY YOUNG ONCE. Re-released as THE
ADVENTURES OF YOUNG DINK STOVER.
     The Cast: Dean Stockwell (John Humperdink Stover), Darryl
Hickman (Tough McCarty), Scotty Beckett (The Tennessee Shad),
Leon Ames (Samuel H. Stover), Margalo Gilmore (Mrs. Stover),
Leo G. Carroll (The Old Roman), Donn Gift (The Big Man), Peter
Thompson (Sambo), Jerry Mickelsen (Cheyenne Baxter), Aline Dine-
hart III (The Coffee Colored Angel), David Blair (The White Mountain
Canary), Danny Mummert (Butsey White), Eddie LeRoy (Poler Beek-
stein), George Chandler (Johnny), Caludia Barrett (Miss Dolly Trav-
ers), Dwayne Hickman, Eleanor Donahue, Tim Wellman (bellringer).
Completed in 1948, released May 24, 1950.

THE NEXT VOICE YOU HEAR (1950) A Metro-Goldwyn-Mayer Pic-
ture. Produced by Dore Schary. Directed by William A. Wellman.
Screenplay: Charles Schnee. Based on the story by George Sumner
Albee. Photography: William Mellor. Art Direction: Cedric Gib-
bons and Eddie Imazu. Set Decoration: Ralph S. Hurst. Assistant
Director: Joel Freeman. Music: David Raksin. Recording Direc-
tor: Douglas Shearer. Editor: John Dunning. Production Manager:
Ruby Rosenberg. 82 minutes.
     The Cast: James Whitmore (Joe Smith), Nancy Davis (Mrs.
Joe Smith), Gary Gray (Johnny Smith), Lillian Bronson (Aunt Ethel),
Art Smith (Mr. Brannan), Tom D'Andrea (Hap Magee), Jeff Corey
(Freddie), George Chandler (traffic cop). Released June 29, 1950.

ACROSS THE WIDE MISSOURI (1951) A Metro-Goldwyn-Mayer Picture. Produced by Robert Sisk. Directed by William A. Wellman.
Screenplay: Talbot Jennings. Based on a story by Talbot Jennings
and Frank Cavett. Suggested by the book by Bernard DeVoto. Photography: William C. Mellor. Music: David Raksin. Art Direc-

tion: Cedric Gibbons and James Basevi. Set Decorations: Edwin
B. Willis. Editor: John Dunning. Recording Director: Douglas
Shearer. 78 minutes.
     The Cast: Clark Gable (Flint Mitchell), Ricardo Montalban
(Ironshirt), John Hodiak (Brecan), Adolphe Menjou (Pierre), J. Car-
roll Naish (Looking Glass), Jack Holt (Bear Ghost), Alan Napier
(Capt. Humberstone Lyon), George Chandler (Gowie), Richard An-
derson (Dick Richardson), Henri Letondal (Lucien Chennault), Douglas
Fowley (Tin Cup Owens), Maria Elena Marques (Kamiah), Louis Ni-
coletti Whitmore (Bit), Russell Simpson (Hoback), John Hartman
(Chip). Released November 6, 1951.

WESTWARD THE WOMEN (1951) A Metro-Goldwyn-Mayer Picture.
Produced by Dore Schary. Directed by William A. Wellman. Screen-
play: Charles Schnee. Based on a story by Frank Capra. Photog-
raphy: William C. Mellor. Art Direction: Cedric Gibbons and Dan-
iel B. Cathcart. Editor: James E. Newcom. Music: Jeff Alexan-
der. 116 minutes.
     The Cast: Robert Taylor (Buck Wyatt), Denise Darcel (Fifi
Danon), Hope Emerson (Patience), John McIntire (Roy Whitman),
Julie Bishop (Laurie Smith), Beverly Dennis (Rose Meyers), Marilyn
Erskine (Jean Johnson), Lenore Lonergan (Maggie O'Malley), Guido
Martufi (Antonio Moroni), Henry Nakamura (Ito), Renata Vanni (Mrs.
Moroni), Bruce Cowling (Cat), Frankie Darro, George Chandler. Re-
leased December 31, 1951.

IT'S A BIG COUNTRY (1952) A Metro-Goldwyn-Mayer Picture. Pro-
duced by Robert Sisk. Directed by William A. Wellman, Richard
Thorpe, John Sturges, Charles Vidor, Don Weis, Clarence Brown,
Don Hartman. Based on a story by Dore Schary. Writers: William
Ludwig, Edgar Brooke, Helen Deutsch, Ray Chordes, Isobel Lennart,
Claudia Cranston, Allen Rivkin, Lucille Schlossberg, Dorothy Kings-
ley, Dore Schary, George Wells, Joseph Petracca, John McNulty.
Photographers: John Alton, Ray June, William C. Mellor, Joseph
Ruttenberg. Editors: Malcolm Brown, William Ferrari, Eddie Ima-
zu, Arthur Lonergan, Gabrel Scognamillo. Recording Director:
Douglas Shearer. Musical Supervisor: Johnny Green. Musical Ar-
rangements: Alberto Colombo, Adolphe Deutsch, Lennie Hayton,
Bronislau Kaper, Rudolph G. Kopp, David Raksin, David Rose,
Charles Wolcott. 89 minutes.
     Wellman directed one of eight stories in this anthology film.
The cast of this one, called THE MINISTER IN WASHINGTON, is:
Van Johnson (Adam Burch), Lewis Stone (Sexton), Leon Ames (Se-
cret Service Man). Released November 16, 1951.

MY MAN AND I (1952) A Metro-Goldwyn-Mayer Picture. Produced
by Stephen Ames. Directed by William A. Wellman. Screenplay:
John Fante and Jack Leonard. Photography: William C. Mellor.
Editor: John Dunning. Art Direction: Cedric Gibbons and James
Basevi. Set Decorations: Edwin B. Willis and Fred MacLean.

Assistant Director: George Rhein. Recording Director: Douglas Shearer. Special Effects: Warren Newcombe. Montage Sequences: Peter Ballbusch. Hairstyles: Sydney Guilaroff. Makeup: William Tuttle. Melodies, "Stormy Weather" by Harold Arlen and Ted Koehler, "Noche de Ronda" by Maria Teresa Lara. Working title: LETTER FROM THE PRESIDENT. 98 minutes.

The Cast: Shelley Winters (Nancy), Ricardo Montalban (Chu Chu Ramirez), Wendell Corey (Ansel Ames/Floyd Hawkson), Claire Trevor (Louise Hawkson), Jose Torvay (Manuel Ramirez), Jack Elam (Celestino), Pascual Garcia Pena (Willie Chung), George Chandler (Frankie), Juan Torena (Vincente Aguilar), Carlos Conde (Joe Mendavio). Released September 5, 1952.

ISLAND IN THE SKY (1953) A Wayne-Fellows Production. Released by Warner Bros. Pictures. Directed by William A. Wellman. Screenplay: Ernest K. Gann. Based on his novel. Photography: Archie J. Stout. Aerial Photography: William Clothier. Editor: Ralph Dawson. Art Director: James Basevi. Music: Emil Newman. Production Manager: Nate H. Edwards. Assistant Director: Andrew V. McLaglen. Narrator: William A. Wellman. 109 minutes.

The Cast: John Wayne (Capt. Dooley), Lloyd Nolan (Stutz), Walter Abel (Col. Fuller), James Arness (McMullen), Andy Devine (Moon), Allan Joslyn (J. H. Handy), James Lydon (Murray), Harry Carey, Jr. (Hunt), Hal Baylor (Stankowski), Sean McClory (Frank Lovatt), Wally Cassell (D'Annunzia), Regis Toomey (Sgt. Harper), Louis Jean Heydt (Fitch), Bob Steele (Wilson), Darryl Hickman (Swanson), Touch [Mike] Connors (Gainer), Gordon Jones (Walrus), Frank Fenton (Capt. Turner), Robert Keys (Major Ditson), Sumner Getchell (Lt. Cord), Paul Fix (Miller), Jim Dugan (Gidley), George Chandler (Rene), Carl Switzer (Hopper), Cass Gidley (Stannish), Guy Anderson (Breezy), Tony DeMario (Ogden), Dawn Bender (Murray's wife), Phyllis Winger (girl in flashback), Ann Doran (Moon's wife), Tim Wellman and Mike Wellman (Moon's sons), Tom Irish, Richard Walsh, Gene Coogan, Johnny Indrisano. Released September 9, 1953.

THE HIGH AND THE MIGHTY (1954) A Wayne-Fellows Production. Released by Warner Bros. Pictures. Directed by William A. Wellman. Screenplay: Ernest Gann, based on his novel. Music composed and conducted by Dimitri Tiomkin. Photography: Archie Stout. Aerial Photography: William Clothier. Photographed in CinemaScope and WarnerColor. Art Direction: Alfred Ybarra. Editor: Ralph Dawson. Assistant Director: Andrew V. McLaglen. Special Effects: Robert Mattey. Production Manager: Nate H. Edwards. 147 minutes.

The Cast: John Wayne (Dan Roman), Claire Trevor (May Holst), Laraine Day (Lydia Rice), Robert Stack (Sullivan), Jan Sterling (Sally McKee), Phil Harris (Ed Joseph), Robert Newton (Gustav Pardee), David Brian (Ken Childs), Paul Kelly (Flaherty), Sidney Blackmer (Humphrey Agnew), Doe Avedon (Miss Spalding), Karen Sharpe (Nell Buck), John Smith (Milo Buck), Julie Bishop (Lillian

Pardee), Pedro Gonzalez-Gonzalez (Gonzalez), John Howard (Howard
Rice), Wally Brown (Lenny Wilby), William Campbell (Hobie Wheel-
er), Ann Doran (Mrs. Joseph), John Qualen (Jose Locota), Paul Fix
(Frank Briscoe), George Chandler (Ben Sneed), Joy Kim (Dorothy
Chen), Michael Wellman (Toby Field), Douglas Fowley (Alsop), Regis
Toomey (Garfield), Carl Switzer (Ensign Keim), Robert Keys (Lt.
Mobray), William DeWolf Hopper (Roy), William Schallert (Dispatch-
er), Julie Mitchum (Susie), Robert Easton, Philip Van Zandt, Dorothy Ford (Tall woman). Released June 31, 1954. Academy Award
for Musical Score (Tiomkin). Nomination for Best Direction, Supporting Actress (Sterling and Trevor), Film Editing, Song ("The High
and the Mighty," lyrics by Ned Washington, music by Tiomkin).

TRACK OF THE CAT (1954) A Wayne-Fellows Production. Released
by Warner Bros. Pictures. Directed by William A. Wellman.
Screenplay: A. I. Bezzerides. Based on the novel by Walter Van
Tilburg Clark. Photography: William H. Clothier. Photographed
in CinemaScope and WarnerColor. Editor: Fred MacDowell. Music:
Roy Webb. Art Direction: Alfred Ybarra. Set Decorations: Ralph
Hurst. Assistant Director: Andrew V. McLaglen. Production Man-
ager: Nate H. Edwards. Script Supervisor: Sam Freedle. Makeup
Supervision: Gordon and George Bau. Sound: Earl Crain, Sr.
Props: Joseph LaBella. Orchestrations: Maurice DePackh. Hair
Stylist: Margaret Donovan. Costumes: Gwen Wakeling. 102 min-
utes.
    The Cast: Robert Mitchum (Curt Bridges), Teresa Wright
(Grace Bridges), Diana Lynn (Gwen Williams), Tab Hunter (Harold
"Hal" Bridges), Beulah Bondi (Ma Bridges), Philip Tonge (Pa
Bridges), William Hopper (Arthur Bridges), Carl Switzer (Joe Sam).
Released December 1, 1954.

BLOOD ALLEY (1955) A Batjac Production. Released by Warner
Bros. Pictures. Directed by William A. Wellman. Screenplay: A.
S. Fleischman. Based on his novel. Photography: William Cloth-
ier. Photographed in CinemaScope and WarnerColor. Production
Designer: Alfred Ybarra. Editor: Fred MacDowell. Music: Roy
Webb. Orchestrations: Maurice DePackh and Gus Levene. Sound:
Earl Crain, Sr. Assistant Director: Andrew V. McLaglen. Cos-
tumes: Gwen Wakeling and Carl Walker. 115 minutes.
    The Cast: John Wayne (Capt. Tom Wilder), Lauren Bacall
(Cathy Grainger), Paul Fix (Mr. Tso), Joy Kim (Susu), Mike Ma-
zurki (Big Han), Berry Kroeger (Old Feng), Anita Ekberg (Wei Long),
Henry Nakamura (Tack), W. T. Chang (Mr. Han), George Chan (Mr.
Sing), Victor Sen Yung (Corporal Wang), Walter Soohoo (Feng's #1
newphew), Eddie Luke (Feng's #2 nephew), Lowell Gilmore (British
Officer). Released October 5, 1955.

GOODBYE MY LADY (1956) A Batjac Production. Released by Warner Bros. Pictures. Produced and Directed by William A. Wellman.
Screenplay: Sid Fleischman. Based on the novel by James Street.

Photography: William Clothier. Art Direction: Donald A. Peters. Editor: Fred MacDowell. Assistant Director: Al Murphy. Music: Laurindo Almeida and George Field. Costumes: Carl Walker. Song by Don Powell and Moris Erby. 95 minutes.

The Cast: Walter Brennan (Uncle Jesse), Phil Harris (Cash Evans), Brandon de Wilde (Skeeter), Sidney Poitier (Gates), William Hopper (Grover), Louise Beavers (Bonnie Dew). Released May 12, 1956.

DARBY'S RANGERS (1958) A Warner Bros. Picture. Produced by Martin Rackin. Directed by William A. Wellman. Screenplay: Guy Trosper. Suggested by the book by Major James Altieri. Music: Max Steiner. Photography: William Clothier. Editor: Owen Marks. Art Director: William Campbell. Sound: Robert B. Lee. Set Decorator: William L. Kuehl. Costumes: Marjorie Best. Orchestrations: Murray Cutter. Technical Advisor: Col. Roy A. Murray, USA, Commander, Fourth Ranger Battalion. Project Training Instructors: Second Lt. Lee Mize and SFC Richard Sandlin, Ranger Dept., USA Infantry School. Makeup: Gordon Bau. Assistant Director: George Veiera. British title: THE YOUNG INVADERS. 121 minutes.

The Cast: James Garner (Major William O. Darby), Etchika Choureau (Angelina DeLotta), Jack Warden (M/Sgt. Saul Rosen), Edward Byrnes (Lt. Arnold Dittman), Venetia Stevenson (Peggy McTavish), Torin Thatcher (Sgt. McTavish), Peter Brown (Rollo Burns), Joan Elan (Wendy Hollister), Corey Allen (Tony Sutherland), Stuart Whitman (Hank Bishop): Murray Hamilton (Sims Delancey), Bill Wellman, Jr. (Eli Clatworthy), Andrea King (Sheilah Andrews), Adam Williams (Heavy Hall), Frieda Inescort (Lady Hollister), Reginald Owen (Sir Arthur), Philip Tonge (John Andrews), Edward Ashley (Lt. Manson), Raymond Bailey (Maj. Gen. Wise), Willis Bouchey (Brig. Gen. Truscott). Released February 12, 1958.

LAFAYETTE ESCADRILLE (1958) A Warner Bros.-First National Picture. A William A. Wellman Production. Produced and Directed by William A. Wellman. Screenplay: A. S. Fleischman. Based on the story "C'est La Guerre" by Wellman. Photography: William Clothier. Music: Leonard Rosenman. Editor: Owen Marks. Production Design: Donald A. Peters. Art Director: John Beckman. Set Decorator: Ralph Hurst. Sound: John Kean. Costume Design: Marjorie Best. Makeup Supervision: Gordon Bau. Orchestrations: Maurice dePackh. Assistant Director: George Veiera. Narrator: William A. Wellman. Working titles: C'EST LA GUERRE, WITH YOU IN MY ARMS. British title: HELL BENT FOR GLORY. 93 minutes.

The Cast: Tab Hunter (Thad Walker), Etchika Choureau (Renee Beaulieu), Marcel Dalio (drill instructor), David Janssen (Reginald "Duke" Sinclair), Paul Fix (American General), Veola Vonn (The Madame), Will Hutchins (Dave Putnam), Clint Eastwood (George Moseley), Bob Hover (David Judd), Tom Laughlin (Arthur Blumenthal), Brett Halsey (Frank Baylies), Henry Nakamura (Jimmy), Maurice

Marsac (Sgt. Parris), Raymond Bailey (Mr. Walker), George Nardelli (Concierge), Bill Wellman, Jr. (Bill Wellman), Jody McCrea (Tom Hitchcock), Dennis Devine (Red Scanlon). Filmed in 1956. Released April 18, 1958.

Wellman contributed uncredited direction to the following films:

THE WAY OF A GIRL (M-G-M, 1925. Dir. Robert Vignola).

ESCAPE (Released as THE EXQUISITE SINNER; M-G-M, 1925. Dir. Josef Von Sternberg and, also uncredited, Phil Rosen).

CHINA SEAS (M-G-M, 1935. Dir. Tay Garnet).

TARZAN ESCAPES (M-G-M, 1936. Dir. Richard Thorpe and, also uncredited, John Farrow and James McKay).

WOMAN CHASES MAN (Goldwyn, 1937. Dir. John G. Blystone).

RING OF FEAR (Batjac, 1954. Dir. James Edward Grant).

It has been reported that Wellman also contributed uncredited direction to VIVA VILLA (M-G-M, 1935. Dir. Jack Conway and, also uncredited, Howard Hawks), GONE WITH THE WIND (Selznick, 1939. Dir. Victor Fleming and, also uncredited, Sam Wood and George Cukor), and DUEL IN THE SUN (Selznick, 1946. Dir. King Vidor). He certainly did no work on the latter two films and it is extremely doubtful that he worked on VIVA VILLA.

Wellman worked as a writer on the following films:

THE LAST GANGSTER (M-G-M, 1937. Dir. Edward Ludwig. Story by Wellman and Robert Carson. Originally titled ANOTHER PUBLIC ENEMY).

THREE GUYS NAMED MIKE (M-G-M, 1951. Dir. Charles Walters. Screenplay by Sidney Sheldon "from an idea by" Wellman).

Wellman and Carson also received screen credit on both remakes of A STAR IS BORN: George Cukor's 1954 version (Warners) and Frank Pierson's 1976 version (Warners).

In 1960, Wellman completed a script called FOOTPRINTS which was never produced.

Television work by Wellman included the following:

LIGHT'S DIAMOND JUBILEE (1954) Produced by David O. Selznick. Assistant to the Producer: Arthur Fellows. Directed by William A. Wellman, King Vidor, Roy Rowland, Christian Nyby, Norman Taurog. Live Sequences Directed by Alan Handley and Allan "Bud" Yorkin. Teleplay: Ben Hecht and David O. Selznick. Based on stories and materials by Robert Benchley, Arthur Gordon, Irwin Shaw, Max Shulman, John Steinbeck, Mark Twain and G. K. Chesterton. Photography: James Wong Howe and Ray June. Production Design: Furth Ullman. Music: Victor Young. 120 minutes.

The Cast: Judith Anderson, David Niven, Lauren Bacall, Walter Brennan, Joseph Cotten, Helen Hayes, Dwight D. Eisenhower, Kim Novak, Guy Madison, George Gobel, Dorothy Dandridge, Robert Benchley, Erin O'Brien Moore, Harry Morgan, Debbie Reynolds. Wellman directed Eisenhower's two-minute introduction to this celebration of the anniversary of Edison's discovery of the incandescent lamp. It was telecast simultaneously on NBC, CBS, ABC and the DuMont television networks on October 24, 1954, at 8:00 EST.

INDEX